EUROPEAN COORDINATION CENTRE
FOR RESEARCH AND DOCUMENTATION IN SOCIAL SCIENCES

CONSUMPTION PATTERNS IN EASTERN AND WESTERN EUROPE

CONSUMPTION PATTERNS IN EASTERN AND WESTERN EUROPE

An Economic Comparative Approach
A Collective Study

Directed by

V. CAO - PINNA
and
S. S. SHATALIN

PERGAMON PRESS

OXFORD · NEW YORK · TORONTO · SYDNEY · PARIS · FRANKFURT

U.K.	Pergamon Press Ltd., Headington Hill Hall, Oxford OX3 0BW, England
U.S.A.	Pergamon Press Inc., Maxwell House, Fairview Park, Elmsford, New York 10523, U.S.A.
CANADA	Pergamon of Canada, Suite 104, 150 Consumers Road, Willowdale, Ontario M2J 1P9, Canada
AUSTRALIA	Pergamon Press (Aust.) Pty. Ltd., P.O. Box 544, Potts Point, N.S.W. 2011, Australia
FRANCE	Pergamon Press SARL, 24 rue des Ecoles, 75240 Paris, Cedex 05, France
FEDERAL REPUBLIC OF GERMANY	Pergamon Press GmbH, 6242 Kronberg-Taunus, Pferdstrasse 1, Federal Republic of Germany

First edition 1979

British Library Cataloguing in Publication Data

Consumption patterns in Eastern and Western Europe.
1. Consumers - Europe
I. Cao-Pinna, V II. Shatalin, S S
III. European Coordination Centre for Research and Documentation in Social Sciences
339.4'7   HC240.9.C6   78-40347
ISBN 0-08-021808-3

In order to make this volume available as economically and as rapidly as possible the authors' typescripts have been reproduced in their original forms. This method unfortunately has its typographical limitations but it is hoped that they in no way distract the reader.

*Printed in Great Britain at
William Clowes & Sons Limited
Beccles and London*

Contents

List of Tables

List of Charts

Foreword

After several years of common work, the participants in a cross-national comparative research project nearly always have the feeling of having raised more questions and problems requiring deeper study than of having provided definite replies, valid from all points of view: theoretical, methodological and practical.

For the first time researchers from Eastern and Western Europe have tried to recognize and compare — by the application of a descriptive and analytical method worked out together — consumption tendencies in Czechoslovakia, France, the German Democratic Republic, Hungary, Italy, Poland, the Soviet Union and Switzerland.

It was not easy task. They had to overcome not only problems posed by the diversity of definitions of a purely statistical nature of the aggregates considered, but also those posed by a deeper diversity resulting from the varied "social" conceptions of the phenomena observed and the function that these phenomena supposedly exercise within the social system and institutional framework of the considered countries.

Thus the reader should not be surprised if significance is placed on the difficulties met with, the diversity of situations, limits of comparison and, above all, on the interpretation of "discovered" tendencies.

This book, however, is not solely a scientific account of the work and problems of a team of European researchers. It is a positive contribution that brings replies — sometimes expected, sometimes less expected — to the questions posed, thus being of undeniable interest for the planners themselves.

May we express, on behalf of the Vienna Centre, our warmest thanks to all members of the team and to the authors of these chapters. Some of them have taken on very difficult tasks which they have fulfilled in a remarkable manner.

The whole project owes its success particularly to the competence, energy and devotion of the two international co-directors: Professor Vera Cao-Pinna of the University of Rome, and Professor Stanislav Shatalin, Vice-President of the Central Institute for Economic Mathematics, U.S.S.R. Academy of Sciences. Their mutual understanding and cooperation with the other participants has given an exemplary scientific and human style to the work of the group. May they find here the expression of our gratitude and the warm appreciation of the Centre's Board of Directors.

                         Professor Adam SCHAFF
                  President of the Board of Directors
March 1976

Preface

Since its origins, economic science has devoted a great deal of its attention to the study and analysis of household consumption. From the start, economists of the classical school were concerned with what could be directly observed in household consumption, that is with goods purchased at a price on the market. This double condition - the existence of a price and a market - has decisively oriented almost the entire research in this field and only the most recent and sophisticated research has not been limited by this framework of hypotheses.

These are highly limiting and misleading hypotheses, when one considers then, since there have always been, and still are, quantities of free, or virtually free, goods consumed by the population outside any market. Examples of these are water and air, education of the young, and health of the population.

Today it is even more difficult to ignore this aspect of houshold consumption of which the State and other public authorities have progressively taken charge, an increasingly important part of those "non-market" goods they spend money to produce and raise taxes to finance.

These few preliminary remarks will perhaps help the reader to grasp the originality of this study which aims to raise this problem at an international level.

There is, in fact, quite a widespread opinion that international comparisons of economic phenomena are rather disappointing, especially if the subjects of such comparisons are based on concepts which diverge from those traditionally accepted and if the countries considered differ greatly in their institutional and political systems. However, the growing interest in criteria and methods of resource allocation which is manifest in all countries seems to justify the risks involved in an attempt to confront the ways in which resources, both individual and collective, are utilized in various countries. Furthermore, scientific curiosity concerning the practical validity of certain more or less gratuitous opinions and impressions of the divergencies between the ways in which the needs of the population are satisfied in socialist and capitalist countries is all the more justified as the necessary empirical bases for testing reality and the validity of these opinions are lacking.

The general purpose of this volume is to provide sufficiently solid statistical bases for answers which serve to meet the practical needs of the public authorities and, at the same time, to satisfy the curiosity of those scientists in Eastern and Western Europe who are concerned with problems of resource allocation.

We obviously do not claim to answer all the questions raised by such critical problems, but this first effort of collaboration between experts of Eastern and Western Europe has shown that remarkable progress can be achieved through a better use of experiences acquired and the exchange of factual information available in the two groups of countries, thus making it possible to correct certain subjective and superficial views, economic or otherwise, put forward by the press.

The study was undertaken under the auspices of the Vienna Centre which aims at promoting multidisciplinary cooperation between experts of different European countries in the field of social sciences. We are very grateful to its president, Professor Adam Schaff, and to the ex-director of the Centre, Mr. Riccardo Petrella, who have attentively followed the work of the group, and to the entire staff of the Centre which has spared no efforts to establish and facilitate contacts between the participants of the different countries on every occasion. Our thanks go especially to the secretaries of research, Messrs. D. Smislov, I. Mitiaev and Y. Kotchetkov, as well as to Miss S. Porges, who was responsible for the organization of discussions between the authors of the various chapters of this volume. Finally, we wish to acknowledge particularly the remarkable translation into English by the economist, Mrs. G. Podbielski, and the excellent translation services, into Russian, provided by Mrs. N.

Novikova.

The chief merit we attribute to this study consists in the wealth of detailed data collected in the countries which participated; these have been rendered comparable by a great effort of revision of the conceptual and statistical conventions established in the countries of Eastern and Western Europe for the elaboration of their respective national accounts.

It must be acknowledged that the harmonization of so vast a collection of data could not have been achieved without first concentrating on the many aspects by which consumption can be analysed from the theoretical point of view before it can be statistically grasped. In this respect we are greatly indebted to the eminent economists who have contributed to the clarification of the theoretical aspects which underlie the elaboration of a common conceptual framework for analysing the structures and methods of financing private and collective consumption. Without their valuable help this work could neither have been started nor completed. They are: Professor J. Bénard of the University of Paris, S. A. Aivasian of the Academy of Science of Moscow, W. Brus of the University of Oxford, and E. Frygies of the Planning Commission of Hungary.

This volume presents a synthesis of the contributions of eight European countries and our warmest thanks go to the eight national monographs. Chapters 2 and 3 are based on the painstaking work undertaken by the experts of Eastern Europe: P. Hronski and J. Stanko (Czechoslovakia), G. Manz (the Democratic Republic of Germany), O. Elteto and E. John (Hungary), S. Rajewski (Poland), I. Korhova (U.S.S.R.), and those of Western European countries: J. Desce (France), A. Santeusanio (Italy) and J.N. Du Pasquier (Switzerland).

The list of eight countries is not the outcome of a deliberate choice or decision made at the beginning of the study; it is rather due to circumstances which have prevented experts of several other countries from undertaking, or completing, the very heavy task involved in the preparation of such a study.

But the differences in demographic size and institutional and political systems, the framework in which the study was developed in the eight countries, offer a sufficiently meaningful sample of similarities and disparities in the consumption structures of Eastern and Western Europe. It is useful to expose the main factors which influence, or condition, these structures in either group of countries.

It is evident that the work required for harmonizing the basic data and interpreting the results has been very substantial and that the results can be of great interest to the readers to whom this study addresses itself. In contrast to what happens when international research aims merely at comparisons of already existing information, this study called for a painstaking preliminary effort of adapting to the new concepts – above all that of "enlarged consumption" – which all the participants in the study had to use to ensure the maximum harmonization of definitions and procedures for an evaluation which can be used to render the results comparable and explainable.

Before the basic data could be assembled it was necessary to organize several meetings of the experts from the two groups of countries, during the course of which data of each country could be progressively rendered homogeneous. The first chapter summarizes the methodology accepted by all the participants. But other meetings had to be arranged after the national monographs had been prepared so as to make them as exhaustive and comparable as possible. The monographs of each country then had to be reassembled in the two synthetic chapters, summarizing the most significant aspects of the structures and methods of financing household consumption in the two groups of countries. The results of this are illustrated in Chapters 2 and 3 respectively.

But the final and most interesting part of the study consisted in attempting a comparative analysis of the results obtained in the two groups of countries: a very delicate task which called for a supplementary effort of interpretation; this was entrusted to a restricted committee whose members had to try and arrive at acceptable interpretations for all the very surprising similarities and differences between the two groups of countries brought to light by the study, and these were finally collected in Chapter 4 by Professor Solari and Mr. Du Pasquier.

Finally, we wish to point out that, as an accompaniment to the present economic study and based on the same principles of international comparison, a sociological analysis has been undertaken. Sociologists of four countries (France, Hungary, Italy and the U.S.S.R.) have investigated the utilization, by households, of four basic services – housing, health, pre-school education and assistance to the elderly – from the point of view of both supply and demand, notably concerning consumer preferences. The economic study could, to some extent, take account of the main results of these analyses which are to be the subject of a subsequent publication of the Vienna Centre.

V. Cao-Pinna, Rome

S. S. Shatalin, Moscow

March 1976

Acknowledgements

The research carried out for this book was organized by the European Coordination Centre for Research and Documentation in Social Sciences in Vienna, with its financial support and the operational costs financed by the national research institutes of the participating countries:

Czechoslovakia	Research Institute on Standard of Living, Bratislava
France	Research and Documentation Centre on Consumption (CREDOC), Paris
Germany (German Democratic Republic)	High School of Economics, Berlin
Hungary	National Planning Office and Central Statistical Office, Budapest
Italy	National Planning Institute, Rome
Poland	Research Centre of the Central Statistical Office, Warsaw
Switzerland	University of Geneva, Department of Econometrics, Geneva
U.S.S.R.	Central Economic Mathematical Institute of the U.S.S.R. Academy of Sciences, Moscow

About the Contributors

Vera CAO PINNA is lecturer on Applied Economics at the University of Rome. She is a leading authority on input-output analysis and on econometric analysis of demand for consumer goods and on forecasting techniques. She has participated in the publication of several collective books and studies organized by national and international organizations on problems of major interest, at multinational, national and regional levels.

Inna KORKHOVA is a senior research member at the Division of the Central Institute of Mathematical Economics (T.S.E.M.I.) of the U.S.S.R. Academy of Sciences, researching into the Standard of Living of the Population.

Stanislaw S. SHATALIN is a corresponding member of the U.S.S.R. Academy of Sciences and joint Director of the Central Institute of Mathematical Economics (T.S.E.M.I.). He is also Dean of the Cybernetical Economics Department at the University of Moscow. As a specialist in the field of mathematical model-building he contributes to the preparation of national economic plans and is author of many scientific articles related to planning problems and methods.

Natasha M. RIMASHEVSKAIA is Head of the Division of the Central Institute of Mathematical Economics (T.S.E.M.I.) of the U.S.S.R. Academy of Sciences for the research on the Standard of Living of the Population. Being a specialist in this field, she is responsible for the Direction of Research concerning Social Welfare. She is author of many studies in this area.

Luigi SOLARI is Director of the Econometric Department, Faculty of Economic and

Social Sciences of the University of Geneva. His major scientific concern is econometric model-building, especially consumption models. He is the editor of a series of scientific papers and books in this field.

Otto SOBEK is a senior member of the Research Institute on Standard of Living in Bratislava. He is also Associated Professor at the High School of Economics in Bratislava. Most of his work and publications have been devoted to distribution and income policy with special regard to financial instruments.

Alain FOULON is one of the research directors of CREDOC (Paris) and Associated Professor at the University of Paris IX (Dauphine). Most of his work and publications are concerned with problems and analysis of income redistribution and methods of estimation for national accounting, especially in the field of health.

Jean-Noel DU PASQUIER is Assistant at the Economic Department, Faculty of Economic and Social Sciences of the University of Geneva.

Filip HRONSKY is Director of the Research Institute on Standard of Living in Bratislava. He is also Professor at the Bratislava Institute of Economics. Most of his works and publications have been devoted to problems of theory and policy of the standard of living.

Jozef STANKO is a senior research member of the Research Institute on Standard of Living in Bratislava. His main field of research is the problems of social consumption funds.

Prof. Dr. Günter MANZ is department chief at the Berlin Institute of Economics, German Democratic Republic.

Eugenia KRZECZKOWSKA is Director of the Research Centre, Central Statistical Office in Warsaw. She is a specialist in the field of international comparisons, especially consumption comparisons. She is author of many scientific studies and articles in this area.

Zenon RAJEWSKI is the scientific secretary of the Research Centre, Central Statistical Office, Warsaw. He is also head of the Research Group of International Comparisons at this Centre.

Teodozja DMOCH is head of the Research Group of Social Development Studies, Research Centre, Central Statistical Office, Warsaw.

Odon ELTETO is deputy chief of section at the Economic Department, Hungarian Central Statistical Office. Most of his work and publications are connected with problems and analysis of income distribution and of consumption models.

Ede JOHN is chief of Department in the Ministry for Light Industry, also adviser to the Hungarian State Planning Office. Publications in the field of the standard of living.

Jean BENARD is Professor at the University of PARIS I and Director of a Research Team of the National Center for Scientific Research (C.N.R.S.). His works of modelization are mainly related with public economy theory and planning.

CHAPTER 1
Methodological Background*

1.1 CONCEPTS AND METHODS OF THE STUDY

Any attempt to merge divisible "market" and "non-market" consumption into a single concept of "enlarged household consumption" and to study its structure and development from various angles raises a number of conceptual and methodological problems. To render international comparison possible, a minimum of harmonization and coherence of instruments of observation and analysis, as well as of the accounting framework, is required.

The substantial differences in the socio-economic structure of capitalist and socialist countries are evidently reflected also in considerable divergencies between their systems of production, of the circulation of goods and services and of income distribution, and between the institutional set-ups for the allocation of national resources. Further, for doctrinal and practical reasons, the methods of constructing national accounts in the two groups of countries are hardly comparable:[1] in particular, while the free services (health, education, etc.) included in consumption in the Material Product Account (MPA) are evaluated on the basis of only the material goods they contain (pharmaceuticals, books, etc.)-that is excluding wages and salaries of persons employed in these services-the evaluation of the same service by the United Nations international system (SNA) includes the goods and wages entering into their production.[2]

To achieve the objectives of the study, it was therefore necessary to ensure that, in spite of different national accounting systems, aggregates and recording and presentation procedures be defined in a sufficiently comparable and homogeneous way. It must be stressed, however, that the study does not propose to question existing national accounting systems but only to redefine those parts of the

---

* This chapter has been prepared by V.Cao-Pinna and A.Foulon with the participation of J.Bernard, J.N.Du Pasquier and L.Solari who have supplied critical comments on earlier versions.
[1] It will be noted, however, that Hungary uses a concept of National Product resembling that of National Income of the SNA simultaneously with the National Income concept of MPA.
[2] In order to facilitate comparison it has been agreed among the participants to use mainly the Western terminology as close as possible to the SNA.

1

conventions and definitions which concern the population's consumption more specifically; it is therefore not intended to analyse explicitly the consequences such modifications may have, either for the concepts of income, savings, financial operations, etc., or for the accounting methods applied to sectors other than consumption. Instead, some sort of partial derivation from existing national accounting systems will be aimed at which is based on the application of specific principles in the field of consumption but does not claim to present an overall scheme of national accounts.

The definition of aggregates,[3] the nomenclature of goods and services of institutions, and the methods of recording and presenting the result constitute the four levels at which the general method of the study is harmonized.

1.2   CONCEPTS AND AGGREGATES

Direct household purchases of marketed goods and services include (i) all purchases made by the household sector from disposable incomes: income from work and capital and from cash transfers (pensions, family allowances, scholarships);(ii) imputed consumption, that is essentially on-farm self-consumption of agricultural products and of housing services covered by imputed rent for owner-occupied dwellings;(iii) income in kind (notably remuneration in kind of collective farmers, etc.)

These direct purchases are recorded "gross" or "net", depending on whether they do or not include reimbursement by Social Security or other public administrations of expenditures incurred by households, in particular for health and housing.

Since, on the one hand, the socialist countries do not resort to reimbursement mechanisms from collective funds and, on the other, the concepts used differ between East and West European countries, the equivalence in the terminology of the two groups of countries can be established (see Table 1.1).

Table 1.1
Direct gross and net households' purchases

Capitalist countries		Socialist countries	
0.1:	Gross Direct Household Purchases	01:	[a]
	less 0.31:Reimbursements		
0.2:	Net Direct Household Purchases =	02:	Direct Household Purchases or Personal Consumption

[a]This concept does not exist or has not been evaluated in the MPA system.

It will be noted that direct purchases are not synonymous with "market consumption" since they include not only consumption which is non-market by definition (imputed rent of owners, self-consumption of food by collective farmers, etc.) but also consumption categories whose market character for the consumer is subject to some reservations (medical expenditure in West European countries).

------

[3]These harmonized definitions are based essentially on the terminology of the SNA system: to clarify the exposition of methods, the way in which these common aggregates are derived from two systems of concepts will be compared.

Social benefits in kind include reimbursements or transfers in kind in the general
sense of the term, that is the direct-total or partial-assumption by collective
funds of part of household market consumption without requiring a simultaneous and
proportional counterpart for the benefits received.

In the West European countries, these social benefits include all allocations in
kind by Social Security[4] and enterprises and the various forms of assistance
specifically granted by the State, local authorities or private administrations
for a predetermined category of consumption. These can take the form of either
reimbursements or of transfers in kind or in the form of services paid directly to
the producer (so-called "third party" payments) with the exclusion of subsidies.
They consist mainly of: (i) payments by Social Security for medical treatment and
partially for housing;(ii) assistance in kind for medical treatment and especially
social services by other public and private administrations; (iii) social benefits
granted by enterprises to their employees, mainly for professional training and
social services and leisure.[5]

In the socialist countries these social benefits consist in the direct but partial
assumption of consumer expenditure by social consumption funds administered by the
State, the Federal or Autonomous Republics, local authorities, trade unions and
possibly enterprises. In many cases they resemble social deliveries in kind
identical to "third party" payments in Western European countries. By contrast,
some of them can be interpreted as deliveries in kind, either of subsidies to
production (excluding subsidies to investments) when-as in the case of dwellings
or collective transport-these benefits are intended to compensate the productive
sector for price or tariff reductions granted to certain categories of households
or indistinctly to the whole population. They concern mainly housing, public
transport, medical and social services and leisure.

Here again an equivalent terminology can be formulated (Table 1.2).

Table 1.2
Social benefits in kind

	Capitalist countries		Socialist countries	
0.31: (plus)	Reimbursements		0.31	_____
0.32:	Transfers in kind or in the form of services		0.32:	Allocations in kind from social consumption funds
0.3:	Social Benefits in kind	=	0.3:	Social Benefits in kind

Private consumption is derived from the additions in Table 1.3 for the two groups
of countries.

Divisible public consumption includes (as stated above) collective services which
have a direct influence on the standard of living of their beneficiaries. They are
produced by public or semi-public administrations but could in principle be
commercialized, that is distributed through the market. They consist of: (i)

---

[4]These social benefits in kind granted by enterprises call for particular accounting procedures (see subsection 1.6.1, Table 1.10, Basic
Table 1, note(c) below.

[5]Social Security systems are understood here as public, separate from
State and Local Authorities, and generally financed by special contributions.

non-market consumption produced by public institutions and distributed to households freely or partially free; (ii) divisible services whose beneficiaries, that is the consumers, can in principle be identified. Excluded in this definition are therefore "pure" (or "indivisible") collective services:[6] the functioning of parliament, foreign affairs, national defence, justice, police[6], etc. Similarly, other services have been omitted in the study-although they satisfy certain household needs and are theoretically "divisible" and "non-market" -since it is in practice extremely difficult and often impossible to identify that part which reaches final household consumption:[7] road and street services, the sanitary control of foodstuffs, territorial planning, etc.

Table 1.3
Private Consumption

	Capitalist countries		Socialist countries
0.2:	Direct Net Household Purchases	0.2:	Direct Household Purchases or Personal Consumption
(plus)		(plus)	
0.3:	Social Benefits in kind	0.3:	Social Benefits in kind
0.4:	Private Consumption[a]	0.4:	Private Consumption

   [a] Whereas in Western European national accounts private household consumption is derived from the addition of direct net purchases and social benefits in kind, official terminology in socialist countries includes under private consumption only direct household purchases in the market, and official collective consumption includes social benefits in kind plus collective consumption (see Table 1.4) and is used as such in Chapter 2.

The nomenclature of all goods and services listed below gives the details of divisible collective services covered in the study. These are: transport, medical goods and services, social services, education,[8] culture, information, leisure and various other services (sports, etc.).

It was, however, impossible to agree among the participants from East and West on the inclusion of services provided by the general administration which are linked to the production of services.[9] For reasons of principles, just as for lack of

---

[6]For the West European countries, however, food supplies in military and prison establishments have been included in total food consumption but not clothing and housing.

[7]In particular, theoretical and statistical difficulties cause problems in separating-within these types of services (notably for the utilization of roads)-that part which can be considered as final collective consumption of households from that which is to be imputed as intermediate collective consumption of the producing agents.

[8]Expenditure on higher education covers a part of university research included in teachers' salaries; however, this expenditure is not analysed here and that for extra-university and autonomous research is also excluded.

[9]These operating costs relate to the administration of collective institutions (Ministry of National Education, Social Security,etc.) which produce divisible non-market services or allocate social transfers. With the exception of a negligible part covering indivisible services (cabinets of ministers, etc.), the bulk of these administrative charges is comparable to the administration costs (management, financial services, etc.) incurred by enterprises in the market sectors for the production of marketed goods and services which are included in market prices: they should, therefore, be included in principle in the factor cost of divisible collective services.

statistics, these services could not be included by the socialist countries (see Chapter 2) although it was recognized that this omission involves an under-estimation of household needs. By contrast, the West European countries present their national data (see Chapter 3) including that part of expenditure on services of the general administration. However, so as not to introduce a bias into the analyses, it was agreed to exclude these services from the East-West comparisons in Chapter 4.

Again, the corresponding terminologies are as in Table 1.4.

Table 1.4
Public and collective consumption

Capitalist countries		Socialist countries	
0.51:	Divisible public consumption[a]	0.51:	Public consumption
(less)			
0.52:	Services of the general administration	0.52:	_____
0.5:	Public Consumption[b]	0.5:	Collective Consumption[b]

[a] Concept used in Chapter 3.   [b] Concept used in Chapter 4.

To render the estimation methods coherent[10] it was necessary to evaluate direct purchases at factor cost and hence to define:

0.7:   Indirect Taxes as relating exclusively to household consumption: turnover taxes (VAT, etc.), specific taxes (taxes on fuel, etc.) and customs duties. They therefore exclude indirect taxation imposed on other household expenditure,whether perceived on current expenditure (registration taxes, etc.) or on investments (VAT on dwelling constrution, etc.)[11].

0.8:   Current Subsidies allocated to products directly. These therefore exclude subsidies paid to producers,notably in France to farmers, on the basis of their social position and not solely in connection with a given specific type of production.[12]

The addition of Private Consumption and Public (or Collective Consumption) gives "Household Consumption" as it is analysed in this study.

However, because of the difficulties of harmonization, due to both differences in economic systems and concepts and the lack of statistical information, enlarged consumption does not have an identical meaning nor is it evaluated in the same terms in the three comparative chapters. Table 1.5. summarizes the way in which

---

[10] See below.

[11] Since only the West European countries were able to supply estimates at factor cost, the harmonization of methods in this field has remained rather superficial, leaving each country relatively free to define the nomenclature of indirect taxes covered in the study according to its own fiscal system and its real incidence on household consumption.

[12] As has been stated above, certain current subsidies can be interpreted as social benefits, particularly in public transport, housing, health services and leisure. For the same reasons as given in note 11, each country was left free to decide on the definition adopted, depending on the institutional set-up through which social benefits and subsidies are granted as well as on national accounting conventions.

Table 1.5

The linking of aggregates in the comparative chapters

Capitalist countries	Socialist countries
0.1: Gross Direct Household Purchases	
(less)	
0-31: Reimbursements	
0.2: Net Direct Household Purchases	0.2: Direct Household Purchases or Personal Consumption
(plus)	(plus)
0.3: Social Benefits (in kind)	0.3: Social Benefits in Kind
0.4: Private Consumption (at market prices)[a]	0.4: Private Consumption (at market prices)
(less)	
0.7: Indirect Taxes	
(plus)	
0.8: Current Subsidies	
0.4 bis: Private Consumption (at factor cost)	
Divisible public consumption (at factor cost)	
(plus)	(plus)
0.51: Public Consumption (excluding services of the general administration at factor cost)	0.5: Collective Consumption (at factor cost)
0.6: Enlarged Household Consumption	0.6: Enlarged Household Consumption
0.6: Enlarged Household Consumption (at factor cost)	
Intra-West comparison (Chapter 3)	Intra-East comparison (Chapter 2)

East-West comparison (Chapter 4)

a See Table 1.3, note(a)

enlarged consumption is defined and arrived at in the three chapters which follow.

Also, a comparative analysis of the structure and development of expanded consumption implied that the structure of financing, not only of social benefits in kind but also of Cash Transfers, be taken into account; the latter are not directly linked to any given consumption but rather to a risk or a precise social position and are intended to compensate for a loss or lack of income. They include the items listed in Table 1.6 for the two groups of countries.

Table 1.6
Social cash transfers

09: Social Cash Transfers

Capitalist countries	Socialist countries
Pensions to retired persons	Old-age pensions
Pensions to the temporarily or perma- nently incapacitated, war veterans, assisted persons, etc.	Pensions to the temporarily or perma- nently incapacitated and war veterans
Family allowances (to large families, households with single wage-earners, etc.)	Family allowances and confinement and maternity grants, allowances to single mothers
Daily sickness, maternity and work accident allowances[a]	Sickness pay
Survivor indemnities	–
Unemployment benefits	–
Scholarships and pre-salaries to students	Scholarships
Other (allowances to repatriated migrants, etc.)	Other

[a]Not included are payments representing a continuation of wages and salaries during sickness paid by employers, notably to government civil servants in France.

Finally, in spite of the limited significance to be attached to annual figures of gross fixed capital formation, the Western participants in the study thought it useful to supply information on this sector so as to compare the structure of private and public Investment finance in the fields of housing, health, education and social services.

1.3   THE NOMENCLATURE OF GOODS AND SERVICES

The coverage and detail of goods and services entering into enlarged consumption depends both on the general content given to the preceding aggregates and on the availability of statistics. As has been seen, the main difficulty in the first case is the inclusion of general administration services in collective consumption; the compromise reached by the participants has been summarized in Section 1.2 above.

As to the breakdown of the nomenclature, a first effort consisted in unifying the classification of private and collective consumption by eighty-two groups of goods and services, regrouped into fourteen categories of needs. In practice the breakdownof private consumption was much more detailed in the West European countries, and the opposite is true for collective consumption in the East European countries.

For this reason it was agreed to harmonize only the content of the fourteen categories of needs, distinguishing between data on "essential" goods and services which each country was asked to supply and specify; for the other categories it was agreed that information could be given in a more aggregate fashion within each category of needs.

The detailed breakdown used by each participant is given in the appendix. At this point only the classification of the fourteen categories of needs is presented, with as much detail as is considered essential for the study.

1.00 Food
       Consumed at home
       Consumed outside the home (in hotels, cafés, restaurants, canteens, hospitals, etc.)
2.00 Beverages
3.00 Tobacco and Matches
4.00 Clothing and Footwear (including maintenance and repairs)
5.00 Personal Care
6.00 Housing
       Imputed rent of owner-occupied dwellings
       Electricity, water, heating
       Household equipment (furniture, electrical appliances, etc.)
7.00 Transportation
       Purchase and repairs of personal vehicles
       Public transport services
8.00 Telecommunications (excluding radio and television)
9.00 Medical Goods and Services
       Treatment in general hospitals (excluding food and beverages, see 1.00 and 2.00)
       Treatment in specialized hospitals (for mental diseases and anti-T.B.) (excluding food and beverages, see 1.00 and 2.00)
       Ambulatory care and home visits
       Services of the general administration of the State, local authorities and Social Security (for West European countries)
10.00 Social Services (excluding food and beverages, see 1.00 and 2.00)
       Establishments for children
       Establishments for incapacitated persons
       Establishments for old people
       Assistance to unemployed
       Services of the general administration of the State, local authorities and Social Security (for West European countries)
11.00 Education and Research (excluding the corresponding services in the armed forces and in prisons)
       Primary education
       Secondary education
       Specialized technical and professional education
       Higher education, advanced engineering schools (Grandes Ecoles) and university research)
       Services of the general administration of the State and local authorities (for West European countries)
12.00 Culture and Information
       Books, newspapers, magazines
       Radio and television
       Museums, cultural centres, clubs, etc.
       Theatres, cinemas, concerts
       Services of the general administration of the State and local authorities (for West European countries)

13.00   Sports, Leisure and Entertainment
        Sports equipment and services, records, musical instruments, toys, hotels
            Cafes, restaurants (excluding food and beverages, see 1.00 and 2.00)
        Services of the general administration of the State and local authorities
            (for West European countries)
14.00   Other Goods and Services (watches, jewellery, travel goods, articles for
            funerals, insurance services for goods and persons, etc.)

1.4   THE INSTITUTIONAL FRAMEWORK

It also seemed important, both for the sake of comparison and for explaining
certain developments, to distinguish the sectors which administer various social
funds in addition to households: that is public, semi-public or private
institutions which supply social benefits and transfers as well as divisible
collective services.

It was therefore decided to subdivide collective deliveries in the tables into the
following sectors:

Central and local administration[13]
Social security institutions[14]
Private non-profit administrations and workers' unions
Private and public enterprises.

It has to be admitted, however, that the only exhaustive data available are those
for the expenditures of the State and Social Security institutions. The
statistical information on the expenditure of local public administrations,
particularly if they are financed from sources other than the central budget, was
highly fragmentary or even non-existent in certain cases. As a result, social
consumption funds are always under-estimated to varying degrees.

Similarly, for the West European countries, the allowances paid and services
rendered by non-profit making private administrations are greatly under-estimated
in Italy and entirely excluded in France and Switzerland.

Little is known in all countries on the benefits in kind granted by enterprises
and these are certainly greatly under-estimated: limited to a few categories of
needs in France, to large enterprises in Italy, not recorded at all in Switzerland
and generally poorly covered in the socialist countries, notably because of
considerable overlapping in this field between enterprises and labour unions.

Finally, it must be noted that in the case of Switzerland (and in the absence of a
generalized Social Security system) a particular institutional framework had to be
considered which takes into account the special feature of a mixed system of
public and private organizations, notably for expenditures on health services.[15]

---

[13] Central government, federal or autonomous republics, cantons, provinces,
   regions, departments, communes, etc.
[14] In the socialist countries the budget for Social Security is included
   in the State budget.
[15] See Chapter 3 and Appendix.

1.5   METHODS OF RECORDING

One of the thorniest problems was that of how to measure the various aggregates. The addition of market (or personal) consumption at market prices and of non-market (social) consumption at factor cost:

  (i) involves more or less substantial double-counting[16] corresponding to the amount of <u>indirect taxes</u> which partly contribute to the financing of public services;

 (ii) omits from market consumption a part of collective financing benefitting consumers to a certain extent in the form of subsidies to production;

(iii) is reflected in an evaluation of enlarged consumption which uses two different and even totally independent measuring rods according to the various items considered.

Conversely, supposing that the subsidies to production intended to reduce production costs are passed on as an equal reduction in the market price in all cases and that they therefore fully benefit the consumer, to ignore them could mean that the collective financing of household consumption is under-estimated.[17]

Thus it seemed necessary either to re-evaluate divisible public consumption at "fictitious" market prices or to estimate all consumption items at factor cost. Apart from the fact that the former procedure appeared theoretically doubtful and in practice often impossible, it had the inconvenience of introducing fictitious (positive or negative) values in the place of those recorded in existing national accounts and on which the estimates of the study had generally been based.

It was therefore agreed to proceed with an overall evaluation at <u>factor cost</u>. But while this procedure was broadly accepted in principle by all the <u>participants</u>, it could not be adopted by the socialist countries which, for theoretical and practical reasons, were not in a position to assess the amount of taxation which falls on final market consumption.

----

[16]The non-allocation of tax receipts to the expenditure of public administrations means that one cannot speak of double counting in the strict sense, and it is therefore impossible to assess the incidence of indirect taxes on market consumption. It is only as a first approximation and for reasons both of the method used and the frequently significant amount of indirect taxes (turnover tax, VAT, etc.) that the double counting has been evaluated in this manner.

[17]To the extent that market mechanisms in price formation and income distribution make it possible for the entrepreneur to absorb the subsidy into profits, the hypothesis of a 100 per cent incidence of the subsidy on the reduction of market prices is partially erroneous. It will be noted, however, that whatever the real and final incidence of subsidies to production, and as long as aggregates are considered, without distinction of categories of the population, the hypothesis according to which the total benefits of the subsidy accrue to consumers does not introduce a very important bias; this is because that part of the subsidy which is transformed into entrepreneurial income is itself consumed significantly by the latter. Such an approach is evidently very schematic but can only be replaced by a precise analysis of the real incidence of the subsidies on prices and incomes which goes far beyond the scope of the present comparison.

The compromise reached by the experts of the participating countries is summarized in Table 1.5 above which shows the two different levels at which enlarged consumption has been estimated in the two groups of countries.

To be entirely satisfactory, a comparative analysis of the development of enlarged household consumption should have been based on both current and constant prices.

For an estimate of the volume of market consumption at market prices, it would have been possible to use current deflators of consumer prices with the help of some approximations.[18]

On the other hand, when current values are given at factor cost, two sets of deflators had to be used: one for market consumption, the other for "divisible" collective consumption. In the former case, no participant disposes of indices of the factor cost of market consumption and their estimation (even indirectly on the basis of consumer price indices and taking into account the development of fiscal pressure and the rate of subsidy by type of product) and so there is a lack of information in various countries which rendered such estimates hazardous. In the case of "divisible" collective consumption it did not seem methodologically correct to apply current deflators to total public consumption since only that part corresponding to "divisible" services whose level and cost structure are very different is considered here:[19] the construction of such indices does not give rise to insoluble conceptual or methodological problems but, as in the previous case, each country represented had to abandon the attempt because of the lack of usable statistics in this field.

It was therefore decided by the various institutes participating in the study to present the results of the harmonized tables only at current prices for three years of a decade-1959 (or 1960), 1965 and 1969.

In the absence of estimates in real (or volume) terms, it was agreed: (i) on the one hand to take into account, if only as a first approximation to qualitative developments, a series of social indicators expressed in physical terms, stressing in particular the categories of health, education, housing, social services and culture and leisure. Each participant had to supply the largest possible number of significant indicators, given the existing statistical apparatus and the system of production and distribution of market and non-market goods and services; (ii) on the other hand , to leave each country free to supplement the analysis with information on the development of prices and costs, making it possible to give a more pertinent definition of "real" factors which explain the trends observed in current values.

---

[18]The price indices applied to: (i) direct purchases, (ii) social benefits in kind and (iii) total private consumptions, respectively, are bound to be different, if only because the composition of the goods and services contained in each of these expenditure categories differs. But most of the time one disposes only of the three groups of deflators (prices of private consumption in the West European countries and prices of personal expenditure in the socialist countries). For the same reasons as in the case of indices at factor cost, it was not possible for the various participating institutes to construct and estimate useful indices for these deflations.

[19]It will be noted in particular that the costs of "divisible" services included in total enlarged consumption cover essentially wage costs and only little intermediary consumption, whereas costs of total public consumption ("divisible" and "indivisible") contain also purchases of military equipment which often represent a significant part of the factor cost of public expenditure.

Table 1.7
Capitalist countries

Households		State, local authorities, Social Security	
Uses	Resources	Uses	Resources
0.4 Private consumption^a (at factor cost)	[Gross wages Incomes from entrepreneurship Income from capital	0.9 Social benefits in cash	0.7 Indirect taxes^a (Direct taxes) -(Social Security contributions) -(Other)
0.7 Indirect taxes^a -(Direct taxes) -Social Security contributions) -(Savings) -(Other)	0.9 Social benefits in cash 0.3 Social benefits in kind 0.8 Subsidies^a -(Other)	0.3 Social benefits in kind 0.8 Subsidies^a 0.5 Divisible collective consumption (at factor cost) -(Indivisible collective consumption) -(Other)	

Items in parentheses indicate operations not analysed in this study.   ^a See Section 1.2 and Table 1.5.

Table 1.8
Socialist countries

Households		State, local authorities, Social Security	
Uses	Resources	Uses	Resources
0.4 Direct household purchases (at market prices) -(Direct taxes) -(Social Security) -(Savings) -(Other)	Remuneration for work 0.9 Cash transfers from social funds -(Others)	-Social consumption funds, of which 0.9 Cash transfers 0.3 Social benefits in kind 0.5 Divisible collective services (at factor cost) -(Indivisible collective consumption) -(Other)	-(Turnover tax) -(Deduction from entrepreurial income) -(Social Security contributions) -(Other taxes)

Items in parentheses indicate operations not analysed in this study.

Table 1.9

East-West comparison—Account of enlarged household consumption

Uses	Resources
Private consumption and consumption of divisible collective services, of which:	Income from work and capital
1.00 Food	0.9 Social services and cash transfers
2.00 Beverages	0.3 Social benefits in kind
3.00 Tobacco and matches	
4.00 Clothing	
5.00 Personal care	0.8 Subsidies to production[b]
6.00 Housing	0.5 Consumption of divisible collective services
7.00 Transport	
8.00 Telecommunications	
9.00 Medical goods and service	
10.00 Social services	
11.00 Education and research	
12.00 Culture and information	
13.00 Sports, leisure and entertainment	
14.00 Other goods and services	
0.7 Indirect taxes on consumption[b]	
−(Direct taxes)	
−(Social Security contributions)	
−(Savings)	
−(Other)	

Column headers (Resources):
0.2 Direct net purchases or consumption of households from personal funds — Consumption of households from social funds — 0.4 Private consumption[a] — 0.6 Enlarged consumption

0.6 *Enlarged consumption*

Items in parentheses indicate operations not analysed in this study.

a See note (a), Table 1.3.

b Intra-West comparison only.

1.6   ACCOUNTING FRAMEWORK AND ANALYTICAL TABLES

The presentation of the basic results of the study and the selection of the most synthetic tables for comparative analyses constituted the final phase of the harmonization of methods. Starting from national accounts which are conceived from a different perspective and with different systems of statistical information, it was necessary: (i) to ensure the homogeneity of breakdowns of the detailed statistics to be supplied by the participants, and (ii) to organize the basic data in a set of more condensed tables which meet the double condition of being comparable between countries and characteristic for the purpose of the study.

1.6.1 Basic tables

Tabulations 1 and 2 summarize in a very simplified fashion how the main economic operations in the national accounting systems of the two groups of countries should be recorded.

They bring out the various discrepancies between the accounts of households and public (or private) administrations, both in the field of consumption and of distribution. In particular:
  (i) while private consumption (0.4) includes services of a collective type
      considered as marketed in West European countries (medical services,
      public transport, etc.), in the socialist countries these figures are
      included at least partly in the consumption of non-market divisible
      collective services (0.5) of the administration;
  (ii) the relationships existing between household and administration accounts
      bring out the resources of social benefits in kind (0.3) which finance
      part of private consumption in West European countries, whereas such
      expenditures form part of the administrations' accounts only in the
      socialist countries.

Tabulation 3 illustrates in a simplified way how these two accounting methods have been at least partially reconciled by aggregating in a single account all the operations which affect the final utilization of goods and services by households, with the exception of their material investments. For a precise analysis of the problems raised by the study, tabulation 3 has been set up in the form of a cross-classification presenting basic data which have been harmonized in the greatest possible detail.

Basic Table 1 distinguishes:

  horizontally, the fourteen categories of needs broken down into as many goods
    and services as available statistics permitted for the 82 items;
  vertically, into the various modalities and sectors for financing enlarged
    consumption.

Basic Table 2 specifies:

  horizontally, the different cash transfers by broad categories of risks covered;
  vertically, the sectors which finance those transfers.

Supposing that the transfers - which are largely allocated to households least favoured in the distribution of primary incomes - are used for market consumption:

this Table supplements and widens the range of information in Basic Table 1 as regards the estimate of that part of direct purchases which is financed from collective funds.

Table 1.10

Basic Table 1. Enlarged household consumption financed by individual and collective resources (in current values)

Categories of wants	Modalities and financing sectors				
	0.2	0.3	0.2+0.3=0.4	0.5	0.4+0.5=0.6
	Direct net household purchases[a]	Social benefits in kind financed by:	Private consumption[d]	Divisible collective consumption[b] financed by:	Enlarged household consumption[d]
		Social Security — State, local authorities — Trade unions — Enterprises[c] (Other social funds)		State, local authorities — Social Security — Other social funds	
1.00 Food					
1.00.A Consumption in the home					
1.01 Bread and cereal products					
....					
14.00 Other Goods and services					
14.01 Watches					
Jewellery					
....					
Total					

a Including transfers in cash. b Not including transfers in cash. c The social benefits in kind provided by the enterprises of the commercial sectors are production expenses included in the factor costs and market prices. They are therefore, at least in part, included in "direct household purchases". Thus they cannot be totalled with the other direct household purchases in section 0.2 at the risk of double counting. d At the factor costs or market prices, depending on whether it is a case of inter-West, inter-East or East-West comparisons (cf. supra 4.5).

Finally, Basic Tables 3 and 4 supply complementary information for the analysis and interpretation of preceding tables on social indicators on the one hand and investments on the other.

Basic Table 3 regroups, for the three years reviewed, the various physical indicators used for estimating in real terms the developments of consumption categories in which collective funds play the most important role.[20]

Finally, Basic Table 4 assembles for each of the three years some aggregate data on the financing of investment in health, education, social services and housing.

1.6.2 Analytical tables

Whereas the basic tables are constructed for the purpose of collecting very detailed information, the analytical tables aim at presenting the aggregates which have been defined above.[21]

They are intended to show synthetic results which eliminate to some extent the minor discrepancies between countries appearing at the more detailed level but, above all, to trace the broad lines in the development of consumption during the 1960s. They aim at bringing to light the changes in the consumption structure in their various aspects and, at the same time, to reveal the orientations of the allocation of collective funds for the satisfaction of the needs of the population during the period.

Analytical Table 1 places the main aggregates of the study in the global economic context of national accounting aggregates for production and income.

Analytical Tables 2 and 3 retrace the various aggregates of enlarged household consumption between 1959 and 1969. In particular they make it possible to assess the evolution of the respective shares of individual and collective financing and of the different forms taken by collective funds.[22] The data are presented in value at current prices, in percentages and in indices.

Analytical Table 4 is identical with Basic Table 2; it distinguishes the detail of social cash transfers by country and by year in a cross-classification with the institutions which pay the transfers. The data are given in current values, percentages of total cash transfers and indices.

Analytical Tables 5 and 6 distinguish by country and year:
  -horizontally, the fourteen categories of needs;
  -vertically, enlarged consumption divided into net direct purchases of households; and consumption financed from collective resources, the latter in turn subdivided into social benefits in kind, subsidies (only in intra-West comparison) and divi sible collective consumption, each category of collective funds distinguishing the institutional origin of financing.

Analytical Table 5 shows developments in the allocation of each of these forms of financing among the fourteen categories of needs (vertically, in percentages).

---

[20] See Section 1.5 above.
[21] See Section 1.2 above.
[22] On the assumption that: (i) all social cash transfers are used for final household consumption and (ii) in intra-West comparisons in Chapter 3 that all benefits in kind, particularly reimbursements, are evaluated at factor cost.

Table 1.11
Basic Table 2.
Social cash transfers allocated to households by financing sectors

| | Financing sectors | | | |
Cash transfers	State and local authorities	Social Security	Other social funds	Total
Pensions[a]				
Family allowances				
Pre-natal and maternity allowances				
Allowances for newborn children				
Allowances to large families				
Allowances to single wage-earners				
Etc.				
Sickness benefits				
Pensions to invalids				
Pensions to temporarily incapacitated				
Etc.				
Unemployment benefits				
Scholarships				
Other				
Assistance				
Etc.				
Total				

[a] Including pensions to war veterans.

Table 1.12
Basic Table 3. Physical indicators

Care of Children under 7 years of age

    Numbers of children under 1 year per thousand newborn children
      (infant mortality rate)
    Percentage of children under 3 years in day nurseries or maternity establish-
      ments

Health

    Percentage of resident population benefitting from free medical care (or covered
      by Social Security)
    Number of doctors per 100,000 inhabitants
    Number of hospital beds per 100,000 inhabitants

Education

    Children aged 6 to 14 in primary schools as percentage of all children in this
      age group
    Children aged 6 to 14 in secondary schools as percentage of all children in this
      age group
    Adolescents aged 15 to 18 in secondary schools as percentage of all adolescents
      in this age group
    Adolescents aged 15 to 18 receiving higher education as percentage of all
      adolescents in this age group
    Number of students receiving higher education per 100,000 inhabitants

Social Services

    Number of children benefitting from free holidays organized by enterprises,
      social services and holiday camps as percentage of the age group 1 to 8
    Number of persons benefitting from paid leave as percentage of the active
      population
    Total pensions as percentage of the gross wage bill (or average pension as
      percentage of the average pay of workers and employees)

Culture and Leisure

    Number of radio sets per 10,000 inhabitants
    Number of television sets per 10,000 inhabitants
    Number of cinema entries per 10,000 inhabitants
    Number of theatre and concert entries per 10,000 inhabitants
    Number of libraries per 10,000 inhabitants

Housing

    Average square meter per inhabitant
    Average number of inhabitants per dwelling
    Percentage of dwellings with electricity
    Percentage of dwellings with running water

Total rentals as percentage of the gross wage bill

Table 1.13
Basic Table 4. Investment expenditures

Investment categories	Sources of financing				
	State budget	Budgets of local au- thorities	Other public admini- strations finance	Other sources of finance	Total
	1	2	3	4	5=1+2+3+4
Health					
Public hospitals					
Private clinics					
Education					
Primary education					
Secondary and technical education					
Higher education and research					
Social services					
Hostels and establishments for old people					
Gross fixed capital formation of social security					
Housing					
New dwellings					
Gross maintenance and repairs					

Table 1.14
Analytical Table 1.
National product, income and enlarged household consumption

		France			....	U.S.S.R.		
		1959	1965	1969		1959	1965	1969
(a)	Gross National Product[a] ⎡Value ⎣Indices							
(b)	National income[b] ⎡Value							
(b')	Enlarged national income[c] ⎣Indices							
(c)	National income per head ⎡Value							
(c')	Enlarged national income per head ⎣Indices							
(d)	Private household consumption[d,f] ⎡Value ⎣Indices							
(e=d/a)	Share of private consumption in gross national product (per cent)							
(f=d/b) (f=d/b)	Share of private consumption in enlarged national income (per cent)							
(g)	Enlarged household consumption[e] ⎡Value ⎣Indices							
(h)	Enlarged consumption per head ⎡Value ⎣Indices							
(i=g/b) (i=g/b')	Share of enlarged consumption in enlarged national income (per cent)							

[a] For the West European countries SNA definition of the UNO.

[b] Definition SNA (for West European countries) and MPA (for socialist countries).

[c] For socialist countries enlarged National Income = National income of the system MPA (b) plus collective services of enlarged consumption.

[d] At market prices.

[e] At factor cost for intra-West comparison.

[f] See note (a), Table 1.3.

Table 1.15
Analytical Table 2. Structure and development of individual and collective
financing of enlarged household consumption in 1959, 1965 and 1969
(in values, percentages and indices)

	Countries					
	France			....	U.S.S.R.	
Aggregates	1959	1965	1969	1959	1965	1969
(a) Direct net household purchases or personal consumption (at market prices)[a]						
(b) less: Indirect taxes[b]						
(c) plus: Subsidies[b]						
(d=a-b+c) Direct net household purchases (at factor cost)[b]						
(e) Social benefits in kind						
(f=d+e) Private consumption[c,e]						
(g) Public consumption of divisible services[d]						
(h=f+g) Enlarged household consumption (h') enlarged consumption per head of resident population						

[a] Used in intra-West and East-West comparisons.

[b] Used in intra-West comparisons only.

[c] At market prices for intra-East and East-West comparisons, at factor cost for intra-West comparisons.

[d] Services of general administration included in intra-West comparison, excluded in intra-East and East-West comparison.

[e] See note (a), Table 1.3.

Table 1.16
Analytical Table 3. Share of enlarged consumption financed directly
or indirectly from collective funds: 1959, 1965 and 1969
(In values, percentages and indices)

		Countries					
		France		....		U.S.S.R.	
	Aggregates	1959	1965	1969	1959	1965	1969
(a)	Social benefits in kind						
	(a1) Reimbursements						
(b)	Public consumption of divisible services[a]						
(c)	Subsidies[b]						
(d)	Social cash transfers						
(e=a+b+c+d)	Total						

[a] See Table 1.15, note (d).

[b] See Table 1.15, note (b).

Analytical Table 6 traces the development of the financing structure for each of the fourteen categories of needs (horizontally, in percentages).

Whereas Analytical Tables 2 and 6 have been conceived with a view of regrouping the various forms of expenditure according to the nature of goods and services, Analytical Table 7 adopts a quasi-functional approach to the social funds which finance household consumption. It is not possible to consider simultaneously, by categories of goods and services, the part of cash transfers for which by definition[23] there is no prior allocation to the acquisition of specific goods and services, on the one hand, and the various benefits in kind which are directly linked to a determined consumption, on the other. By contrast, the allocation of collective funds in cash or in kind aims more or less explicitly not only at reducing the disparities of consumption between social groups but also at counterbalancing risks incurred, notably that of a loss of income through sickness, old age, etc. In this sense, the benefits, transfers and collective consumption categories can be regrouped under the heading of general functions: health, social services, education, etc., on behalf of which the collective funds operate in various preferential forms.

---

[23] But at least part of these transfers is consumed (see footnote 22) and included in "direct purchases" of households: it is therefore not possible to add total collective funds including cash transfers and direct purchases without double-counting.

Table 1.17

Analytical Tables 5 and 6.

Structure of enlarged consumption and its financing by categories of needs (percentages)

Countries:	France										U.S.S.R.									
	Net direct house-hold pur-chases	Collective funds								Enlarged consump-tion	Net direct house-hold pur-chases	Collective funds								Enlarged consump-tion
		Social benefits in kind			Subsi-dies[c]			Collec-tive di-visible con.				Social benefits in kind			Subsi-dies[d]			Collec-tive di-visible con.		
Categories of needs		Social Security	State and local auth.	Other	Social Security	State and local auth.	Other	Social Security	State and local auth.	Other		Social Security	State and local auth.	Other	Social Security	State and local auth.	Other	Social Security	State and local auth.	Other	
1.00 Food 1959																					
1965																					
1969																					
2.00 Beverages 1959										100[b]											
1965										100[b]											
1969										100[b]											
⋮																					
14.00 Other goods and services 1959																					
1965																					
1969																					
15.00 Total 1959										100[a]											
1965										100[a]											
1969										100[a]											

a Analytical Table 5.
b Analytical Table 6.
c For intra-West comparison only.
d Empty columns for socialist countries.

This is why Analytical Table 7 presents the following cross-classification (in values and percentages):

- vertically, the various categories of collective funds allocated to households-cash transfers, social benefits in kind, subsidies (only in intra-West comparison), and divisible collective consumption broken down by institutional origin;
- horizontally, categories of needs interpreted here in terms of functions. To the extent that only collective funds are considered, it seemed preferable to stress mainly: health (9.00), social services (10.00) and education (11.00). The other categories (1.00 to 8.00 and 12.00 to 14.00) are given in their aggregates with some exceptions.

Various cash transfers have been broken down by functions according to the following conventions:

9.00   Health: daily sickness indemnity and pensions to incapacitated persons;

10.00   Social services: old-age pensions, family allowances, pre-natal and maternity allowances, unemployment benefits and other (assistance in cash to the needs, aid to children, etc.);

11.00   Education: Scholarships, pre-salaries for students;

1.00 to 8.00   Other needs: Allocations for loss of income of military
    and   personnel, various cash benefits (allocations to repatriated
12.00 to 14.00   persons in France, etc.).

1.7   CONCLUSIONS AND COMMENTS ON METHODS

A mass of statistics has been supplied by each participant but the economic, social and institutional structures differ all the more - even within a group of countries with similar socio-economic principles and political ideologies - the more the analysis enters into detail. There was no a priori reason to expect that the information on the period 1959 to 1969 would reveal parallel orientations of private and collective consumption in all countries and identical preoccupations in these respects on the part of the various public authorities. Conversely, as it appears from Chapter 4, some striking similarities appear from the results of this study.

Unless one were to sketch a large fresco which would merely set the different countries side by side without attempting a real comparison or deriving major results, the only possible course to be adopted had to be a flexible one: (i) the preparation of national reports which bring out the various facets of the social policies pursued in each country; (ii) the formulation of two syntheses for the socialist and West European countries; (iii) a tentative global analysis of both groups of countries (Chapter 4).

The harmonized pattern of the Basic and Analytical Tables provides a common denominator for the synthesis and interpretation of developments in the following fields:

- the share of enlarged consumption in national resources (Analytical Table 1);
- the allocation of this consumption between "market" and "non-market" forms of acquiring goods and services (Analytical Tables 2 and 6);
- the structure of enlarged consumption by categories of needs and goods and services (Analytical Table 5);
- the pattern of financing the satisfaction of needs from individual or collective resources (Analytical Tables 2,3 and 6);
- institutional structures and the forms taken by collective funds allocated to household incomes and consumption (Analytical Tables 4,6 and 7).

Table 1.18

Analytical Table 7.   Structure of all collective funds benefitting households
(In values and percentages)

Countries:		France						U.S.S.R.				
	Categories of wants (functions)	Cash transfers (Social Security / State and local auth. / Other)	Social benefits in kind (Social Security / State and local auth. / Other)	Subsidies[a] (Social Security / State and local auth. / Other)	Divisible collective con. (Social Security / State and local auth. / Other)	Total	Cash transfers (Social Security / State and local auth. / Other)	Social benefits in kind (Social Security / State and local auth. / Other)	Subsidies[a] (Social Security / State and local auth. / Other)	Divisible collective con. (Social Security / State and local auth. / Other)	Total
	9.00 Health 1959 / 1965 / 1969										
	10.00 Social Services 1959 / 1965 / 1969										
	11.00 Education 1959 / 1965 / 1969										
	1.00 to 8.00 + / 12.00 to 14.00 Other Needs 1959 / 1965 / 1969										
	15.00 Total 1959 / 1965 / 1969										

a Intra-West comparison only.

But starting from this common approach, the syntheses for East and West have sometimes stressed more precise aspects, either because available information made this possible onle for one group of countries or because they represented important factors in social policy during the period. It must be noted in particular that among socialist countries the expansion of paid personal services is more deeply studied. The intra-West comparison devotes instead more attention to the modalities of financing from collective funds and to the evolution of the institutional structures of public and semi-public funds.

In spite of the efforts made to tackle the problems raised in the study in their aggregate as well as to harmonize the concepts and methods of comparison, it must be admitted that important gaps remain:

  (i) An inadequate representation of Western Europe compared with the presence among the five socialist participants of the most important countries of the group makes for a certain imbalance in the East-West comparison. While the representative character of the group of socialist countries cannot be questioned, the many similarities between France and Italy and the particular case of Switzerland makes it impossible to arrive at generalized conclusions for the whole of Western Europe without taking into account the Anglo-Saxon countries, the Federal Republic of Germany and Scandinavia.

 (ii) As to the methods adopted, the limits to a harmonization of concepts, nomenclature, estimates at factor cost and of volume have already been stated and need not be repeated at this point.

(iii) Finally, it must be stressed that one important aspect of the study has not been dealt with here: namely, the different consumption patterns of various categories of the population. With the exception of Hungary and France, the comparisons do not refer, or only in a highly fragmentary and sporadic fashion, to the question of whether the intervention by the public authorities, either in income formation, in market consumption or in the production of non-market services, succeeds in reducing-and by how much-social and economic inequalities in the fields of housing, transport, health, education,etc.

In other words, this comparison reveals neither the precise objectives of socio-economic policies which have been pursued with the help of the mechanisms described nor what the redistributive effects of collective funds allocated to households have been.

However, in spite of these limitations and the necessarily global character of such a study, the comparisons of the following chapters have the merit of throwing a new light on certain aspects of social and economic policy for the satisfaction of population needs with the help of more precise methods and a better harmonization than existing systems of national accounting have so far been able to do.

CHAPTER 2

A Comparative Study of the Structure and Development of Enlarged Consumption in Czechoslovakia, German Democratic Republic, Hungary, Poland and the U.S.S.R.*

2.1   INTRODUCTION: BASIC CONCEPTS

2.1.1   Aim and object of the study

This study was undertaken under the auspices of the European Coordination Centre for Research and Documentation in Social Sciences within the framework of an international project on "Personal and Collective Consumption in some East and West European Countries: A comparative study" (PLAN/CONS).

The purpose of the project is to devise a methodology for the formulation of criteria, making it possible to optimize the consumption pattern of the population and to define the qualitative content of consumption. The study aims to establish the principles for a breakdown of consumption by sources from which it is financed (family budgets or centralized funds), by allocation procedures for consumer goods (according to work performed or needs from social funds) and by forms of organization for the satisfaction of need (individual or collective).

The breakdown of consumption into its main components, correctly defined, provides a basis for scientifically founded forecasts of economic development, the formulation of socio-economic policies and the centralized determination of the consumption structure.

A specific feature of this study is that it is based on an analysis of "expanded household consumption" of the population which includes all goods and services, irrespective of the method of their allocation, the forms of their exchange and the organization of their consumption. This approach was adopted so as to permit a study of the consumption structure as a whole and not only of that part which is most easily regulated by central decisions. Although, seen from the point of view of the consumer, the centralized determination of the consumption structure affects only social services directly, all the components of the system are closely interdependent and influence each other. Further, even though the State cannot exert a direct influence on the structure of individual consumption, it nevertheless disposes powerful means of indirect action such as the system of price formulation, publicity, etc.

---

*This chapter has been prepared by: Dr. O. Sobek and Dr. J. Stanko, Czechoslovakia; Prof. G.Manz, G.D.R.; Dr. E. John, Dr. O. Elteto, Hungary; Dr. Z. Rajewski, Dr. T. Dmoch, Poland; and Prof. S. Shatalin, Prof. N. Rimashevskaya and Dr. I. Korkhova, U.S.S.R.

This chapter presents the results of a statistical analysis of the structure of "enlarged consumption" in the light of its development in each of the participating socialist countries.

From such an analysis it is possible, in principle:

   (i) to derive the major components of enlarged consumption, broken down into personal and collective consumption, market and nonmarket forms of the allocation of a product, individual and collective forms of the organization of consumption, consumption in the form of goods and services, etc.;
  (ii) to trace in detail (depending on the information available) the changes in the consumption pattern for each category of needs;
 (iii) to assess the role of social consumption funds and of the centralized mechanism for the allocation of consumer goods in total consumption;
  (iv) to identify the main factors which influence changes in the composition of enlarged consumption.

An interpretation of certain tendencies in the evolution of enlarged consumption (derived empirically and taking into account the factors which influence it), the determination of their interaction and effects, as well as their formalization with the help of appropriate mathematical models, can provide useful elements for forecasting. Such tendencies are more significant if they emerge from a comparative study of a number of countries, even though this analysis is bound to be conventional in many respects.

An examination of the allocation and consumption processes, seen from the consumer's viewpoint, makes it possible to study the problems of feed-back, that is the effects of conditions of life and of allocation patterns on production, economic activity and growth. A study of the allocation of social funds to socio-economic groups of the population constitutes the basis for an analysis and evaluation of the attitudes of various strata of society towards different ways of satisfying needs and for arriving at a set of individual preferences.

The results of the study are preliminary and-although useful as far as they go-insufficient for the purposes outlined above. Additional research would therefore be required to complete the study.

2.1.2   Main concepts and procedures for the calculation of indicators

Enlarged consumption is not an official indicator in socialist countries but it has been evaluated and analysed in a series of studies undertaken in the Soviet Union and the other socialist countries. This chapter deals with enlarged consumption according to the methods formulated in the PLAN/CONS project, to the extent that an overall scheme can be fitted into national accounting systems.

Various aggregates of enlarged consumption have also been estimated with the help of this method but they differ from the statistical indicators published in socialist countries. Thus, paid leave is not included in social consumption funds; the amounts allocated from social funds to education, health, etc., do not include expenditure on food and capital investment. Certain items have been regrouped, and this again makes for differences between the data presented here and official statistics.

The concept of enlarged consumption used in this study relates to current consumer expenditure rather than to the volume of goods actually consumed; thus it does not include the utilization of stocks of durable consumer goods, and their consumption is therefore under estimated. On the other hand, the consumption of durables is evaluated on the basis of the sums spent on purchases in the course of a year whereas their consumption extends over a longer period. Clearly, expenditure and consumption do not coincide in time; thus, strictly speaking, the consumption of durables should be evaluated on the basis of their utilization in a year. But such an evaluation comes up against insurmountable statistical difficulties. That is why the consumption of durables is conventionally calculated on the basis of actual current expenditure for their purchase.

The meaning of consumption is that the population appropriates, in individual or collective form, material goods and services produced and allocated within the setting of the existing productive system.

It is logical to distinguish between main consumption categories according to the mechanism which shapes the consumption pattern and the factors which influence it:

   (i) personal consumption, financed by households (from all incomes, including cash payments from social funds) and social consumption, that is free or partially free (in the form of goods and services supplied from social funds); if self-consumption is excluded, this breakdown does, in fact, coincide with the division into market and non-market consumption;[1]

 (ii) consumption classified by different needs of population (food, clothing, housing, health and education and other goods and services);

(iii) consumption financed from wage funds and from social funds according to the forms (and procedures) of the allocation of consumer goods.

In a socialist economy, the breakdown into categories and into forms of consumption is based on different criteria and the respective components do not coincide since they reflect different economic mechanisms and processes. This relationship between market and non-market consumption reflects exchange relationships which are formed in the process of social reproduction and which characterize consumption from the viewpoint of the production channels of the goods and services consumed. Market consumption takes place within the market sphere and the process which determines its structure is covered up by the price mechanism and the use of money as a universally accepted means of exchange. Non-market consumption falls outside money-commodity exchanges in the strict sense and takes place within the framework of directly allocated social services. In the scheme adopted, the latter covers that part of social funds which the population receives as benefits in the form of freely supplied goods and services. The two categories-market and non-market consumption-do not coincide with the breakdown of personal consumption and consumption financed from social funds. In this context, food consumption from privately owned plots of land by workers, employees and members of agricultural cooperatives (so-called "self-consumption") as well as on-farm consumption in kind of collective farmers, all constitute consumption categories which are placed outside the market although they have nothing in common with consumption from social funds. For the sake of simplification they are included in personal market consumption. By contrast, one part of transfers from social consumption funds passes through the market. This is why the breakdown of consumption into a personal and a social component adopted in the project is of limited significance from the viewpoint of interpreting social consumption. It is with this reservation in mind that the relationship between personal and social consumption shown in Tables 2.2, 2.6 and 2.7 must be viewed.

---

[1]Personal and social consumption must be distinguished from individual and collective forms of the organization of consumption. The latter subdivision delimits social services and self-service.

The need to consider the consumption of goods and services in its aggregate is self-evident. It must be stressed that only by means of such an approach is it possible to study the adaptation of the consumption structure to the pattern of collective needs. A detailed analysis of the consumption structure is presented in Tables 2.13 and 2.17.

The wage fund is allocated to individuals in proportion to their productive contribution and in accordance with the quantity and quality of work performed by the various participants in social production; the material and cultural goods supplied from social consumption funds are allocated according to the needs of all members of society and without a direct link with their contribution to gross national product. This is why the consumption of pensioners paid for from their pensions, that of students from their scholarships and that of the temporarily unemployed from their incapacity allowances, etc., while it is considered as market consumption from the point of view of the method of exchange, is linked to social funds from the point of view of the allocation process since it is financed from social sources and supplied according to needs. In examining the role of social funds in enlarged consumption from the viewpoint of the individual consumer, only material goods and services, the consumption of which can be clearly individualized, have been considered. All consumption which falls outside this definition serves the satisfaction of the needs of society as a whole; it therefore belongs to the category of public (indivisible) consumption and is not covered in this study. The latter consumption category includes the general administration, justice, defence, internal affairs, the maintenance of roads, bridges, gardens and parks, the protection against fire and the operating costs of social service institutions.

Central social consumption funds-and these predominate-are fed mainly from the State budget; the administrations, social organizations, agricultural coopera-tives,etc., supply the decentralized sources of finance. The population does not directly contribute to social consumption funds.[2]

As a source of income to consumers, the social funds take the form of:

    cash transfers-pensions, scholarships and allowances;
    free goods and services (education, health, culture, etc.);
    goods and services supplied on favourable terms (housing, transport, etc.).

Before reaching the consumer, the goods and services in the first category take the form of unallocated household incomes, and pass through the family budget and are acquired through money-commodity exchanges. In their second and third forms the social funds reach consumers directly via the system of social services supplied outside the family budget and the market. In this context the goods and services allocated from social funds are evaluated on the basis of their production costs (factor costs).

In examining consumption according to the satisfaction of needs or the form of organization, one can distinguish between individual consumption on the basis of concrete household purchases (considered as the primary individual consumption unit) on the one hand, and collective consumption within the setting of appropriate institutions for the provision of health services, instruction, culture, child education, public catering, etc., which in some way take over the functions of household consumption, on the other. The different forms of the satisfaction of food requirements are a striking illustration of this distinction. A meal taken in the home represents an individual form of consumption whereas meals taken in hospitals, schools, canteens, nurseries, etc., must be included in col-lective consumption.

---

[2]In Hungary a part of the pension fund is financed from contributions of earners.

It is evident that the classification of enlarged consumption and of its components outlined above is to a large extent conventional, and the same applies to any other statistical classification. The delimitation of the different categories is relative and flexible and depends on the purpose for which the classification has been made. Further, each group contains composite forms of consumption which cannot be attributed to any class in a precise way.

2.1.3   Sources of information and difficulties of a comparative analysis

A comparative analysis of the development and structure of enlarged consumption in Czechoslovakia, the G.D.R., Hungary, Poland and the U.S.S.R. in the years 1960, 1965, 1969 was made on the basis of a series of analytical tables which will be examined below. These tables were derived from basic tables for each country (see Appendix B); a common pattern for their presentation has been formulated by Professor V. Cao-Pinna.

All countries adopted a common concept in preparing the documentation, and the statistical information was presented on the basis of a jointly agreed tabulation; even so, serious difficulties were constantly encountered because of the specific national characteristics of the data and the peculiar features of needs and of statistical accounting methods; in each country the way in which the data are obtained differs, and the social institutions which allocate goods and services have characteristics of their own.

But the difficulties in arriving at a comparative analysis stem above all from the different content of the items listed in the analytical tables. Thus, in contrast to other countries, the items "Education, culture, sports, leisure and entertainment" are lumped together in the Hungarian data.

In the G.D.R., for instance, enlarged consumption does not include self-consumption of agricultural products. The item 4.00 "Clothing and shoes" does not include repairs and made-to-measure clothing, and item 3.00 "Medical goods and services" does not cover the cost of staying in sanatoria and rest homes, while the relevant figures have been estimated for the other countries.

In Poland, item 11.00 "Education" does not include the purchase of school books by individual consumers, and the same applies to the U.S.S.R.; these expenditures figure under item 12.00 "Culture and information".

In contrast to the classification adopted, expenditure on beverages and "self-consumption" of food does not figure under those headings in the U.S.S.R. data. Beverages are included in item 1.00 "Food products" and self-consumption of food in item 14.00 "Other goods and services". Item 6.00 "Housing" excludes State expenditure for housing freely supplied to certain categories of workers: railway workers, doctors and teachers in rural regions, etc. Item 7.00 "Transport" does not cover the cost of vehicles which social security institutions put at the free disposal of invalids; nor does it cover the free transport services from which certain categories of the population (war invalids, certain groups of pensioners, transport workers, etc.) benefit. Item 13.00 "Sports, leisure and entertainment" does not include free performances for children and the cost of tourism and hotel services. These expenditure items figure in item 14.00. Such peculiarities of the U.S.S.R. data give rise to notable differences between the information presented and the adopted classification.

In the tables on Czechoslovakia all expenditure from social funds is covered from a unique source-the State budget; this means that the part of the population's consumption paid for by society is considerably under-valued. Further,nurseries and orphanages are included in item 9.00 "Public health" and kindergardens in item 11.00 "Education", whereas they figure under 10.00 "social services in all the other countries.

Many other examples of this kind could be quoted. However, it was impossible to eliminate such discrepancies. The difficulties in interpreting the statistical information are accentuated by differences in the prices of consumer goods and services.

Even though the methods and main categories of allocation are identical in socialist countries, considerable differences exist in the organization of institutions responsible for the provision of social services and, especially, in statistical accounting systems.

All these features reduce the comparability of the data, when broken down in detail, both as to level and composition, even within one group of countries. The subsequent analysis must therefore be considered only as an attempt to compare general tendencies and broad patterns in each country and to explain their deviation from general trends.

Another convention of the study concerning longer-term tendencies and, notably, an evaluation at constant prices, must not be lost sight of. The present study is based entirely on current prices and this has certain implications for all the conclusions which have been drawn.

2.2   GENERAL ANALYSIS OF ENLARGED CONSUMPTION

2.2.1   Enlarged consumption and national income

Enlarged consumption is closely linked to the national income produced by society; it is therefore of considerable interest to observe the development of the two series side by side (see Table 2.1). In socialist countries the growth of national income is the material basis for enlarged consumption and for the improvement of living standards in all its various aspects.

The table shows that in all countries the rate of growth of national income accelerated and was more rapid in the second than in the first sub-period (1965-1969 and 1960-1965 respectively). The only exception is Poland, where the rate of increase remained virtually unchanged in the two periods. Poland achieved the highest rate of growth over the whole period, followed by the U.S.S.R., Hungary and Czechoslovakia, with the G.D.R. occupying last place (see Chart 2.1).

The data are given in current prices and these tend to be stable.

Consumer price indices

	1960 = 100	1965	1969
Czechoslovakia	100	101	107
G.D.R.	100	100	100
Hungary	100	102	105
Poland	100	106	113
U.S.S.R.	100	100	100

Between 59 and 75 per cent of the national income of socialist countries (varying between countries and periods) is absorbed by the consumption funds for the satisfaction of material and cultural needs and the performance of various socio-economic tasks. It is not surprising that the rates of increase of expanded consumption tend to reflect those of national income in all countries and phases of development. However, a certain decline in the share of the consumption fund in national income is a common feature in all countries except for the U.S.S.R. where it remained practically unchanged. This means that the accumulation fund in these

Table 2.1

Main indicators of economic development In national currencies at current prices and indices (1960–100)

		Czechoslovakia			G.D.R.			Hungary			Poland			U.S.S.R.		
		1960	1965	1968	1960	1965	1969	1960	1965	1968	1960	1965	1969	1960	1965	1969
I. National income	values	157.5	175.1	245.7	71.0	84.2	102.9	147.1	176.1	229.8	375.1	527.6	686.2	145.0	193.5	261.9
	indices	100.0	111.2	156.0	100.0	118.6	144.8	100.0	119.8	156.3	100.0	140.7	182.9	100.0	133.4	180.6
II. Enlarged national income[a]	values	173.8	188.0	277.2	83.2	99.0	120.6	160.2	193.3	249.2	420.0	595.0	760.0	160.5	217.6	294.2
	indices	100.0	108.1	159.5	100.0	118.6	145.0	100.0	120.7	155.6	100.0	141.5	180.7	100.0	136.0	183.5
III. Consumption funds of households	values	100.4	116.3	146.0	52.9	60.5	70.8	107.1	129.4	157.4	256.3	342.5	439.4	102.1	136.1	181.3
	indices	100.5	115.8	145.4	100.0	115.6	137.7	100.0	120.8	147.0	100.0	133.6	171.6	100.0	133.3	177.6
IV. Share of household consumption in national income (per cent)		64.6	70.2	58.6	74.5	71.9	68.8	72.6	73.5	68.5	68.3	64.2	64.1	70.4	70.4	69.2
V. Enlarged consumption	values	120.9	147.3	185.6	63.8	73.3	87.5	115.5	140.2	170.5	292.8	398.2	517.9	117.0	158.0	217.1
	indices	100.0	121.8	153.5	100.0	114.9	137.1	100.0	121.4	147.6	100.0	136.0	176.9	100.0	135.0	185.5
VI. Share of enlarged consumption in expanded national income (per cent)		69.5	78.3	66.9	76.7	74.0	72.6	72.1	72.5	68.4	69.7	66.9	68.1	72.9	72.6	73.8
VII. Enlarged consumption per head	values	8857	10403	12922	3708	4312	5146	11567	13812	16620	9875	12644	15907	550.8	688.1	906.0
	indices	100.0	117.4	145.9	100.0	116.2	138.3	100.0	119.4	143.7	100.0	128.3	161.1	100.0	124.9	164.4

a Including services rendered to the population (as for expanded consumption).

countries increased more rapidly than the consumption fund. In the U.S.S.R. both funds increased at the same rate.

In Czechoslovakia the share of the consumption fund rose substantially above its 1960 level in 1965 but in 1968 it registered an even more marked decline. This is due to the fact that national income remained virtually stationary between 1960 and 1965, whereas the consumption fund continued to grow. National income rose sharply towards 1968 while the consumption fund experienced only a moderate rise. It must be recalled that the changes in the consumption fund follow their own particular rules; its development is notably influenced by demographic factors (increasing numbers of pensioners, for instance) which may cause its rapid expansion even though national income increases only slowly. This is what happened in Czechoslovakia at the beginning of the 1960s.

In all countries the behaviour of the share of the expanded consumption fund in expanded national income closely follows the evolution of the share of the consumption fund in national income. Thus the latter indicator largely determines the total volume and structure of consumption.

Enlarged national income (including the services which figure in enlarged consumption) increased in all countries somewhat more rapidly than national income measured by material production. This was due to more rapid growth of the tertiary sector than of material product.

In the period reviewed, the share of the enlarged consumption fund in enlarged national income declined somewhat in all countries except for the U.S.S.R., and the share of the consumption fund in national income followed the same tendency. In the U.S.S.R. a small increase in that share was accounted for by a more rapid rate of expansion of the tertiary sector.

The enlarged consumption fund per head of the population rose continuously in all countries, more particularly in the U.S.S.R. and Poland, corresponding to its more rapid global growth in the two countries.

2.2.2   The structure of enlarged consumption according to methods of distribu-
          tion and forms of allocation (see Tables 2.2, 2.3, 2.4)

The classification of the enlarged consumption structure adopted in Tables 2.2-2.4 is not entirely clear-cut. The methods of primary and secondary income distribution overlap with the forms of exchange of goods and services. This is due to some extent to the construction of a unique tabulation scheme for countries with different economic systems and hence also different mechanisms of distribution and institutional arrangements. In a socialist economy the social consumption funds must in the first place be considered as a means of allocating the goods and services produced by society, although they are also largely linked to the form of exchange of consumer goods and services. It follows that the conventional character of the indices used (due entirely to the manner in which the tables have been constructed) as well as terminological peculiarities must be borne in mind when examining the data in Tables 2.2-2.4.

The major part of national income spent on enlarged consumption reaches the population as remuneration for work in the form of wages and salaries and the retribution of members of agricultural cooperatives. At the same time the population receives an increasing number of goods and services from social consumption funds.

Table 2.2

The sources of financing (individual or collective) of enlarged consumption in 1960
(in national currencies and percentages)

	Czechoslovakia		G.D.R.		Hungary		Poland		U.S.S.R.	
	values	%	values	%	values	%	values	%	values	%
1. Direct household purchases in the market (at market prices)[a]	105.3	87.1	51.5	80.7	102.0	88.3	262.3	89.6	101.9	87.1
2. Social benefits in kind (at factor cost)	15.6	12.9	12.3	19.3	3.4	2.9	6.2	2.1	2.8	2.4
3. Public consumption (at factor cost)					10.1	8.8	24.3	8.3	12.3	10.5
4. Enlarged consumption	120.9	100.0	63.8	100.0	115.5	100.0	292.8	100.0	117.0	100.0
(a) collective consumption (2 + 3)	15.6	12.9	12.3	19.3	13.5	11.7	30.5	10.5	15.1	12.9
(b) cash payments from collective funds	20.0	16.6	6.3	9.9	8.3	7.2	23.1	7.9	10.4	8.9
(c = a+b) financed from collective funds	35.6	29.5	18.6	29.2	21.8	18.9	53.6	18.4	25.5	21.8

a Including self-consumption and consumption in kind received as remuneration of work; this item covers all individual consumption.

Table 2.3

The sources of financing (individual or collective) of enlarged consumption in 1965
(in national currencies and percentages)

	Czechoslovakia		G.D.R.		Hungary		Poland		U.S.S.R.	
	values	%	values	%	values	%	values	%	values	%
1. Direct household purchases in the market (at market prices)[a]	128.9	87.5	58.6	79.9	122.1	87.1	353.7	88.8	133.4	84.4
2. Social benefits in kind (at factor cost)	18.4	12.5	14.7	20.1	4.8	3.4	10.2	2.6	5.1	3.2
3. Public consumption (at factor cost)					13.3	9.5	34.3	8.6	19.5	12.4
4. Enlarged consumption	147.3	100.0	73.3	100.0	140.2	100.0	398.2	100.0	158.0	100.0
(a) collective consumption (2 + 3)	18.4	12.5	14.7	20.1	18.1	12.9	44.5	11.2	24.6	15.6
(b) cash payments from collective funds	24.3	16.5	8.3	11.3	12.6	9.0	32.9	8.3	14.9	9.4
(c = a+b) financed from collective funds	42.7	29.0	23.0	31.4	30.7	21.9	77.4	19.5	39.5	25.0

a Including self-consumption and consumption in kind received as remuneration of work: this item covers all individual consumption.

Table 2.4

The sources of financing (individual or collective) of enlarged consumption in 1969
(in national currencies and percentages)

	Czechoslovakia		G.D.R.		Hungary		Poland		U.S.S.R.	
	values	%	values	%	values	%	values	%	values	%
1. Direct household purchases in the market (at market prices)[a]	161.2	86.8	69.8	79.8	148.6	87.2	457.0	88.2	183.1	84.4
2. Social benefits in kind (at factor cost)					6.0	3.5	13.7	2.6	6.8	3.1
3. Public consumption (at factor cost)	24.4	13.2	17.7	20.2	15.8	9.3	47.2	9.2	27.1	12.5
4. Enlarged consumption	185.6	100.0	87.5	100.0	170.5	100.0	517.9	100.0	217.1	100.0
(a) collective consumption (2 + 3)	24.4	13.2	17.7	20.2	21.8	12.8	60.9	11.8	33.9	15.6
(b) cash payments from collective funds	30.9	16.6	10.1	11.6	17.7	10.4	47.7	9.2	21.6	10.0
(c = a+b) financed from collective funds	55.3	29.8	27.8	31.8	39.5	23.2	108.6	21.0	55.5	25.6

a Including self-consumption and consumption in kind received as remuneration of work; this item covers all individual consumption.

Ignoring the conventional character of the calculations, it can be seen that the share of goods and services in total enlarged consumption obtained from social funds ranges between 21 and 32 per cent and tended to increase in all countries.

Social consumption funds play the most important role in the G.D.R. (see Chart 2.2) because of the larger volume of consumption in kind supplied free or partially free in that country. This in turn is due to the operation of a highly developed system of freely supplied goods and services from social consumption funds. In particular, the G.D.R. supplies a larger number of free services to children than do other socialist countries: compulsory ten-year school attendance is generalized, pupils take their meals at school at reduced prices and there are numerous pre-school institutions. The G.D.R. ranks among the first in the field of medical services, notably with respect to the number of hospital beds per 10,000 inhabitants and the number of places in sanatoria and rest homes; in addition the population receives free medicines (on doctor's prescription).

In Czechoslovakia a large proportion of the social fund in enlarged consumption is spent on cash payments.[3] This is due not only to the demographic structure of the population (for details, see below) but also to the State assuming greater responsibility than elesewhere, for persons unable to work, by providing pensions, family allowances, etc.

Social consumption funds contribute least to enlarged consumption in Poland for the following reasons:

(i) in the period under review, the owners of individual farm units and their families (that is 23 per cent of the population in 1969) were not covered by free medical assistance;[4]
(ii) there were relatively few pre-school institutions;
(iii) for demographic reasons (the youngest population), the proportion of pensioners to the total population is the lowest among socialist countries.

The rate of increase of social consumption funds (see Chart 2.3) was highest in the U.S.S.R. (9.0 per cent), followed by Poland (8.1 per cent), Hungary (7.7 per cent), Czechoslovakia (5.6 per cent) and finally the G.D.R. (4.6 per cent). The development of social funds is largely determined by a range of functional tasks assumed by this allocation mechanism in each of the socialist countries. In a socialist society these funds have several socio-economic tasks. Above all they provide material support to members of society unable to work and with no other independent means of livelihood: children, old persons, the temporarily incapacitated and students who prepared themselves for jobs and received appropriate training; the latter group must be considered as "socially" and not physically unable to work. In carrying out these functions, the social funds contribute towards an equalization of conditions of life and standards of consumption of the various strata of the population, whatever the family burdens borne by the active members of a household.

The second-and no less important-function of social funds consists in ensuring, for all members of society, equal opportunities for the satisfaction of a series of socio-cultural needs such as the protection of health, instruction, the education of children, leisure, etc.; and this independently of their material conditions and of income differentials arising "objectively" from the principle of distributing incomes according to work performed. This function derives from the

---

[3]The share of social consumption funds in Czechoslovakia is underestimated in Table 2.2 and the following tables because the data cover only financing from the State budget.
[4]Since 1972 medical assistance has been rendered freely to the whole population.

necessity for society to stimulate the development of each of its members within the setting of the productive and cultural levels attained and by promoting a harmonious development of the individual, to consolidate the socialist way of life.

It is with the help of social funds that society exercises its influence on the consumption structure with a view to improving and rationalizing it. Finally, the social funds contribute to the expansion of collective forms of consumption and of social services. Social development is promoted not only by means of an expansion of production but also through an increasing satisfaction of needs in its collective and social forms. In this way consumption is rendered more efficient and economical and its organization more rational.

Economic development and increased production in socialist countries favour the extension and consolidation of these functions and the latter is, in turn, promoted by the growing range of potential beneficiaries of goods and services supplied from social funds. This results not only from natural demographic factors such as ageing population and an increase in the number of persons unable to work. It also arises from the scientific and technical revolution, the increased role of education, of qualified manpower, the rapid obsolescence of knowledge acquired, etc.-all of which prolong the span of time devoted to study in the life of an individual and raise the number of persons of working age who withdraw from social production to acquire new knowledge and skills.

In addition, in the period under review, the socialist countries have witnessed an increase in the number of beneficiaries of goods and services supplied from social funds as a result of new measures adopted to promote welfare.

In Czechoslovakia, for instance, during the period reviewed, old-age pensions have been raised regularly, the system of sickness pay and of old-age pensions for members of agricultural cooperatives has been considerably improved, and family allowances have been raised. Salaries of personnel working in the fields of education and health have been increased.

In Hungary all categories of pensioners had their pensions raised between 1960 and 1969 and legislation has been passed which grants women the right to abstain from work during the three years following the birth of a child while receiving family child allowances.

In the G.D.R. old-age pensions and birth premia have been increased; the quantity of food supplies in primary and secondary schools has been raised.

In Poland all categories of retired persons have had their pensions increased; compulsory school attendance of twelve years-from 7 to 19-has been introduced.

In the U.S.S.R. salaries of teaching and medical personnel have been raised considerably involving larger outlays in these fields; a system of State-financed pensions for collective farmers has replaced the previous pensions paid by the collective farms themselves, and their level has been considerably raised; the retirement age of collective farmers has been lowered from 65 to 60 years for men and from 60 to 55 years for women; compulsory school attendance of eight years has been generalized.

The increase in the number of pupils in the various types of schools and of children in pre-school establishments is shown in Table 2.5. The increase in the number of persons benefitting from health services is given in Table 2.27.

Table 2.5
Indicators of the development of education (in thousands)

	Czechoslovakia			G.D.R.			Hungary			Poland			U.S.S.R.		
	1960	1965	1968	1960	1965	1969	1960	1965	1969	1960	1965	1969	1960	1965	1969
1. Number of pupils in primary and secondary schools	2227	2334	2077	2059	2426	2615	1392	1414	1255	5272	5815	5961	36051	47991	49080
2. (a) Total number of teachers	93	103	105	86	102	134	57.0	62.0	63.0	193	227	265	1994	2382	2472
(b) for 1000 pupils	41.0	44.0	50.5	41.7	42.0	51.2	41.1	44.0	49.8	36.7	46.4	44.5	55.3	49.7	50.4
3. Number of pupils in secondary schools	238	298	283	171	143	176	156	237	228	380	815	838	2060	3659	4302
4. (a) Total number of teachers	10.2	13.1	15.4	7.1	6.7	7.3	8.8	12.1	13.0	39.7	61.7	66.6	32.0	134.0	175.0
(b) for 1000 pupils	42.1	43.9	54.4	41.5	46.8	41.4	56.5	51.0	56.8	104.4	75.7	79.4	39.8	36.6	40.6
5. Number of students in higher education	94	145	134	102	109	123	45	94	79	166	252	322	2396	3861	4550
6. (a) Total number of teachers	10.5	15.4	16.6	11.8	14.1	17.0	5.6	8.4	9.2	19.2	23.0	30.0	128	201	264
(b) For 1000 students	111.7	106.2	123.8	115.7	129.3	138.2	126.4	89.9	117.2	72.2	91.3	93.7	53.4	52.5	58.0
7. (a) Number of children in pre-school establishments	329	398	450	563	697	817	269	260	264	502	607	706	4428	7673	9072
(b) Per 10,000 children of pre-school age	2333	2992	3413	3112	3624	4566	2618	3341	3272	1286	2320	3075	1033	1507	1948

2.2.3   The structure of social consumption funds according to the form of allo-
         cation to beneficiaries (see Tables 2.6-2.8)

The social funds are homogeneous in their allocation but not in the form in which
they are granted to beneficiaries.

That part of the fund which is principally intended for the support of the passive
members of society-pensions to incapacitated persons, scholarships and various
allowances-is paid in cash. Another part takes the form of services rendered on
favoured conditions with the beneficiary reimbursing part of the cost. These
include housing, institutions for children (holiday camps, kindergartens and
nurseries, orphanages, boarding schools), sanatoria, rest homes, etc. A third
portion of the fund is devoted to the free supply of material goods and services
by educational, public health and cultural institutions.

Since not all countries show each of these forms of allocating goods and services
by social funds, the analysis is in principle limited to a comparison of two
magnitudes only: cash transfers, on the one hand, and free or partially free goods
and services, on the other.

The share of cash transfers in the total varies substantially from country to
country and from year to year, ranging from 36 per cent in the G.D.R. to 56 per
cent in Czechoslovakia. The differences arise largely from government transfer
policies as well as from divergencies in the age structure of the population which
will be dealt with in more detail in the following chapter. Differences in the
composition of this indicator from one country to another also have a certain
effect.

The share of cash transfers increased in all countries except Czechoslovakia and
the U.S.S.R.: it rose from 38.3 to 44.8 per cent in Hungary, from 33.9 to 36.4 per
cent in the G.D.R. and from 43.1 to 43.9 per cent in Poland. In the U.S.S.R. and
Czechoslovakia this share declined somewhat from 40.8 to 38.8 and from 56.3 to
55.8 per cent respectively, whereas the share of free consumption in kind
increased (see Chart 2.4).

The average annual rates of increase in the absolute value of cash transfers
varied from one country to another, They were highest in Hungary (9.8 per cent),
in the U.S.S.R. (8.5 per cent), Poland (8.4 per cent), followed at some distance
by Czechoslovakia (5.6 per cent) and the G.D.R. (5.4 per cent) (see Chart 2.5).
These differences arose primarily from changes in the structure of transfers
during the period.

2.2.4   The strucutre of cash transfers from social consumption funds

The structure of cash transfers from social funds is similar in the various
countries (see Table 2.9). Pensions account for the major part (58 to 84 per cent)
and allowances come next with family, sickness and maternity allowances
constituting the most important items. Scholarships occupy third place. But this
general pattern is shaped in different ways in the different countries.

Pensions account for a similar share in all countries except the G.D.R. The higher
share in that country is due to particular features of its demographic structure.
Thus old people of more than 60 years made up 21.9 per cent of the population
compared to 12.9 per cent in Poland, 11.8 per cent in the U.S.S.R., 16.5 per cent
in Czechoslovakia and 16.6 per cent in Hungary. These percentages have a direct
bearing on the number of pensioners in each country. In 1969 they accounted for
21.7 per cent of the population in the G.D.R. and 6.7 per cent in Poland. In
Poland the share of pensioners was substantially lower than that of old persons
because at that time, the pension system did not cover a large part of the active
population in agriculture. Also retirement age in Poland is higher than in the
majority of socialist countries-65 years for men and 60 years for women.

Table 2.6
Destination of collective consumption funds in 1969
(in national currencies and percentages)

	Czechoslovakia		G.D.R.		Hungary		Poland		U.S.S.R.	
	values	%	values	%	values	%	values	%	values	%
1. Cash payments to the population from social funds	20.0	56.3	6.3	33.9	8.3	38.3	23.1	43.1	10.4	40.8
2. Social benefits in kind	15.6	43.7	12.3	66.1	3.4	15.4	6.2	11.6	2.8	10.9
3. Public consumption					10.1	46.3	24.3	45.3	12.3	48.3
4. Total (2+3)	(15.6)	(43.7)	(12.3)	(66.1)	(13.5)	(61.7)	(30.5)	(56.9)	(15.1)	(59.2)
5. Total receipts of the population from collective funds (1+4)	35.6	100.0	18.6	100.0	21.8	100.0	53.6	100.0	25.5	100.0

Table 2.7

Destination of collective consumption funds in 1965

(in national currencies and percentages)

	Czechoslovakia		G.D.R.		Hungary		Poland		U.S.S.R.	
	values	%	values	%	values	%	values	%	values	%
1. Cash payments to the population from social funds	24.3	56.8	8.3	35.9	12.6	41.0	32.9	42.5	14.9	37.8
2. Social benefits in kind					4.8	15.5	10.2	13.2	5.1	12.9
3. Public consumption	18.4	43.1	14.7	64.1	13.3	43.5	34.3	44.3	19.5	49.3
4. Total (2+3)	(18.4)	(43.1)	(14.7)	(64.1)	(18.1)	(59.0)	(44.5)	(57.5)	(24.6)	(62.2)
5. Total receipts of the population from collective funds (1+4)	42.7	100.0	23.0	100.0	30.7	100.0	77.4	100.0	39.5	100.0

Table 2.8

Destination of collective consumption funds in 1969
(in national currencies and percentages)

	Czechoslovakia		G.D.R.		Hungary					
	values	%	values	%	values	%	values	%	values	%
1. Cash payments to the population from social funds	30.9	55.8	10.1	36.4	17.7	44.8	47.7	43.9	21.6	38.8
2. Social benefits in kind					6.0	15.2	13.7	12.6	6.8	12.2
3. Public consumption	24.4	44.2	17.7	63.6	15.8	40.0	47.2	43.5	27.1	49.0
4. Total (2+3)	24.4	44.2	17.7	63.6	21.8	55.2	60.9	56.1	33.9	61.2
5. Total receipts of the population from collective funds (1+4)	55.3	100.0	27.8	100.0	39.5	100.0	108.6	100.0	55.5	100.0

The high proportion of pensions in cash transfers in the G.D.R. is also due to the fact that other payments from social funds are of less importance than in the other countries: children, babies and their mothers and invalids benefit mainly from free services in kind (as can be seen from Table 2.2) rather than from cash payments.

The considerable divergencies in the share of allowances in total cash transfers are due primarily to differences in the systems of allocation and the ways in which they are granted. This applies mainly to family allowances.

In Czechoslovakia, Poland and Hungary, where the share of family allowances in the total is highest, the ways in which they are granted are identical. In Czechoslovakia and Poland permanent allowances are paid for all children, and in Hungary from the second child onwards, whatever the income of the parents. The amounts of the allowance increase with the number of children: in Poland up to the third child (from the fourth child the amount remains unchanged) and in Czechoslovakia up to the fourth child. In Poland an allowance is paid to non-working women who attend to the upbringing of their children. In Hungary, non-working women have received an allowance for children up to the age of 3 years since 1967. (In Czechoslovakia such an allowance has been granted to women with two children since 1969.)

In the G.D.R. permanent family allowances are paid to one of the parents as an addition to his or her wage or salary. Allowances increase with the number of children. Substantial allowances are paid as a lump sum with the birth of every child.

In the U.S.S.R. family allowances are paid as a lump sum. Permanent allowances are granted to mothers of large families-that is with more than four children. Single mothers receive a permanent allowance for all their children.[5]

The rate of increase of transfers (pensions and allowances) from social funds is presented in Chart 2.5. Hungary has the highest rat of growth of total cash transfers-212.2 per cent from 1960 to 1969-followed by the U.S.S.R. with 207.7 per cent, Poland with 206.4 per cent, the G.D.R. with 161 per cent and finally Czechoslovakia with 153.7 per cent. As shown in Table 2.12, the differences in the rate of increase of expenditures on pensions reflect differences in the growth of the number of pensioners and in the size of pensions.

Table 2.12
Number of retirements and average monthly pensions

	Number of retirements as per cent of total number of inhabitants			Amount of pension in national currencies		
	1960	1969	1969/1960	1960	1969	1969/1960
Czechoslovakia	16.2	20.1	124.1	645	820	127.1
G.D.R.	17.0	21.7	127.6	145	179	123.4
Hungary	7.6	13.1	172.4	486	694	142.8
Poland	4.6	6.7	145.6	620	1058	170.6
U.S.S.R.	9.9	16.3	164.6	34	39	114.7

[5] Since 1974 all families with an average monthly income of less than 50 roubles per capita are entitled to child allowances in the U.S.S.R.

Table 2.9

Structure of social transfers according to the nature of their allocation in 1960
(percentages)

	Czechoslovakia		G.D.R.		Hungary	Poland	U.S.S.R.	
	from the state budget	from all sources	from all sources	from the state budget	from all sources	from all sources	from all sources	from the state budget
1. Pensions	56.6	74.4		71.0	54.9	47.9	69.2	63.6
2. Family allowances and pre-natal and maternity allowances	23.3	3.5a		3.4a	17.1	35.9	25.0	12.9
3. Sickness benefits	12.7	15.2		17.6	20.2	9.6		17.1
4. Scholarships	1.4	6.4		7.4	2.2	3.7	5.8	6.5
5. Other	6.0	0.5		0.6	5.6	2.9	...	...
6. Total	100.0	100.0		100.0	100.0	100.0	100.0	100.0
7. of which: financed from state and social security budgets		86.6					74.9	
8. from enterprise funds, trade unions, etc.		13.4					25.1	

a Only pre-natal and maternity allowances.

Table 2.10

Structure of social transfers according to the nature of their allocation in 1965
(percentages)

| | Czechoslovakia | | G.D.R. | | Hungary | Poland | U.S.S.R. | |
	from the state budget	from all sources	from all sources	from the state budget	from all sources	from all sources	from all sources	from the state budget
1. Pensions	62.6	81.6		79.5	61.4	53.4	71.1	66.8
2. Family allowances and pre-natal and maternity allowances	22.7	3.0[a]		2.9[a]	12.5	28.2	23.1	9.7
3. Sickness benefits	12.9	10.5		12.0	18.1	10.1		17.7
4. Scholarships	1.2	4.5		5.5	2.5	3.9	5.5	5.8
5. Other	0.6	0.4		0.1	5.5	4.4		
6. Total	100.0	100.0		100.0	100.0	100.0	100.0	100.0
7. of which: financed from state and social security budgets		87.3					74.3	
8. from enterprise funds, trade unions, etc.		12.7					25.7	

a Only pre-natal and maternity allowances.

Table 2.11

Structure of social transfers according to the nature of their allocation in 1969
(percentages)

	Czechoslovakia		G.D.R.		Hungary	Poland	U.S.S.R.	
	from the state budget	from all sources	from all sources	from the state budget	from all sources	from all sources	from all sources	from the state budget
1. Pensions	61.8		84.1	81.9	58.4	61.5	69.4	65.3
2. Family allowances and pre-natal and maternity allowances	22.1		1.3[a]	1.3[a]	16.2	18.9	24.6	7.7
3. Sickness benefits	14.7		9.6	11.1	15.7	11.1		20.9
4. Scholarships	0.9		4.5	5.2	1.9	3.4	6.0	6.1
5. Other	0.5		0.5	0.5	7.8	5.1	...	...
6. Total	100.0		100.0	100.0	100.0	100.0	100.0	100.0
7. of which: financed from state and social security budgets		86.8	81.9				74.0	
8. from enterprise funds, trade unions, etc.		13.2	13.2				26.0	

[a] Only pre-natal and maternity allowances.

2.2.5   The structure of personal and social consumption by categories of goods
         and services (see Tables 2.13 and 2.17)

The data presented in Tables 2.13-2.15 reveal the difficulties of a detailed
comparison of the consumption structure in different countries. The variations of
expenditure on food are due to differences in the composition of the indicator
rather than actual differences in food consumption.

Through an analysis of enlarged consumption by categories it is possible to arrive
at several conclusions on the hierarchy of wants which reflects individual and
collective preferences only to a limited extent.

Needs classified according to their share in personal consumption in four
socialist countries give some idea of the individual preferences of the population
after taking into account existing levels of prices and incomes and supply
conditions.

Table 2.16 shows an identical "hierarchy" of needs in all countries except
Czechoslovakia, where the item "Culture and information" figures in fifth place
instead of "Sports, leisure and entertainment". Such an identity reflects a common
degree of urgency for different physiological and social wants in the various
countries. To a certain extent it is also conditioned by the type of social supply
of services and the role played by centralilzed funds in the allocation of free
goods and services serving par excellence the satisfaction of such important wants
as education, health, etc. This "hierarchy of preferences" has not changed between
1960 and 1969.

From a tabulation of consumption categories or wants according to their share in
collective consumption, the following collective preferences emerge (see Table
2.20).

Table 2.16
"Hierarchy" of individual consumption in 1969 (percentages)

Position:	Czechoslovakia	G.D.R.	Hungary	Poland	U.S.S.R.
I	Food 49.1	Food 45.0	Food 51.9	Food 54.7	Food 45.0
II	Clothing and footwear 17.9	Clothing and footwear 14.6	Housing 15.2	Clothing and footwear 15.7	Clothing and footwear 21.4
III	Housing 12.9	Housing 14.3	Clothing and footwear 13.2	Housing 11.4	Housing 9.9
IV	Transport and communications 6.3	Transport and communications 6.4	Transport and communications 6.3	Transport and communications 5.4	Transport and communications 5.2
V	Culture, sports, leisure 4.0	Culture leisure and entertainment 5.0	Culture, leisure and entertainment 5.1	Sports, leisure and entertainment 4.1	Sports, leisure and entertainment 4.2

For all countries beverages are included under food.
For the G.D.R. and U.S.S.R. food does not include self-consumption.

Table 2.13

Structure of enlarged consumption by categories of needs in 1960 (percentage)

	Czechoslovakia			G.D.R.			Hungary			Poland			U.S.S.R.		
	Personal consumption	Collective consumption	Total	Personal consumption	Collective consumption	Total	Personal consumption	Collective consumption	Total	Personal consumption	Collective consumption	Total	Personal consumption	Collective consumption	Total
1.00 Food	47.8	2.6	41.8	36.2	6.1	30.4[a]	43.3	14.5	40.0	50.4	11.5	46.3	44.2	8.0	39.5[a]
2.00 Beverages	8.0	–	7.0	7.3	–	5.9	10.0	1.1	9.0	8.4	–	7.5	1.5	–	1.3
3.00 Tobacco and matches	0.1	6.6	0.9	4.8	–	3.9	2.0	–	1.7	3.3	–	3.0	–	–	–
4.00 Clothing and footwear	14.7	28.4	3.8	16.0	–	12.9	16.4	2.5	14.8	16.8	–	15.0	21.9	–	19.1
5.00 Personal care	3.7	–	1.5	3.8	–	3.1	1.2	–	1.0	1.6	–	1.4	1.1	–	1.0
6.00 Housing	6.0	7.3	9.1	15.7	18.0	14.6	14.6	9.3	14.0	8.7	5.6	8.3	9.3	8.2	9.1
7.00 Transport	0.4	1.3	5.4	6.7	–	5.1	4.4	–	3.9	4.1	–	3.7	4.2	1.3	3.8
8.00 Telecommunications	0.5	–	0.3	0.7	–	0.6	0.5	–	0.4	0.5	–	0.4	0.5	–	0.4
9.00 Medical goods and services	0.1	36.9	5.2	0.4	18.3	3.9	0.5	31.1	4.1	1.2	36.7	4.9	0.9	31.1	4.8
10.00 Social services	0.7	37.7	0.1	0.3	8.9	1.9	–	8.2	1.0	0.1	5.4	0.7	0.3	6.4	1.0
11.00 Education and research	2.4	7.3	5.5	0.4	32.9	6.7	0.7	26.8	3.7	0.1	35.0	3.8	–	37.1	4.8
12.00 Culture and information	1.1	–	3.1	2.2	8.1	3.3	3.7	6.4	4.0	0.9	1.6	1.0	1.5	3.7	1.8
13.00 Sports, leisure and entertainment	3.6	–	0.9	4.8	2.6	4.5	–	–	–	3.0	3.3	3.1	3.6	0.3	3.2
14.00 Other goods and services	4.5	6.5	4.1	0.7	5.1	3.2	2.7	–	2.4	0.9	0.9	0.9	11.0	3.9	10.2
15.00 Enlarged consumption	100.0	100.0	100.0	100.0	100.0	100.0	100.0	100.0	100.0	100.0	100.0	100.0	100.0	100.0	100.0

A brace in the left margin links categories 5.00 (Personal care) and 6.00 (Housing) for Czechoslovakia with the figures 3.3 and 4.5.

[a] Self-consumption is not included.

Table 2.14

Structure of enlarged consumption by categories of needs in 1965 (percentages)

	Czechoslovakia			G.D.R.			Hungary			Poland			U.S.S.R.		
	Personal consumption	Collective consumption	Total	Personal consumption	Collective consumption	Total	Personal consumption	Collective consumption	Total	Personal consumption	Collective consumption	Total	Personal consumption	Collective consumption	Total
1.00 Food	44.5	9.6	39.5	36.0	6.2	30.0[a]	41.7	14.9	38.2	46.2	11.2	42.2	46.8	8.5	40.8[a]
2.00 Beverages	8.2	–	7.2	8.5	–	6.8	10.8	1.0	9.5	9.3	–	8.3	1.4	–	1.2
3.00 Tobacco and matches	0.2	6.7	1.0	4.8	–	3.9	2.3	–	2.0	3.0	–	2.7	–	–	–
4.00 Clothing and footwear	0.9	28.4	4.5	14.8	–	11.8	14.5	1.5	12.8	15.7	–	13.9	20.2	–	17.0
5.00 Personal care	1.6	–	1.4	3.8	–	3.1	1.3	–	1.1	1.9	–	1.7	1.2	–	1.0
6.00 Housing	10.5	7.4	10.2	14.6	5.9	14.8	14.9	8.4	14.1	10.6	6.2	10.1	10.1	9.4	10.0
7.00 Transport	5.3	5.1	5.3	5.8	–	4.5	4.9	–	4.3	4.5	–	3.9	4.5	0.9	3.9
8.00 Telecommunications	0.4	–	0.3	0.7	–	0.5	0.5	–	0.5	0.5	–	0.5	0.6	–	0.5
9.00 Medical goods and services	0.6	34.1	4.8	0.6	18.8	4.2	0.6	33.5	4.8	1.1	36.4	5.1	0.8	26.7	4.9
10.00 Social services	0.1	–	0.1	0.3	9.3	2.1	0.1	8.9	1.2	0.1	4.8	0.6	0.3	7.7	1.5
11.00 Education and research	0.7	37.9	4.9	0.4	34.4	7.4	1.0	26.2	4.3	0.1	35.1	4.0	–	37.1	5.9
12.00 Culture and information	3.0	6.6	3.4	2.2	8.6	3.5	4.4	5.6	4.5	1.1	1.6	1.2	1.6	6.9	2.2
13.00 Sports, leisure and entertainment	1.3	–	1.1	5.3	2.1	4.7				4.1	4.7	4.2	4.1	0.2	3.4
14.00 Other goods and services	4.3	5.9	4.3	2.2	4.9	2.7	3.0	–	2.6	1.8	0.1	1.6	8.5	3.6	7.7
15.00 Enlarged consumption	100.0	100.0	100.0	100.0	100.0	100.0	100.0	100.0	100.0	100.0	100.0	100.0	100.0	100.0	100.0

[a] Self-consumption is not included.

Table 2.15

Structure of enlarged consumption by categories of needs in 1969 (percentages)

		Czechoslovakia			G.D.R.			Hungary			Poland			U.S.S.R.		
		Personal consumption	Collective consumption	Total	Personal consumption	Collective consumption	Total	Personal consumption	Collective consumption	Total	Personal consumption	Collective consumption	Total	Personal consumption	Collective consumption	Total
1.00	Food	40.4	3.3	35.6	36.1	6.4	30.1[a]	40.7	15.2	37.4	44.2	9.7	40.1	45.0	7.2	39.1[a]
2.00	Beverages	6.6	–	7.6	8.9	–	7.1	11.2	0.8	9.8	10.5	–	9.4	1.4	–	1.0
3.00	Tobacco and matches	3.2	–	2.8	4.5	–	3.6	2.3	0.1	2.1	2.9	–	2.6	21.4	–	18.0
4.00	Clothing and footwear	17.9	0.6	15.6	14.6	–	11.7	13.2	2.0	11.8	15.7	–	13.8	1.3	–	1.0
5.00	Personal care	1.5	–	1.3	4.2	–	3.3	1.3	–	1.2	1.9	–	1.7	9.9	9.6	9.8
6.00	Housing	12.9	7.1	12.1	14.3	13.0	14.0	15.2	7.8	14.2	11.4	3.5	10.5	4.5	0.7	3.9
7.00	Transport	5.9	6.2	5.9	5.8	–	4.6	5.8	–	5.1	4.9	–	4.3	0.7	–	0.5
8.00	Telecommunications	0.4	–	0.3	0.6	–	0.5	0.5	–	0.4	0.5	–	0.4	0.9	27.8	5.2
9.00	Medical goods and services	0.7	31.9	4.8	0.5	17.7	3.9	0.5	34.7	4.9	1.0	37.4	5.3	0.2	7.3	1.4
10.00	Social services	0.1	–	0.1	0.3	15.9	3.4	0.1	8.4	1.2	0.2	5.0	0.7	–	35.8	5.6
11.00	Education and research	0.6	38.3	5.6	0.4	31.9	6.8	1.0	25.8	4.1	0.1	37.0	4.5	1.7	7.8	2.7
12.00	Culture and information	2.7	6.8	3.3	2.0	8.6	3.4	5.1	5.2	5.1	1.2	1.8	1.2	4.2	0.1	3.6
13.00	Sports, leisure and entertainment	1.3	–	1.1	5.0	1.6	4.3				4.1	5.4	4.3	8.8	3.7	8.2
14.00	Other goods and services	3.7	6.0	3.9	2.8	4.9	3.3	3.1	–	2.7	1.4	0.2	1.2			
15.00	Enlarged consumption	100.0	100.0	100.0	100.0	100.0	100.0	100.0	100.0	100.0	100.0	100.0	100.0	100.0	100.0	100.0

[a] Self-consumption is not included.

"Education" and "health" occupy the two first positions in the system of collective preferences. The items "housing", "culture and information" and "social services" take up the following three places but in combinations which vary between countries. Hungary with "food" in third place and Czechoslovakia with "transport" in fifth place are the only exceptions.

It must be noted that the data (derived from the analytical Table 2.13) reflect not only the real proportions which the different categories of collective needs assume in total collective consumption in the various countries, but they are also influenced by the different "content" of the items shown; had it been possible to make the composition of each item identical, the hierarchy of collective needs would perhaps have turned out differently. For the U.S.S.R., items IV and V would probably change places since "Social services" are somewhat under-valued as they include neither services supplied by establishments for old people nor the services of performances for children.

For Czechoslovakia, "Social services" do not figure in the tabulation since the relevant expenditure is included with "Education" and "Health".

The scale of individual and collective preferences depends a great deal on the sources from which the various wants are financed: that is family incomes or social consumption funds. In this respect the situation is more or less identical in all countries (see Tables 2.17-2.19).

The consumption of food, clothing, transport and articles of personal hygiene is almost entirely financed from family budgets. Goods and services for leisure, sports and entertainment are financed by households to the extent of between 85 per cent (Poland) and 99 per cent (U.S.S.R.). These relatively large differences arise partly from differences in the interpretation and grouping of the items concerned. In the U.S.S.R. performances financed from social sources figure in item 12.00 "Culture and information", it follows that item 13.00 is undervalued while item 12.00 is over-valued. The same applies to Czechoslovakia, where all services which form part of 13.00 "Sports, leisure and entertainment" are included in item 12.00; in Hungary the two categories are merged into one.

Table 2.17

Share of personal and collective consumption in the various categories of goods and services, in 1960 (percentages)

	Czechoslovakia			G.D.R.			Hungary			Poland			U.S.S.R.		
	Personal consumption	Collective consumption	Total	Personal consumption	Collective consumption	Total	Personal consumption	Collective consumption	Total	Personal consumption	Collective consumption	Total	Personal consumption	Collective consumption	Total
1.00 Food	98.8	1.2	100.0	96.2	3.8	100.0	95.8	4.2	100.0	97.4	2.6	100.0	97.4	2.6	100.0
2.00 Beverages	100.0	-	100.0	100.0	-	100.0	98.5	1.5	100.0	100.0	-	100.0	100.0	-	100.0
3.00 Tobacco and matches	100.0	-	100.0	100.0	-	100.0	100.0	-	100.0	100.0	-	100.0	100.0	-	100.0
4.00 Clothing and footwear	99.4	0.6	100.0	100.0	-	100.0	98.0	2.0	100.0	100.0	-	100.0	100.0	-	100.0
5.00 Personal care	100.0	-	100.0	100.0	-	100.0	100.0	-	100.0	100.0	-	100.0	100.0	-	100.0
6.00 Housing	89.6	10.4	100.0	76.2	23.8	100.0	92.2	7.8	100.0	93.1	6.9	100.0	88.	11.5	100.0
7.00 Transport	96.9	3.1	100.0	100.0	-	100.0	100.0	-	100.0	100.0	-	100.0	95.5	4.5	100.0
8.00 Telecommunications	100.0	-	100.0	100.0	-	100.0	100.0	-	100.0	100.0	-	100.0	100.0	-	100.0
9.00 Medical goods and services	8.5	91.5	100.0	9.5	90.5	100.0	11.3	88.7	100.0	21.3	78.7	100.0	15.9	84.1	100.0
10.00 Social services	100.0	-	100.0	11.0	89.0	100.0	12.2	87.8	100.0	15.9	84.1	100.0	20.9	79.1	100.0
11.00 Education and research	11.5	88.5	100.0	5.3	94.7	100.0	14.4	85.5	100.0	3.6	96.4	100.0	0.5	99.5	100.0
12.00 Culture and information	69.3	30.7	100.0	53.6	46.4	100.0	81.2	18.8	100.0	82.4	17.6	100.0	78.5	21.5	100.0
13.00 Sports, leisure and entertainment	100.0	-	100.0	88.6	11.4	100.0				88.8	11.2	100.0	99.9	0.1	100.0
14.00 Other goods and services	80.5	19.5	100.0	77.9	21.1	100.0	100.0	-	100.0	89.6	10.4	100.0	94.6	5.4	100.0
15.00 Enlarged consumption	87.1	12.9	100.0	80.8	19.2	100.0	88.3	11.7	100.0	89.5	10.5	100.0	87.1	12.9	100.0

(For Hungary, rows 12.00 Culture and information and 13.00 Sports, leisure and entertainment are grouped together: 81.2 personal, 18.8 collective.)

Table 2.18

Share of personal and collective consumption in the various categories of goods and services, in 1965 (percentages)

	Czechoslovakia			G.D.R.			Hungary			Poland			U.S.S.R.		
	Personal consumption	Collective consumption	Total	Personal consumption	Collective consumption	Total	Personal consumption	Collective consumption	Total	Personal consumption	Collective consumption	Total	Personal consumption	Collective consumption	Total
1.00 Food	99.3	0.7	100.0	95.9	4.1	100.0	95.0	5.0	100.0	97.1	2.9	100.0	96.6	3.4	100.0
2.00 Beverages	100.0	–	100.0	100.0	–	100.0	98.6	1.4	100.0	100.0	–	100.0	100.0	–	100.0
3.00 Tobacco and matches	100.0	–	100.0	100.0	–	100.0	100.0	–	100.0	100.0	–	100.0	100.0	–	100.0
4.00 Clothing and footwear	94.4	5.6	100.0	100.0	–	100.0	98.5	1.5	100.0	100.0	–	100.0	100.0	–	100.0
5.00 Personal care	100.0	–	100.0	100.0	–	100.0	100.0	–	100.0	100.0	–	100.0	100.0	–	100.0
6.00 Housing	90.8	9.2	100.0	78.7	21.3	100.0	92.7	7.3	100.0	93.1	6.9	100.0	85.4	14.6	100.0
7.00 Transport	88.0	12.0	100.0	100.0	–	100.0	100.0	–	100.0	100.0	–	100.0	96.2	3.8	100.0
8.00 Telecommunications	100.0	–	100.0	100.0	–	100.0	100.0	–	100.0	100.0	–	100.0	100.0	–	100.0
9.00 Medical goods and services	11.5	88.5	100.0	10.9	89.1	100.0	10.4	89.6	100.0	19.9	80.1	100.0	14.8	85.2	100.0
10.00 Social services	100.0	–	100.0	10.5	89.5	100.0	17.4	82.6	100.0	17.9	82.1	100.0	19.9	80.1	100.0
11.00 Education and research	4.0	96.0	100.0	6.0	94.0	100.0	17.6	82.4	100.0	3.2	96.8	100.0	0.5	99.5	100.0
12.00 Culture and information	75.7	24.3	100.0	50.6	49.4	100.0	84.0	16.0	100.0	83.9	16.1	100.0	59.2	40.8	100.0
13.00 Sports, leisure and entertainment	100.0	–	100.0	91.0	9.0	100.0	100.0	–	100.0	87.4	12.6	100.0	99.2	0.8	100.0
14.00 Other goods and services	82.6	17.4	100.0	73.8	26.2	100.0	99.6	0.4	100.0	99.6	0.4	100.0	94.4	5.6	100.0
15.00 Enlarged consumption	87.5	12.5	100.0	79.9	20.1	100.0	87.1	12.9	100.0	88.8	11.2	100.0	84.5	15.5	100.0

Table 2.19

Share of personal and collective consumption in the various categories of goods and services, in 1969 (percentages)

	Czechoslovakia			G.D.R.			Hungary			Poland			U.S.S.R.		
	Personal consumption	Collective consumption	Total	Personal consumption	Collective consumption	Total	Personal consumption	Collective consumption	Total	Personal consumption	Collective consumption	Total	Personal consumption	Collective consumption	Total
1.00 Food	99.2	0.8	100.0	96.6	3.4	100.0	94.8	5.2	100.0	97.2	2.8	100.0	97.1	2.9	100.0
2.00 Beverages	100.0	-	100.0	100.0	-	100.0	99.0	1.0	100.0	100.0	-	100.0	100.0	-	100.0
3.00 Tobacco and matches	100.0	-	100.0	100.0	-	100.0	99.2	0.8	100.0	100.0	-	100.0	100.0	-	100.0
4.00 Clothing and footwear	100.0	-	100.0	100.0	-	100.0	97.9	2.1	100.0	100.0	-	100.0	100.0	-	100.0
5.00 Personal care	100.0	-	100.0	100.0	-	100.0	100.0	-	100.0	100.0	-	100.0	100.0	-	100.0
6.00 Housing	92.3	7.7	100.0	81.4	18.6	100.0	93.0	7.0	100.0	96.0	4.0	100.0	85.9	15.1	100.0
7.00 Transport	86.2	13.8	100.0	100.0	-	100.0	100.0	-	100.0	100.0	-	100.0	97.0	3.0	100.0
8.00 Telecommunications	100.0	-	100.0	100.0	-	100.0	100.0	-	100.0	100.0	-	100.0	100.0	-	100.0
9.00 Medical goods and services	12.1	87.9	100.0	10.3	89.7	100.0	9.4	90.6	100.0	16.6	83.4	100.0	14.8	85.2	100.0
10.00 Social services	100.0	-	100.0	6.0	94.0	100.0	19.4	80.6	100.0	18.8	81.2	100.0	20.3	79.7	100.0
11.00 Education and research	9.2	90.8	100.0	5.1	94.9	100.0	16.9	83.1	100.0	2.3	97.7	100.0	0.4	99.6	100.0
12.00 Culture and information	73.2	26.8	100.0	46.0	54.0	100.0	87.0	13.0	100.0	83.0	17.0	100.0	54.3	45.7	100.0
13.00 Sports, leisure and entertainment	100.0	-	100.0	92.7	7.3	100.0				85.3	14.7	100.0	99.5	0.5	100.0
14.00 Other goods and services	79.8	20.2	100.0	76.7	23.3	100.0	100.0	-	100.0	97.5	2.5	100.0	92.3	7.7	100.0
15.00 Enlarged consumption	86.8	13.2	100.0	79.8	20.1	100.0	87.2	12.8	100.0	88.2	11.8	100.0	84.4	15.6	100.0

Table 2.20
"Hierarchy" of collective consumption in 1969 (percentages)

Place:	Czechoslovakia	G.D.R.	Hungary	Poland	U.S.S.R.
I	Education 38.3	Education 31.9	Health 34.7	Health 37.4	Education 35.8
II	Health 31.9	Health 17.7	Education 25.8	Education 37.0	Health 27.8
III	Housing 7.1	Social Services 15.9	Food 15.2	Food 9.7	Housing 9.6
IV	Culture and information 6.6	Housing 13.0	Social services 8.4	Sports, leisure, entertain- ment 5.4	Culture and information 7.8
V	Transport 6.2	Culture and information 8.6	Housing 7.8	Social services 5.0	Social services 7.5

In the financing of housing needs the share of social sources ranges from 7 per cent (Hungary) to 20 per cent (G.D.R.). Such a relatively unimportant contribution (except for the G.D.R.) is due to the fact that housing includes not only actual expenditure for the maintenance of the public housing stock (rent and State subsidies) but also imputed rent, that is the maintenance cost of the individual housing stock incurred by the owners of dwellings. The item "Housing" includes also municipal services and expenditures on furniture and household equipment. The two latter expenditure categories are also covered from family budgets.

Between 83 and 90 per cent of expenditure on health is financed from social funds. The remaining 10 to 17 per cent is paid for by households and represents expenditure on medicines and payment for accomodation in sanatoria and rest homes. Educational needs are satisfied by society to the extent of between 91 per cent (Czechoslovakia) and 99.6 per cent (U.S.S.R.); such differences as exist can be explained by the fact that the cost of school books and supplies paid for by the population is included in "Education" in Czechoslovakia and the G.D.R. but in "Culture and information" in the U.S.S.R. and Poland. In addition, in the case of Hungary, "Education" covers purchased educational services such as: the fees paid for accomodation in a number of colleges and universities fees for certain courses (e.g.language courses) and the amounts paid for private lessons (in the other countries this type of expenditure is not included).

Any comparison of item 10.00 "Social services" and 12.00 "Culture and information" remains purely conventional in view of the differences in the interpretation and grouping of their components mentioned above.

Table 2.21

Development of the structure of individual consumption (percentages)

	Czechoslovakia			G.D.R.			Hungary			Poland			U.S.S.R.		
	1960	1965	1968	1960	1965	1969	1960	1965	1968	1960	1965	1969	1960	1965	1969
1.00 Food	100.0	100.0	100.0	100.0	100.0	100.0	100.0	100.0	100.0	100.0	100.0	100.0	100.0	100.0	100.0
1 Bread and cereals	19.0	17.9	16.1	14.6	15.3	14.0	15.3	14.7	12.7	15.7	14.7	13.4	25.6	20.4	18.4
2 Meat and poultry	25.8	26.4	28.6	25.8	26.0	24.9	25.9	24.2	27.3	23.9	24.7	27.1	17.9	19.2	20.4
3 Fish	1.4	1.4	1.5	2.5	2.2	1.8	0.6	0.6	1.0	1.6	1.9	2.1	5.7	5.3	5.2
4 Milk, butter, cheese, eggs	15.6	16.7	17.2	24.8	23.5	22.1	13.5	13.0	12.7	24.2	23.5	23.0	8.9	16.0	17.5
5 Oils and fats	6.3	5.3	4.6				13.8	11.5	9.4	6.9	6.7	5.3	10.0	9.5	8.5
6 Potatoes and vegetables	4.7	3.9	5.1	6.8	7.2	9.5	10.0	10.9	10.8	14.0	14.8	15.4	4.7	5.0	5.5
7 Fruit	3.8	5.1	4.3				6.4	6.7	7.6				4.3	4.5	5.3
8 Sugar, confectionary	14.0	12.7	11.8	10.3	10.3	9.6	8.8	9.3	7.7	9.2	8.8	8.1	22.9	20.1	19.2
9 Other	9.4	10.6	10.8	15.2	15.5	18.5	5.7	9.1	10.8	4.5	4.9	5.6	–	–	–
2.00 Beverages	100.0	100.0	100.0	100.0	100.0	100.0	100.0	100.0	100.0	100.0	100.0	100.0	100.0	100.0	100.0
1 Non-alcoholic	11.4	11.2	10.0	8.0	9.9	10.0	3.5	4.2	4.6	4.1	5.2	5.4	...	...	...
2 Alcoholic	88.6	88.8	90.0	92.0	90.1	90.0	96.5	95.8	95.4	95.9	94.8	94.6	...	...	...
4.00 Clothing and footwear	100.0	100.0	100.0	100.0	100.0	100.0	100.0	100.0	100.0	100.0	100.0	100.0	100.0	100.0	100.0
1 Clothing and repairs	82.0	80.4	84.8	87.6	83.2	83.3	87.2	79.5	81.8	90.0	92.5	93.8	82.2	79.9	80.1
2 Footwear and repairs	18.0	19.6	15.2	12.4	16.8	16.7	18.8	20.5	18.2	10.0	7.5	6.2	17.8	20.1	19.9
5.00 Personal care	100.0	100.0	100.0	100.0	100.0	100.0	100.0	100.0	100.0	100.0	100.0	100.0	100.0	100.0	100.0
1 Toilet articles, cosmetics and perfumes	75.7	77.2	79.1	...	...	...	43.6	48.5	46.5	80.4	77.7	78.7	77.3	74.9	76.8
2 Hairdressing and beauty treatment	24.3	22.8	20.9	...	...	...	56.4	51.5	53.5	19.6	22.3	21.3	22.7	25.1	23.2
6.00 Housing	100.0	100.0	100.0	100.0	100.0	100.0	100.0	100.0	100.0	100.0	100.0	100.0	100.0	100.0	100.0
1 Real rent	10.6	17.0	14.4	22.3	20.1	18.9	10.5	10.3	10.6	7.9	8.5	12.2	6.5	6.6	6.1
2 Imputed rent	17.6	19.8	20.2	11.3	9.3	8.0	10.2	10.0	8.9	10.5	7.1	6.0	27.6	27.6	24.1
3 Energy, water and heating	12.4	12.5	9.5	7.4	8.9	10.4	22.8	24.9	24.1	26.2	46.2	43.6	20.2	22.3	23.7

Table 2.21 (cont.)

4 Furniture and equipment	42.3	35.6	38.0	57.0	59.3	60.3	48.7	48.1	49.1	55.4	38.2	38.2	38.1	39.4	41.5
of which: electrical equipment	(15.8)	(12.1)	(10.3)	...	...	...	...	...	...	...	...	...	(4.2)	(7.5)	(10.1)
5 Goods and services for construction and repairs	17.1	15.1	27.9	2.0	2.4	2.4	7.8	6.7	7.3	...	...	...	7.6	4.1	4.6
7.00 Transport	100.0	100.0	100.0	100.0	100.0	100.0	100.0	100.0	100.0	100.0	100.0	100.0	100.0	100.0	100.0
1 Purchases and repairs of individual vehicles	30.4	26.9	41.0	42.8	43.1	55.0	31.7	33.6	43.8	39.4	43.6	40.9	17.0	17.3	17.2
2 Public transport services	69.6	73.1	59.0	57.2	56.9	45.0	68.3	66.4	56.2	60.6	56.4	59.1	83.0	82.7	82.8
12.00 Culture and information	100.0	100.0	100.0	100.0	100.0	100.0	100.0	100.0	100.0	100.0	100.0	100.0	100.0	100.0	100.0
1 Books, newspapers, periodicals	53.0	47.3	61.1	53.6	50.6	46.0	...	...	...	68.7	59.9	57.1	72.6	59.1	54.2
2 Cultural education services	3.9	15.9	3.6												
3 Arts, radio, television	43.1	36.8	35.3	46.4	49.4	54.0	...	...	...	31.3	40.1	42.9	27.4	40.9	45.8
13.00 Sports, leisure ane entertainment	100.0	100.0	100.0	100.0	100.0	100.0	100.0	...	...	100.0	100.0	100.0	100.0	100.0	100.0
1 Articles for leisure and entertainment	32.4	29.0	32.9	...	...	...	...	...	...	71.4	71.5	69.5	39.5	47.2	50.1
2 Sports articles	37.3	40.6	38.1	...	...	...	...	...	...	...	...	...	6.4	6.2	6.4
3 Entertainments	4.5	4.6	4.9	...	...	...	...	...	...	...	...	...	29.6	22.3	18.4
4 Cafés, restaurants, canteens, etc.	25.8	25.8	24.1	...	...	...	...	...	...	28.6	28.5	30.5	24.5	24.3	25.1

2.3   DETAILED ANALYSIS OF THE STRUCTURE AND FINANCING OF ENLARGED CONSUMPTION
        BY CATEGORIES OF NEEDS

2.3.1   Developments in the structure of individual consumption (see Table 2.21)

An analysis of the dynamics of personal consumption in the countries reviewed
reveals a qualitative improvement in its composition. Several marked tendencies
emerge:

There are, in the first place, the changes in the composition of food consumption.
But it must be remembered that differences in the level and composition of food
consumption in the various countries are caused not only by their levels of economic development but also by their demographic, geographical and natural
environment and the tastes and habits of their population. The changes which
accompany increasing welfare in socialist countries are analogous and consist in a
shift of consumption to high-quality goods; thus the proportion of products with a
high protein content, particularly of animal origin, increases while that of food
with a high carbohydrate content diminishes.

The composition of food consumption changes broadly as follows:

  (i) the proportion of bread and cereals, sugar and sweets and oil declines;
 (ii) that of meat and poultry, milk and other dairy produce, eggs and fruit
      and vegetables increases;
(iii) fish and fishery products maintain about the same proportion.[6]

Several specific tendencies can be observed in each country. In the G.D.R. meat
consumption remains virtually unchanged while the share of fish drops substantially; the share of milk, other dairy produce, eggs and oil consumption contracts and
that of fruit and vegetables expands. In Poland there is a shift away from an
already very high level of milk and other dairy produce consumption. Milk represents a large proportion of total dairy produce consumption, whereas its
derivatives (for instance, cheese) are consumed less. In contrast to other
countries, Poland has a high level of fish consumption due to the widespread
supply of sea fish.

Some clarification of the method of grouping food products is perhaps required at
this point. In analysing food consumption in socialist countries, it would be a
mistake to lump together potatoes and vegetable consumption in a same group, since
there is a long-term tendency for the consumption of potatoes to fall off and that
of vegetables to increase. The absolute volume of per capita consumption of these
two foodstuffs developed as in Poland and the U.S.S.R. as shown in Table 2.22.

These tendencies represent a qualitative improvement of the diet, since potatoes
belong to the group of products with a predominantly carbohydrate content whereas
vegetables contain large amounts of vitamins and salts which are essential for the
human body. The fluctuations in vegetable consumption in Poland in some years are
accounted for by crop variations.

In Hungary the consumption of protein foods of animal origin (meat and fish)
increased at a rapid rate since 1965. In 1968, 41 grams of animal proteins were
consumed daily. The proportion of vegetables in food consumption was higher than
in the other countries already at the outset and this explains its relatively

------

[6]It must be recalled, however, that consumption is valued at current
prices, and that in countries where relative prices of food have changed
this may partly account for changes in composition.

Table 2.22
Consumption of potatoes and vegetables in Poland and the U.S.S.R.

| | Annual per capita consumption in kilos | | | | | |
| | Poland | | | U.S.S.R. | | |
	1960	1965	1969	1960	1965	1969
Potatoes	223	215	199	143	142	131
Vegetables and cucurbits	82.0	94.4	86.6	70	72	76

small increase during the period, while the proportion of fruit rose quite fast. Coffee and tea consumption expanded most rapidly: the former from 140 grams per capita in 1960 to 1.2 kg in 1968, and the latter more than doubled.

In the consumption of beverages consisting of between 80 and 90 per cent of alcoholic beverages there has been a tendency for the demand for soft drinks to rise more rapidly; this was not sufficient, however, to change the proportions of the two categories substantially.

The structure of consumption for the satisfaction of housing needs develops in a specific way in socialist countries. A considerable part of the housing stock is owned by the State and, in addition, the population benefits from large subsidies paid out of social funds to cover the maintenance costs of the socialized housing stock (two-thirds in the U.S.S.R.). Imputed rent is attributed to dwellings which are owned by households and represents their estimated maintenance cost. The State does not contribute to the financing of this expenditure. This is why the share of imputed rent in personal expenditure for housing is higher than real rent.

Expenditure connected with housing is largely financed from social sources but municipal services and household equipment are entirely paid for from household budgets. This must be borne in mind when analysing item 6.00 "Housing".

Except for Poland and Czechoslovakia, the following tendencies are identical for all countries: the proportion of real and imputed rent declines while that of expenditure on household equipment increases. This is due to the increasing role played by durable stocks in the equipment of dwellings and to the decline of the private housing stock accompanied by a fall in imputed rent (which constitutes a major part of housing costs).

The declining proportion of durable household goods for cultural and other purposes in the total expenditure on housing in Poland is primarily due to the increases in municipal services and rent, which occurred in 1965. The higher proportion of rent was in turn caused by a change in the composition of the housing stock. According to 1970 data, 35 per cent of the housing stock was State-owned, 7.3 per cent belonged to cooperatives and 60 per cent to private owners. During more recent years cooperative construction accelerated. Thus in 1971, out of 190,600 dwellings completed, public construction accounted for 23 per cent and cooperative and private building for 49 and 28 per cent, respectively. Similar tendencies were typical also for other socialist countries. On 1 January 1970 out of a total of 3,145,000 dwellings in Hungary, 75 per cent were personally owned (including cooperative ownership) and 25 per cent belonged to the State. In the period 1971 it was envisaged that another 400,000 dwellings would be completed: 185,000 by the State and the rest by housing cooperatives.

Even so, the purchases of household durables continued to increase and the stock of durables for cultural and other uses registered substantial advances (Table 2.23).

Table 2.23

Stocks of household durables for cultural and other uses per 100 households

		Radios	Television sets	Refrigerators	Washing machines	Vacuum cleaners
G.D.R.[a]	1963	–	42	16	18	–
	1970	–	82	65	58	101
Poland[a]	1960	82	52	16	72	27
	1970	91	77	47	81	52
U.S.S.R.	1960	46	8	4	4	3
	1970	72	51	32	52	12
Czech.	1960	80	20	10	50	25
	1970	150	80	50	80	50
Hungary	1960	72.2	3.4	1.2	14.7	3.5
	1970	75.7	57.9	31.6	55.0	34.3

[a] Only in the State and cooperative sector (except for individual farmers).

Higher standards of living of the population in this field obviously involve a considerable increase in current expenditures.

Transport requirements of the population can be met by two means: the promotion of public transport and the purchase of private vehicles.

In all countries except the U.S.S.R., transport needs are satisfied, in roughly the same proportion, by public and private transport (see Table 2.21). In the U.S.S.R. collective transport plays a much more important role on account of the vast size of the territory and the large distances to be covered. From 1955 to 1969 the expenditure on transport services and the number of passengers (passengers/km) have increased more than threefold, air passenger traffic 25.5 times and road traffic 8.8 times.

All countries without exception show a tendency for the proportion of public transport to decline, but the extent of these changes varies from one country to another.

In the U.S.S.R. and in Poland, the rates of increase of expenditure on public and individual transport are very similar but with a somewhat more rapid expansion of individual transport in Poland.

In the U.S.S.R. the average rate of increase of individual transport expenditure was almost double that of public transport. In 1965 there has been a slowing down in the former rate but it rose again in 1970; since then it has remained substantially higher than the 1960–1969 average.

In contrast to other countries, expenditure on public transport rose in Czechoslovakia in 1965, whereas that on individual transport declined. In 1968 the situation was reversed and the proportion of public transport in the total dropped considerably.

Among the goods and services for the satisfaction of cultural and information needs, the consumption of services, that is the part which is essentially financed by the State (cultural education, museums, radio and television), increased in all countries. This tendency is particularly marked in the U.S.S.R. where the proportion of services in the total group rose from 27.4 to 45.8 per cent in the period.

2.3.2   Consumption structure, by broad social functions (Tables 2.24-2.26)

So far only the two consumption categories relating to social consumption in kind or in the form of services supplied by social funds have been examined. It is also of interest, however, to analyse the composition of consumption according to public functions, whether financed by private means or social funds, including transfers. The latter (as with consumption in kind) relate to education and take the form of scholarships, to health (allowances for temporary incapacity to work) and to social services (old-age pensions and allowances).

Tables 2.24-2.26 show that in all the countries reviewed education accounts for the major part of State-financed consumption. If all social consumption of that group is equal to 100, personal consumption in 1969 amounted to a mere 0.4 per cent in the U.S.S.R. and 9.8 per cent in Czechoslovakia. Household contributions consist of partial payments for boarding schools and schools with after-lesson supervision. In the G.D.R. and Hungary school books must be added. The relatively high contribution of household expenditure in Czechoslovakia is attributable to the fact that payments for kindergartens are included, but these figure in the item "Social services" in other countries.

The household share in expenditure on education declined progressively in all countries since the State assumed an increasing responsibility for education and the social importance of education has been continuously raised.

Expenditure on education is divided into two groups according to its content and destination: (a) general aducation and (b) professional training. This division is logical as the functions of the two categories, as well as the factors which determine their progress, differ.

The growing expenditure on general education is primarily influenced by the needs of the population which depend on changes in its demograhpic structure. Expenditure on professional training, on the other hand, is determined, among other factors, by the requirements of the economy for workers with specific professional qualifications and special skills which, in turn, depend on changes in the production structure.

The rapid increase in expenditure on education (see Chart. 2.8) is due not only to demographic growth but also to an improvement in the standards of instruction and a change in the composition of pupils (see Table 2.5).

Czechoslovakia is the only exception to this general trend: for demographic reasons the number of pupils in educational establishments declined in that country from 1960 to 1969.

The share of social funds in the financing of consumption is second largest for social services. Personal consumption as a ratio of social consumption in this group ranges from 1.6 per cent in Poland to 6.3 per cent in Hungary. But differences in coverage in the various countries render comparison tenuous. The share of personal consumption has declined in Hungary and the G.D.R., and has remained virtually unchanged in Poland and has risen somewhat in the U.S.S.R.

Table 2.24

Expenditure according to the nature of social needs, 1960 (percentages)

	Czechoslovakia				G.D.R.				Hungary				Poland				U.S.S.R.			
	Transfers	Free consumption in kind	Total	Personal consumption	Transfers	Free consumption in kind	Total	Personal consumption	Transfers	Free consumption in kind	Total	Personal consumption	Transfers	Free consumption in kind	Total	Personal consumption	Transfers	Free consumption in kind	Total	Personal consumption
9.00 Medical services	30.7	69.3	100.0	6.4	29.4	70.6	100.0	7.4	28.8	71.2	100.0	9.1	16.4	83.6	100.0	22.4	22.1	77.1	100.0	14.7
10.00 Social services	...	...	...	...	81.5	18.5	100.0	2.9	90.3	9.7	100.0	13.8	92.2	7.8	100.0	1.3	89.4	10.6	100.0	2.8
11.00 Education	4.6	95.4	100.0	12.3	8.9	77.9	100.0	5.8	4.7	95.3	100.0	18.0	6.9	93.1	100.0	3.4	3.0	97.0	100.0	0.4
15.00 Expanded consumption	61.6	43.7	100.0	295.7	33.0	67.0	100.0	279.2	38.4	61.5	100.0	465.7	43.1	56.9	100.0	489.3	40.1	59.9	100.0	400.0

Table 2.25

Expenditure according to the nature of social needs, 1965 (percentages)

	Czechoslovakia				G.D.R.				Hungary				Poland				U.S.S.R.			
	Transfers	Free consumption in kind	Total	Personal consumption	Transfers	Free consumption in kind	Total	Personal consumption	Transfers	Free consumption in kind	Total	Personal consumption	Transfers	Free consumption in kind	Total	Personal consumption	Transfers	Free consumption in kind	Total	Personal consumption
9.00 Medical services	27.2	72.8	100.0	8.6	23.6	76.4	100.0	9.3	27.4	72.6	100.0	8.5	16.9	83.1	100.0	20.5	23.0	77.0	100.0	13.5
10.00 Social services	89.2	10.8	...	...	83.5	16.5	100.0	1.9	90.1	9.9	100.0	9.0	93.1	6.9	100.0	1.6	86.1	13.9	100.0	3.5
11.00 Education	5.7	96.3	100.0	4.0	6.7	93.3	100.0	5.9	4.8	95.2	100.0	24.1	7.7	92.3	100.0	3.0	8.2	91.8	100.0	0.5
15.00 Expanded consumption	56.8	43.2	100.0	301.5	35.5	64.5	100.0	255.3	41.1	58.9	100.0	397.7	42.5	57.4	100.0	456.9	37.0	63.0	100.0	341.5

Table 2.26

Expenditure according to the nature of social needs, 1969 (percentages)

	Czechoslovakia				G.D.R.				Hungary				Poland				U.S.S.R.			
	Transfers	Free consumption in kind	Personal consumption	Total	Transfers	Free consumption in kind	Personal consumption	Total	Transfers	Free consumption in kind	Personal consumption	Total	Transfers	Free consumption in kind	Personal consumption	Total	Transfers	Free consumption in kind	Personal consumption	Total
9.00 Medical services	36.9	63.1	4.4	100.0	23.7	76.3	8.7	100.0	26.9	73.1	7.7	100.0	18.9	80.1	16.1	100.0	26.2	73.8	12.9	100.0
10.00 Social services	...	...	...	...	75.4	24.6	2.5	100.0	91.8	8.2	6.3	100.0	93.1	6.9	1.6	100.0	86.7	13.3	3.3	100.0
11.00 Education	5.2	94.8	9.8	100.0	7.5	92.5	4.9	100.0	6.0	94.0	22.5	100.0	6.7	93.3	2.0	100.0	9.6	90.4	0.4	100.0
15.00 Expanded consumption	44.8	55.2	291.2	100.0	36.1	63.9	252.3	100.0	44.6	55.4	376.2	100.0	43.9	56.1	423.2	100.0	38.1	61.9	341.7	100.0

Table 2.27

Indicators for the development of health services (number per 10,000 inhabitants)

	Czechoslovakia			G.D.R.			Hungary			Poland			U.S.S.R.		
	1960	1965	1969	1960	1965	1969	1960	1965	1969	1960	1965	1969	1960	1965	1969
Number of beds in hospitals and clinics	71.1	76.6	80.3	119	121	112	67.2	72.3	76.8	70.3	73.8	73.6	80	96	106
Number of doctors	15.3	19.2	22.2	12.2	15.1	19.3	15.3	18.9	22.0	12.7	16.2	18.5	20.0	23.9	26.6
Number of beds in sanatoria and other health establishments	57.6	54.6	53.1	72.0	71.0	67.0	47.7	52.1	63.9	30.5	51.5	95.8	23.5	27.6	30.4

In this classification health occupies the third position. The share of private consumption ranges from 22.4 per cent in Poland (where in the period reviewed part of the rural population was not covered by free medical assistance) to 6.4 per cent in Czechoslovakia. This low figure for Czechoslovakia is due to the fact that not only all health services, but also the stay in most sanatoria, are supplied free of charge. In addition, medicines are distributed freely upon doctors' prescription.

In all socialist countries health services are increasingly financed by society. The most rapid advances in this respect were registered in Poland and the U.S.S.R. (see Chart 2.7); they were due to the creation of hospitals and an improvement in the quality of treatment. The development of health services is illustrated in Table 2.27. It is shown that the number of doctors and hospital beds (per 10,000 inhabitants) are expanding constantly. At the same time the places available in sanatoria and rest homes tend to decline in the countries where they have attained the highest absolute level (G.D.R. and Czechoslovakia), reflecting an increasing preference of the population for travel, tourism, etc., financed from household incomes.

Since 1972, practically the whole Polish population has benefited from freely rendered health services, whereas in the period reviewed persons not covered by health insurance (self-employed and some other categories of the population) were not entitled to them and had to pay for these services out of their incomes. In addition, there exist in Poland dispensaries and cooperative polyclinics as well as private doctors who give curative and preventive assistance. These services are also paid for from household incomes. Out of 7837 dispensaries and polyclinics existing in Poland, 681 or about 9 per cent were cooperative. The proportion of private practice is insignificant. There were 12,000 doctors, that is close to 20 per cent of the medical corps, in that category in 1969. It must be noted that private practice is only a supplementary occupation since all doctors are employed in public medical establishments. In Poland about 70 per cent of medicines are freely supplied from social funds. In all countries there is a tendency for the proportion of the social satisfaction of health needs to increase. The only exception is the G.D.R. where this proportion registered a progressive although moderate decline. This is due to the fall in the share of allowances for the temporarily incapacitated and not to a decline in the volume of health services rendered.

The structure of social funds according to the form of their allocation has been examined in Section 2.3 of this chapter. Tables 2.24-2.26 show the broad categories broken down into the most important needs. Social consumption is shown in the tables as the aggregate of transfers plus the free consumption of goods and services in kind. The share of transfers is largest in item 10.00 "Social services"; this shows that pensions and allowances are the most important form of the satisfaction of social wants. The proportion of transfers in the consumption from social funds ranges from 93.1 per cent in Poland to 76.4 per cent in the G.D.R.

Social funds finance health services with the help of transfers (invalidity allowances) and goods and services supplied freely by medical establishments.

In 1969 transfers accounted for from 36.9 per cent of social consumption in Czechoslovakia to 18.9 per cent in Poland. The relatively low ratio in Poland is due to the fact that individual farmers did not benefit from invalidity allowances.

In the field of education, transfers take the form of scholarships in secondary and higher educational establishments. In 1969 the proportion of scholarships in total expenditure on education ranged from 7.5 per cent in the G.D.R. to 2.8 per cent in Czechoslovakia.

In 1969 total transfers accounted for the following proportions in the total consumption financed by social funds: 56.3 per cent in Czechoslovakia, 43.1 per cent in Poland, 40.1 per cent in the U.S.S.R., 38.4 per cent in Hungary and 33 per cent in the G.D.R. These figures suggest that transfers predominate in Czechoslovakia (except for scholarships) while consumption in kind is more important in the G.D.R. The other countries occupy an intermediate position.

The share of transfers and consumption in kind have shifted in favour of transfers in the majority of countries but have remained virtually unchanged in Poland and Czechoslovakia.

2.4 CONCLUSIONS

This study of the standards of welfare in terms of enlarged consumption by categories of needs, methods of allocation and forms of organization of consumption has given a fairly detailed picture of the ways in which the living standards of the population develop and has made it possible to arrive at a number of novel conclusions. The peculilarities of national statistics and the differences in price relationships have sometimes prevented direct comparisons of the level and structure of consumption between countries. But the desire of the participating countries to achieve a maximum possible comparability of data created a sound basis for tracing the main tendencies in the behaviour of the welfare indicators and the causes and factors responsible for the discrepancies observed in some respects, even in countries with similar productive systems.

The analysis of the development and structure of enlarged consumption shows that the socialist countries have common rules for the formation of incomes and consumption derived from the similarity of socialist productive systems, the identical methods of allocation of material and cultural goods and the common objectives of social development. In socialist countries individual and collective consumption have assumed equal proportions, and the structure and hierarchy of personal and social needs are virtually identical.

Steady growth of social product and national income provided the basis for promoting enlarged consumption and all the parameters of well-being directly connected with it. These advances in welfare took place in a setting of stable prices and full employment.

A major part of material and cultural goods produced by society, i.e. 68 to 79 per cent, is supplied to the population as a counterpart of income from work. The share of consumption financed from social funds ranges from 21 to 32 per cent in the various countries. During the period under review, this share continued to increase: from 18.9 to 23.2 per cent in Hungary, 29.2 to 31.8 per cent in the G.D.R., 18.4 to 21 per cent in Poland, 21.8 to 25.6 in the U.S.S.R. and 29.6 to 29.8 per cent in Czechoslovakia. The State budget is the main source of finance for all social consumption funds; they therefore rely predominantly on central finance; decentralized finance consists of contributions by enterprises, agricultural cooperatives and social institutions but represents only a small proportion of the social consumption funds. The income of the population does not participate directly in the formation of social funds which are created at the distribution and redistribution stage of national income.

In all the countries considered, the relationship between personal consumption financed from labour income, pensions or derived from individually owned plots of land, on the one hand, and social consumption of free or partially free goods and services financed from social funds, on the other, has shifted in favour of the social consumption funds. Thus in the period 1960 to 1969 the share of the latter component of consumption rose in the G.D.R. from 19.3 to 20.2 per cent, in Poland from 10.5 to 11.8 per cent, in the U.S.S.R. from 12.9 to 15.5 per cent and in Czechoslovakia from 12.9 to 13.2 per cent.

This tendency stems from the growing role of social funds in the performance of important socio-economic tasks for the development of socialist countries: the growth of social funds becomes increasingly necessary for their economic and social progress. The centralized consumption funds serve the promotion of education and technical training, the protection of health and the extension of the network of health institutions, and the improvement of housing conditions for workers. They ensure not only an increasingly complete satisfaction of the needs of the population but contribute also to enlarging the supply of more highly qualified manpower and to raising social productivity.

The more rapid rates of increase of the consumption funds than of income from work are caused not only by the extension of the social functions of this mechanism of allocation in socialist economies but also from a steady increase in the number of potential "consumers" of goods and services allocated through social channels.

The indicators of various forms of allocation of consumer goods from social funds differ very much from country to country. This applies, for instance, to the pension system which is a function of the modalities of granting pensions and of the demographic structure of the population.

In all countries the five most important categories of enlarged consumption are food, clothing and footwear, health, education and transport. Only the relative importance of the last three items varies between countries. The demand for food, clothing, housing and transport is covered mainly from family budgets whereas education, the protection of health and social services are essentially provided by social consumption funds.

The consumption structure of goods and services by categories of needs has changed in the following directions:

(i)   there has been a growing tendency towards a reduction of the share of foodstuffs together with a shift in their composition: the consumption of meat and meat products, vegetables, fruit, milk and other dairy produce has increased and that of bread, cereals, potatoes and sugar has declined;
(ii) cultural and other household durables and municipal services have taken on an increasing importance in the satisfaction of household needs, following the qualitative improvement of housing standards;
(iii) the satisfaction of transport needs has come to rely increasingly on private vehicles, although the pace of this change has varied considerably from one country to another.

The differences between the indicators in question arise from the system and form of allocation of the social consumption funds as well as from the level and nature of their allocation. This applies both to the part of consumption financed from social funds and to the share of cash transfers in the total amount of these funds.

The future development of consumption in socialist countries is likely to be characterized by a higher rate of increase of the social funds than of income from work. This tendency is to be expected from the promotion of the social functions of the funds as a method of allocation as well as from the increase in the number of potential "consumers" of goods and services distributed from centralized sources.

The following changes in the consumption patterns of goods and services can be foreseen:

  (i) a marked tendency for a reduction in the total proportion of food and a change in the composition of food consumption in the direction of an improvement in the quality of the products consumed;
 (ii) for non-food consumption, a tendency for more rapid increases in the consumption of cultural and other household goods and of consumer durables which are connected with tourism, recreation and leisure;
(iii) a substantial increase in the demand for vehicles and other means of private transport-motor-cycles, scooters and bicycles.

It must be remembered that these general tendencies in the development of consumption in socialist countries emerge from the study of a period which ended six years ago. Since then a number of measures to improve welfare have been introduced, thus changing the conditions which prevailed in the period 1960 to 1969.[7]

This reservation is all the more significant since the analysis is based on rather dynamic indicators; this applies in the first place to the share of social funds in total consumption, the structure of consumption by categories of needs, etc.

Thus, in Hungary, the conditions which determined the amount of pensions have been changed; the monthly amounts of family allowances and allocations granted to non-working women with children less than 3 years old have been substantially raised; salaries of kindergarten personnel and of primary and secondary school teachers, doctors, chemists and nurses have been increased, and this has led to an increase in expenditure on education and health.

In the G.D.R., incomes of old-age pensioners have been substantially raised due to new modalities of calculating the increase in pensions, and the monthly minimum has been raised to 150 marks. Allocations for newly born children have been increased. Salaries have been increased for certain categories of personnel in health services, teachers in orphanages, kindergartens and nurseries, and this has raised total expenditure on health and social welfare.

In Poland, free medical assistance has been extended to individual farmers and their families who represent close to 20 per cent of the population; minimum old-age and invalidity pensions have been increased; family allowances to families with modest incomes and sickness benefits as well as scholarships for higher education have been raised.

In the U.S.S.R. workers, employees and collective farmers had the minimum amount of their old-age pensions raised. At present collective farmers receive pensions on the same basis as workers and employees and their families: pensions for invalids and family survivors have been increased; the amounts of scholarships in higher education and specialized secondary schools have been considerably raised

---

[7]Only the measures directly linked with the promotion of social consumption funds are mentioned here.

(by 25 and 50 per cent respectively); pre-natal and maternity leave for working women is now fully paid (previously the amount was fixed in accordance with the length of employment); families whose average total income is below 50 roubles per person and per month benefit from a child allowance of 12 roubles per month for each child under 8 years old.

In Czechoslovakia the minimum pension was raised; the same applies to permanent family allowances; paid leave of two years is granted to women with at least two children from the second child onwards.

In the U.S.S.R. a new increase in all consumption indicators was expected to result from the policy to promote the welfare of the population. National income was expected to increase in 1975 by 39 per cent above its 1970 level, and the corresponding consumption funds 40.6 per cent. The latter will account for 27.5 per cent of the enlarged consumption of the population. The volume of paid services will double, on average, in the whole country, and almost triple in rural regions.

But the conclusions of this analysis are of considerable importance for the solution of methodological questions concerning the study of standards of living of the population independently of the time span covered. This applies to the general approach to the study of consumption, based as it is on the quantification of the "enlarged" concept, and also to the structural relationships examined in this project.

However, it is also true that the results of the analysis would have been more far- reaching, had it been based on a longer time span and a larger number of observations. It would then have been possible to apply more effective econometric methods permitting a quantitative (and not only qualitative) evaluation of the impact of different factors on the changes in the level and structure of consumption.

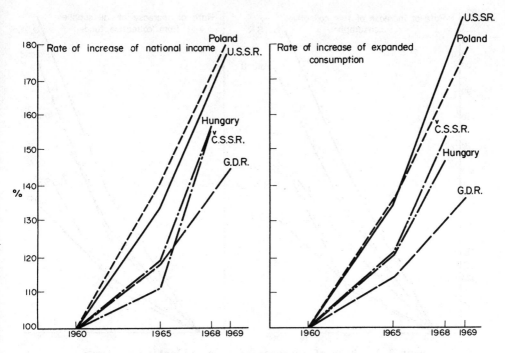

Chart 2.1.   Rate of increase of national income; rate of
             increase of enlarged consumption.

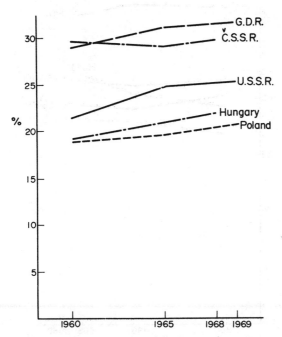

Chart 2.2.   Share of collective funds in enlarged con-
             sumption.

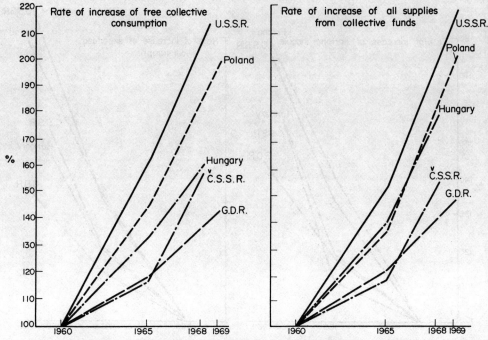

Chart 2.3. Rate of increase of free collective consumption; rate of increase of all supplies from
collective funds.

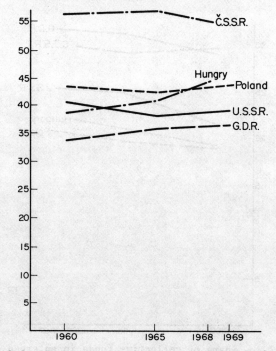

Chart 2.4.   Share of cash payments from collective funds.

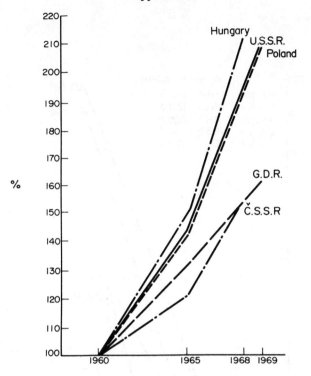

Chart 2.5.   Rate of increase of cash payments.

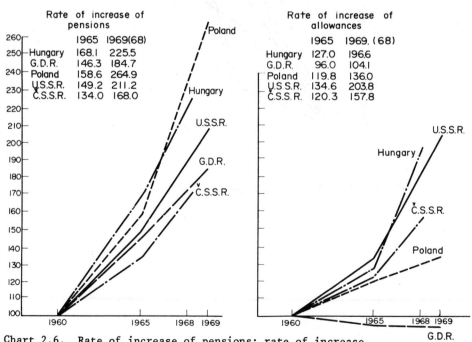

Rate of increase of pensions	1965	1969(68)
Hungary	168.1	225.5
G.D.R.	146.3	184.7
Poland	158.6	264.9
U.S.S.R.	149.2	211.2
Č.S.S.R.	134.0	168.0

Rate of increase of allowances	1965	1969. (68)
Hungary	127.0	196.6
G.D.R.	96.0	104.1
Poland	119.8	136.0
U.S.S.R.	134.6	203.8
Č.S.S.R.	120.3	157.8

Chart 2.6.   Rate of increase of pensions; rate of increase
             of allowances.

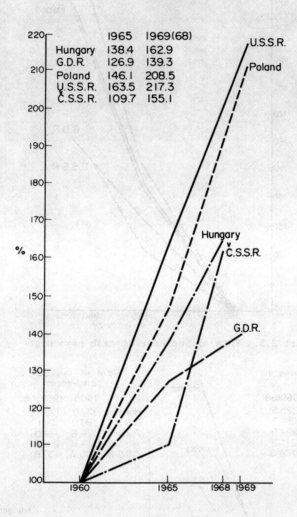

Chart 2.7. Rate of increase of health expenditure.

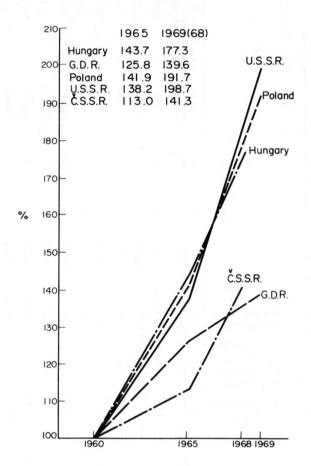

Chart 2.8.   Rate of increase of expenditure on education.

APPENDIX B

Basic Table B1. Enlarged consumption of households financed from individual and collective resources
(In millions of current crowns)
Č.S.S.R.

Goods and services by categories of needs of the population	1960			1965			1968		
	Direct household purchases	Consumption in kind financed from the State budget	Total household consumption						
	1	2	3	4	5	6	7	8	9
1.00 *Food*	50,166	381	50,547	57,875	425	58,290	65,079	805	65,884
1.01 Bread and cereals	8038	–	8038	9094	–	9094	9089	–	9089
1.02 Meat and poultry	10,862	–	10,862	13,417	–	13,417	16,109	–	16,109
1.03 Sea food	600	–	600	740	–	740	880	–	880
1.04 Milk, cheese, eggs, butter	6575	–	6575	8470	–	8470	9673	–	9673
1.05 Oils and fats	2647	–	2647	2673	–	2673	2596	–	2596
1.06 Potatoes and vegetables	1973	–	1973	1980	–	1980	2902	–	2902
1.07 Fresh and dried fruit	1594	–	1594	2617	–	2617	2415	–	2415
1.08 Sugar, chocolate, confectionery	5900	–	5900	6431	–	6431	6657	–	6657
1.09 Other food products	3985	–	3985	5404	–	5404	6068	–	6068
1.10 Self-consumption	7992	–	7992	7049	–	7049	8690	–	8690
1.11 Food consumption outside the home*)	–	381	381	–	425	425	–	805	805

*) Included in 100, 1.10

Basic Table B1. *Č.S.S.R.* (*cont.*)

	1960			1965			1968		
	1	2	3	4	5	6	7	8	9
2.00 *Beverages*	8401	–	8401	10,549	–	10,549	14,069	–	14,069
–Non-alcoholic	961	–	961	1182	–	1182	1402	–	1402
–Alcoholic	7440	–	7440	9367	–	9367	12,667	–	12,667
3.00 *Tobacco and matches*	3787	–	3787	4194	–	4194	5188	–	5188
4.00 *Clothing and footwear*	15,489	96	15,585	20,900	132	21,032	28,894	149	29,043
4.01 Clothing (and repairs)	12,704	64	12,768	17,439	66	17,505	24,499	75	24,574
4.02 Footwear (and repairs)	2785	32	2817	3461	66	3527	4395	74	4469
5.00 *Personal care*	1771	–	1771	2075	–	2075	2489	–	2489
5.01 Toilet articles, cosmetics and perfume	1340	–	1340	1602	–	1602	1698	–	1698
5.02 Hairdresser and other aesthetic care services	431	–	431	473	–	473	521	–	521
6.00 *Housing*	9890	1143	11,033	13,588	1373	14,961	20,771	1740	22,511
6.01 Real rent	1043	–	1043	2316	–	2316	3246	–	3246
6.02 Imputed rent of owners	1741	–	1741	2689	–	2689	4531	–	4531
6.03 Energy, water and urban heating	1229	–	1229	1695	–	1695	2142	–	2142
6.04 Furniture and other household equipment (including repairs)	4187	–	4187	4843	–	4843	6316	–	6316

Basic Table B1. *Č.S.S.R.* (cont.)

6.05	of which: electrical equipment	1566	–	1566	1646	–	1646	2145	–	2145
6.05	Product and services for construction and repairs of dwellings	1690	1143	2833[c]	2045	1373	3418[c]	4536	1740	4536[c]
7.00	*Transport*	6299	200	6499	6795	933	7728	9491	1521	11,012
7.01	Purchase of vehicles and repairs	1918	–	1918	1831	–	1831	3887	–	3887
7.02	Public transport services	4381	200	4581	4964	933	5897	5604	1521	7125
8.00	*Telecommunications* (excluding radios and television sets)	452	–	452	488	–	488	544	–	544
9.00	*Medical goods and services*	532	5742	6274	816	6274	7090	1077	7791	8868
9.01	Pharmaceuticals (including medical apparatus)	425	1293	1718	483	1538	2021	651	1297	1948
9.02	Establishments for prophylactic treatment (hospitals, clinics, ambulatories)	107	4449	4556	252	4736	5069	289	6494	6920
9.03	Sanitary-prophylatic establishments (anti-epidemic and disinfection stations, institutions for sanitary education)									
9.04	Sanatoria, health institutions and dietectic feeding					137				
10.00	*Social services*	92	...	92	162	...	162	123	...	123
10.01	Pre-school establishments	37[a]	...[a,b]		69[a]	...[a,b]	69	69[a]	...[a,b]	69
10.02	Children's homes	9	...[b]	9	20[b]	...[b]	20	...[b]	...[b]	...
10.03	Holiday colonies (holiday camps, extra-school establishments, etc.)	46	...	46	73	...	73	54	...	54

Basic Table B1. Č.S.S.R. (cont.)

	1960			1965			1968		
	1	2	3	4	5	6	7	8	9
11.00 *Education and research*	762	5872	6634	884	6984	7868	946	9346	10,292
11.01 Primary and secondary schools of which schools for adult education									
11.02 Boarding schools									
11.03 Specialized secondary schools (technicums, technical and professional training)	762	5872	6634	884	6984	7868	946	9346	10,292
11.04 Higher education and university research									
11.05 Professional technical schools (crafts, apprenticeships, schools for agricultural mechanization)									
12.00 *Culture and information*	2556	1130	3686	3797	1219	5016	4417	1621	6038
12.01 Books, newspapers, periodicals including manuals, copybooks, school and office supplies	1353	269	1622	1796	194	1990	2698	158	2856
12.02 Activities of cultural education (cultural universities, clubs, cultural centres, libraries)	98	861	959	603	1025	1628	160	1463	3182
12.03 Fine arts, radio and television	1105	–	1105	1398	–	1398	1559		
13.00 *Sports, leisure and entertainment*	1185	–	1185	1616	–	1616	2015	–	2015
13.01 Articles for leisure and entertainment (radio apparatus, records, musical instruments, toys)	384	–	384	469	–	469	663	–	663

Basic Table B1. *Č.S.S.R.* (cont.)

13.02	Sport equipment and services	442	–	442	656	–	656	768	–	768
13.03	Theatres, cinemas, concert halls and other spectacles and entertainment	53	–	53	74	–	74	98	–	98
13.04	Restaurant, bar and café services	306	–	306	417	–	417	486	–	486
14.00	*Other goods and services*	3980	1007	4987	5131	1078	6209	6046	1461	7507
15.00	*Enlarged consumption*	105,362	15,571	120,933	128,870	18,418	147,288	161,149	24,434	185,583

a Kindergartens are included in 11.00 to 11.05.

b Nurseries and children's homes are included in 9.02 to 9.04.

c Individual house construction is included.

Basic Table B2. Gross social benefits
(In millions of current crowns)
Č.S.S.R.

Social benefits	From all sources		
	1960	1965	1969
A. Social benefits in kind or in the form of services	15,571	18,418	24,434
B. Social cash transfers	20,056	24,319	30,891
1. Old-age pensions			
2. Invalidity pensions	11,352	15,210	19,076
3. Allowances (of which)	7210	8675	11,379
Family allowances			
Maternity allowances	4666	5531	6830
Allowances for newborn children			
Sickness allowances	2544	3144	4549
4. Scholarships	284	291	269
5. Other social transfers	1210	143	167
C. Total expenditure for social benefits and transfers (A + B)	35,627	42,737	55,325

APPENDIX B

Basic Table B3.   Indicators of the development of public services
Č.S.S.R.

		1960	1965	1969
	1	2	3	4

I.   *Public concern with children up to 7 years*

1.	Children up to 7 years benefiting from free medical services as percentage of all children in this age group	99.0	99.0	100.0
2.	Children in pre-school establishments as percentage of all children up to 7 years	18.9	24.4	27.0
3.	Number of children up to 1 year per 1000 of newborn children	969.4	992.7	970.7

II. *Education*

1.	Number of children aged 7 to 15 attending primary and secondary schools as percentage of all children in this age group	100.0	100.0	100.0
2.	Number of adolescents aged 16 to 19 attending secondary schools as percentage of all adolescents in this age group	26.1	29.3	28.4
3.	Number of adolescents aged 16 to 19 attending technical professional schools as percentage of all adolescents in this age group	17.8	19.3	18.9
4.	Number of pupils in special secondary schools per 10,000 inhabitants	106.6	137.3	136.6
5.	Number of students in higher education per 10,000 inhabitants	67.5	100.7	93.5

III. *Public Health*

1.	Number of persons benefiting from free medical services as percentage of total population	99.0	99.0	100.0
2.	Medical personnel per 10,000 inhabitants	84.5	92.8	96.7
	(a) of which doctors and specialists	17.5	20.5	22.5
3.	Number of beds in hospitals and clinics per 10,000 inhabitants	76.1	79.7	80.2
4.	Number of beds by doctors employed in hospitals and polyclinics	17.0	18.1	15.9

IV. *Social Security and Insurance*

1.	Number of children placed free of charge (totally or partially) in holiday camps as percentage of pupils in classes 1 to 9	17.0	22.6	24.7
2.	Average length of paid leave of adult workers and employees in working days	-	-	-
3.	Average amount of old-age pensions as percentage of the average wage of workers and employees	40.3	39.6	36.6

Basic Table B3. *Č.S.S.R.* *(cont.)*

	1	1960	1965	1969
		2	3	4
V.	*Cultural Services and Leisure*			
1.	Number of persons benefiting from organized leisure (sanatoria, boarding houses, health establishments, in per cent)	7.0	8.1	8.4
2.	Average number of theatre entries per 10,000 inhabitants	9347	7848	6781
3.	Average number of cinema entries per inhabitant	12.9	9.1	8.3
4.	Number of owners of radio sets per 10,000 inhabitants	2586	2632	2762
5.	Number of owners of television sets per 10,000 inhabitants	582	1493	1994
6.	Average number of readers per library	135.1	143.1	150.6
7.	Number of libraries per 10,000 inhabitants	10.1	9.0	8.2
VI.	*Housing Services*			
1.	Average surface per urban inhabitant in towns with more than 1 million inhabitants	10.6	–	–
2.	Average surface per inhabitant in the whole country	9.5	10.5	11.2
3.	Total rent as percentage of the wage fund of workers and employees	1.3	2.2	˙2.5
4.	Percentage of dwellings with:			
	–running water	58.7	67.7	73.1
	–electricity	97.2	97.9	98.3

Basic Table B1. Enlarged consumption of households financed from individual and collective resources
(In millions of current marks)
G.D.R.

Goods and services by categories of needs of the population	1960				1965				1969			
	Direct household purchases	collective funds	the State budget	Total household consumption								
	1	2	3	4	5	6	7	8	9	10	11	12
1.00 *Food*	18,652	746	146	19,398	21,100	913	213	22,013	25,240	1110	310	26,350
1.01 Bread and cereals	2718	–	–	2718	3218	–	–	3218	3531	–	–	3531
1.02 Meat and poultry	4804	–	–	4804	5489	–	–	5489	6260	–	–	6260
1.03 Sea food	474	–	–	474	476	–	–	476	460	–	–	460
1.04 Milk, cheese, eggs, butter	4627	–	–	4627	4949	–	–	4949	5574	–	–	5574
1.05 Oils and fats												
1.06 Potatoes, vegetables, fruit	1269	–	–	1269	1525	–	–	1525	2400	–	–	2400
1.07 Sugar, chocolate and confectionery	1915	–	–	1915	2165	–	–	2165	2425	–	–	2425
1.08 Other food products	6610	–	–	6610	8238	–	–	8238	10,750	–	–	10,750
1.09 Food consumption outside the home	(864)	446	146	(1610)	(1094)	913	213	(2007)	(1621)	1110	310	(2731)

Note: Columns 2, 3 (and corresponding) headed "Consumption in kind financed from:"

Basic Table B1. *G.D.R.* (*cont.*)

	1960				1965				1969			
	1	2	3	4	5	6	7	8	9	10	11	12
2.00 *Beverages*	3765	–	–	3765	4960	–	–	4960	6160	–	–	6160
2.01 Non-alcoholic	299	–	–	299	490	–	–	490	610	–	–	610
2.02 Alcoholic	3466	–	–	3466	4470	–	–	4470	5550	–	–	5550
3.00 *Tobacco and matches*	2504	–	–	2504	2820	–	–	2820	3150	–	–	3150
4.00 *Clothing and footwear*	8249	–	–	8249	8663	–	–	8663	10,205	–	–	10,205
4.01 Clothing (and repairs)	7227	–	–	7227	7213	–	–	7213	8497	–	–	8497
4.02 Footwear (and repairs)	1022	–	–	1022	1450	–	–	1450	1708	–	–	1708
5.00 *Personal care*	1980	–	–	1980	2267	–	–	2267	2916	–	–	2916
6.00 *Housing*	8094	2215	2080	10,309	8547	2310	2160	10,857	9963	2284	2100	12,247
6.01 Real rent	1584	2215	2080	3799	1712	2310	2160	4022	1887	2284	2100	4171
6.02 Imputed rents of owners[a]	800	–	–	800	800	–	–	800	800	–	–	800
6.03 Energy, water, urban heating	524	–	–	524	760	–	–	760	1039	–	–	1039
6.04 Furniture and other household equipment (including repairs)	4046	–	–	4046	5075	–	–	5075	6008	–	–	6008
6.05 Products and services for construction and repairs of dwellings	140	–	–	140	200	–	–	200	229	–	–	229

Basic Table B1. *G.D.R.* *(cont.)*

7.00	*Transport*	3230	–	–	3230	3332	–	–	3332	4038	–	–	4038
7.01	Purchase and repairs of vehicles	1384	–	–	1384	1438	–	–	1438	2222	–	–	2222
7.02	Public transport services	1846	–	–	1846	1894	–	–	1894	1816	–	–	1816
8.00	*Telecommunications* (excluding radios and television sets)	372	–	–	372	390	–	–	390	480	–	–	480
9.00	*Medical goods and services*	235	2241	2181	2476	340	2774	2694	3114	354	3103	3009	3457
9.01	Pharmaceuticals (including medical apparatus)	235	–	–	235	340	–	–	340	354	–	–	354
9.02	Establishments for prophylactic treatment (hospitals, clinics, ambulatories)	...	2044	1984	2044	–	2401	2321	2401	–	2970	2878	2970
9.03	Sanitary-prophylactic establishments (anti-epidemics and dis-infection stations, institutions for sanitary education)		197	197	197	–	373	373	373	–	131	131	131
9.04	Santoria, health establishments, dietectic feeding												
10.00	*Social services*	135	1090	870	1225	161	1372	1072	1533	180	2810	2465	2990
10.01	Pre-school establishments, children's homes	71	931	711	1002	102	1190	890	1292	127	2580	235	2707
10.02	Old people's homes	64	159	159	223	59	182	182	241	53	230	230	283
11.00	*Education and research*	224	4035	3035	4259	322	5083	3583	5405	300	5634	3934	5934
11.01	Books and school equipment	224	...	39	...	322	...	31	...	300	...	40	...

Basic Table B1. *G.D.R. (cont.)*

	1960				1965				1969			
	1	2	3	4	5	6	7	8	9	10	11	12
11.02 Primary and secondary schools	—	1357	1357	1357	—	1794	1794	1794	—	1915	1915	1915
-Higher education	—	1015	1015	1015	—	1046	1046	1046	—	1130	1130	1130
-Professional and specialized schools	—	...	624	...	—	...	712	...	—	...	849	...
12.00 *Culture and information*	1145	991	856	2136	1302	1269	1119	2571	1363	1599	1415	2962
1. Books, newspapers, periodicals	949	...	...	...	894	...	...	...	855	...	...	...
2. Radio and TV services	196	...	...	...	408	...	...	...	508	...	...	...
3. Museums	...	16	16	...	...	14	14	...	...	65	65	...
4. Other services	...	...	840	...	...	...	1105	...	...	...	1350	...
13.00 *Sports, leisure and entertainment*	2504	322	202	2726	3100	307	167	3407	3500	274	114	3774
14.00 *Other goods and services*	1424	630	—	2054	1255	730	—	1985	1987	845	—	2832
15.00 *Enlarged consumption*	51,513	12,270	9370	63,783	58,559	14,758	11,008	73,317	69,836	17,659	13,347	87,495

aProbable figures.

Basic Table B2. Gross social benefits
(In millions of current marks)
G.D.R.

Social benefits	From all sources		
	1960	1965	1969
A. Social benefits in kind or in the form of services	12,270	14,758	17,659
B. Social cash transfers	6286	8280	10,101
1. Old-age pensions	4560	6669	8424
2. Invalidity pensions	1147	1101	1095
3. Allowances (of which)	1147	1101	1095
Family allowances			
Maternity allowances allowances for newborn children	214	245	131
Sickness allowances	933	856	964
4. Scholarships	393	365	455
5. Other social transfers	186	145	127
C. Total expenditure for social benefits and transfers (A + B)	18,556	23,028	27,760

Basic Table B3. Indicators of the development of public services
G.D.R.

		1960	1965	1969
	1	2	3	4

I. *Public concern with children up to 7 years*

1. Children up to 7 years benefiting from free medical services as percentage of all children in this age group — 100 / 100 / 100
2. Children in pre-school establishments as percentage of the number of all children up to 7 years — 42 / 45 / 55
3. Number of children up to 1 year per 1000 of newborn children — 966 / 979 / 983

II. *Education*

1. Number of children aged 7 to 15 attending primary and secondary schools as percentage of all children in this age group — 100 / 100 / 100
2. Number of adolescents aged 16 to 18 attending secondary schools as percentage of all adolescents in this age group — 31 / ... / 53
3. Number of adolescents aged 14 to 19 in technical professional schools as percentage of all adolescents in this age group — 50 / 68 / 58
4. Number of pupils in specialized secondary schools per 10,000 inhabitants — 73 / 66 / 88
5. Number of students in establishments for higher education per 10,000 inhabitants — 59 / 64 / 72

III. *Public Health*

1. Number of persons benefiting from free medical services as percentage of total population — 100 / 100 / 100
2. Medical personnel per 10,000 inhabitants
   (a) of which doctors and specialists — 12.2 / 15.1 / 19.3
3. Number of beds in hospitals and clinics per 10,000 inhabitants — 119 / 121 / 112

IV. *Social Security and Insurance*

1. Number of children placed free of charge (totally or partially) in holiday camps as percentage of pupils in classes 1 to 9 — ... / 42 / ...
2. Average duration of paid leave of adult workers and employees in number of working days — 16 / 16 / 17
3. Average amount of old-age pensions as percentage of the average wage of workers and employees — 27.2 / 26.7 / 26.5

Basic Table B3. *G.D.R (cont.)*

			1960	1965	1969
		1	2	3	4

V. *Cultural Services and Leisure*

1.	Number of the population benefiting from organized leisure (sanatoria, boarding houses, and health establishments, in per cent)		...	20.2	...
2.	Average number of theatre and concert entries per 10,000 inhabitants		9300	7500	7250
3.	Average number of museum entries per 10,000 inhabitants		...	...	...
4.	Average number of cinema entries per inhabitant		14	7	5
5.	Number of owners of radio sets per 10,000 inhabitants		3230	3370	3510
6.	Number of owners of television sets per 10,000 inhabitants		600	1890	2510
7.	Average number of readers per public library		175	161	230

VI. *Housing Services*

1.	Average surface per urban inhabitant in towns with more than 1 million inhabitants		...	...	15.4
2.	Total rent as percentage of the wage fund of workers and employees		5.3	4.8	3.3
3.	Percentage of dwellings with				
	-running water		66	...	82
	-electricity		100	100	100

Basic Table B1. Enlarged consumption of households financed from individual and collective resources
(In millions of Forints)

Hungary

Goods and services by categories of needs of the population	Direct household purchases	Consumption in kind financed from:		Total household consumption	Direct household purchases	Consumption in kind financed from:		Total household consumption	Direct household purchases	Consumption in kind financed from:		Total household consumption
		collective funds	the State budget			collective funds	the State budget			collective funds	the State budget	
	1960				1965				1968			
	1	2	3	4	5	6	7	8	9	10	11	12
1.00 *Food*	44,191	1950	1950	46,141	50,914	2690	2690	53,604	60,531	3323	3323	63,854
1.01 Bread and cereals	6783	282	282	7065	7489	389	389	7878	7665	481	481	8146
1.02 Meat and poultry	11,430	695	695	12,125	12,322	961	961	13,283	16,532	1185	1185	17,717
1.03 Seafood	262	11	11	273	317	15	15	332	588	18	18	606
1.04 Milk, cheese, eggs, butter	5976	202	202	6178	6607	277	277	6884	7703	342	342	8045
1.05 Oils and fats	6078	170	170	6248	5844	235	235	6079	5711	290	290	6001
1.06 Potatoes and vegetables	4417	210	210	4627	5530	288	288	5818	6557	358	358	6915
1.07 Fresh and dried fruit	2822	147	147	2969	3431	203	203	3634	4597	251	251	4848
1.08 Sugar, chocolate, confectionery	3877	130	130	4007	4745	180	180	4925	4687	222	222	4909
1.09 Other food products	1686	103	103	1789	3259	142	142	3401	4793	175	175	4968
1.10 Food consumption outside the home	860	(1950)	(1950)	(2810)	1370	(2690)	(2690)	(4060)	1700	(3323)	(3323)	(5123)

Basic Table B1. *Hungary* *(cont.)*

2.00 *Beverages*	10,234	151	38	10,385	13,199	186	35	13,385	16,617	165	45	1678
2.01 -Non-alcoholic	355	38	38	393	555	35	35	590	763	45	45	808
2.02 -Alcoholic	9879	113	–	9992	12,644	151	–	12,795	15,854	120	–	15,974
3.00 *Tobacco and matches*	2006	–	–	2006	2776	–	–	2776	3483	27	27	3510
4.00 *Clothing and footwear*	16,746	344	344	17,090	17,680	264	264	17,944	19,634	427	427	20,061
4.01 Clothing	10,310	283	283	10,593	11,010	207	207	11,217	12,578	351	351	12,929
4.02 Footwear	2822	61	61	2883	3379	57	57	3436	3591	76	76	3667
4.03 Repairs of clothing and footwear	1645	–	–	1645	1373	–	–	1373	1265	–	–	1265
4.04 Accessories	1969	–	–	1969	1918	–	–	1918	2200	–	–	2200
5.00 *Personal care*	1195	–	–	1195	1575	–	–	1575	1998	–	–	1998
5.01 Toilet articles, cosmetics and perfume	521	–	–	521	764	–	–	764	929	–	–	929
5.02 Hairdresser and other aesthetic care services	674	–	–	674	811	–	–	811	1069	–	–	1069
6.00 *Housing*	14,897	1256	–	16,153	18,188	1523	–	19,711	22,546	1704	–	24,250
6.01 Real rent (including repairs)	1561	1256	–	2817	1872	1523	–	3395	2388	1704	–	4092
6.02 Imputed rents of owners	1522	–	–	1522	1819	–	–	1819	1997	–	–	1997
6.03 Electricity	664	–	–	664	1073	–	–	1073	1380	–	–	1380
6.04 Water, gas, urban heating	2738	–	–	2738	3457	–	–	3457	4043	–	–	4043

Basic Table B1. *Hungary* (*cont.*)

	1960				1965				1968			
	1	2	3	4	5	6	7	8	9	10	11	12
6.05 Furniture and other household equipment	7253	-	-	7253	8750	-	-	8750	11,081	-	-	11,081
6.06 Products and services connected with housing	1159	-	-	1159	1217	-	-	1217	1657	-	-	1657
7.00 *Transport*	4519	-	-	4519	6047	-	-	6047	8618	-	-	8618
7.01 Purchase of vehicles	953	-	-	953	1068	-	-	1068	2283	-	-	2283
7.02 Repair of vehicles	480	-	-	480	962	-	-	962	1488	-	-	1488
7.03 Public transport services	3086	-	-	3086	4017	-	-	4017	4847	-	-	4847
8.00 *Telecommunications* (excluding radios and television sets)	458	-	-	458	629	-	-	629	708	-	-	708
9.00 *Medical goods and services*	535	4182	3847	4717	707	6072	5549	6779	789	7576	6876	8365
9.01 Pharmaceuticals (including medical apparatus)	402	921	921	1323	507	1623	1623	2130	576	2069	2069	2645
9.02 Hospitals, clinics	-	1786	1786	1786	-	2443	2443	2443	-	2975	2975	2975
9.03 Polyclinics, ambulatories	-	1140	1140	1140	-	1483	1483	1483	-	1832	1832	1832
9.04 Other medical services	133	335	-	468	200	523	-	723	213	700	-	913
10.00 *Social services*	124	896	896	1020	254	1207	1207	1461	321	1337	1337	1658
10.01 Pre-school establishments, children's homes	124	582	582	706	254	890	890	1144	321	977	977	1298

Basic Table B1. Hungary (cont.)

10.02	Old people's homes	–	314	314	314	–	317	317	317	–	360	360	360
11.00	Education and research	644	3821	3821	4465	1107	5131	5131	6238	1245	6131	6131	7376
11.01	School books and equipment	318	–	–	318	571	–	–	571	645	–	–	646
11.02	Primary schools	74	2174	2174	2248	168	2573	2573	2741	193	2931	2931	3124
11.03	Secondary and specialized schools	226	1126	1126	1352	274	1600	1600	1874	309	2021	2021	2330
11.04	Higher education and university research	26	521	521	547	94	958	958	1052	98	1179	1179	1277
12.00 13.00	Culture, information / Sports	3725	865	–	4590	5322	1012	–	6324	7538	1127	–	8665
12.01	Books, newspapers, periodicals	971	–	–	971	1377	–	–	1377	1825	–	–	1825
12.02	Radio and TV services	661	–	–	661	1152	–	–	1152	2239	–	–	2239
12.03	Articles for recreation	199	–	–	199	194	–	–	194	232	–	–	232
12.04	Sports equipment and toys	278	–	–	278	405	–	–	405	441	–	–	441
12.05	Other goods	112	–	–	112	139	–	–	139	110	–	–	110
12.06	Cultural and sports services	1504	865	–	2369	2055	1012	–	3067	2691	1127	–	3818
14.00	Other goods and services	2745	–	–	2745	3676	–	–	3676	4612	–	–	4612
14.01	Goods	772	–	–	772	995	–	–	995	1290	–	–	1290
14.02	Services	1973	–	–	1973	2681	–	–	2681	3322	–	–	3322
15.00	Enlarged consumption	102,019	13,465	10,103	115,484	122,074	18,055	13,591	140,159	148,639	21,817	16,660	170,456

Basic Table B2. Gross social benefits
(In millions of forints)
Hungary

Social benefits	From all sources		
	1960	1965	1969
A. Social benefits in kind or in the form of services	13,465	18,085	21,817
B. Social cash transfers	8350	12,599	17,718
1. Old-age pensions			
2. Invalidity pensions	4587	7712	10,343
3. Allowances (of which)	3583	4547	7040
Family allowances	1432	1575	2868
Maternity allowances for newborn children and others	465	700	1394
Sickness allowances	1686	2272	2778
4. Scholarships	180	340	335
C. Total expenditure for social benefits and transfers (A + B)	21,815	30,684	39,535

Basic Table B3. Indicators of the development of public services
Hungary

	1960	1965	1969
1	2	3	4
I. *Public concern with children up to 7 years*			
1. Children in pre-school establishments as percentage of the number of children up to 3 years	6.8	9.6	8.7
3 to 5 years	33.7	47.1	53.9
2. Number of children up to 1 year per 1000 of newborn children	952	961	964
II. *Education*			
1. Number of children aged 6 to 14 attending primary schools as percentage of all children in this age group	98.5	98.8	98.7[a]
2. Number of adolescents aged 14 to 19 attending secondary or professional schools as percentage of all adolescents in this age group	47.7	59.8	60.6[a]
3. Number of young men aged 20 to 24 attending establishments for higher education as percentage of all young men in this age group	4.2	6.9	6.7
4. Number of students in establishments for higher education per 10,000 inhabitants	44.6	89.8	76.6
III. *Public Health*			
1. Number of persons benefiting from free medical services as percentage of total population	85.0	97.0	97.0
2. Medical personnel per 10,000 inhabitants	15.3	18.9	22.0
3. Number of hospital beds in clinics per 10,000 inhabitants	71.1	76.6	80.3
4. Number of doctors per 100 beds in hospitals and clinics	7.7	9.1	9.3
IV. *Social Security and Insurance*			
1. Number of beds in old people's home per 10,000 inhabitants	20.2	22.9	25.3
2. Number of children placed free of charge (totally or partially) in holiday camps, etc., as percentage of the age group 6 to 14	9.9	8.1	10.8
3. Number of persons (including children) benefiting from organized free holidays	5.0	5.8	6.9
4. Average amount of old-age pensions as percentage of average wage of workers and employees	30.0	32.3	35.4[b]
V. *Cultural Services and Leisure*			
1. Average number of theatre and concert attendance per 10,000 inhabitants	6865	6564	6444
2. Average number of museum entries per 10,000 inhabitants	3646	5512	6311

Basic Table B3. *Hungary* *(cont.)*

		1960	1965	1969
1		2	3	4
3.	Average number of cinema seats per 10,000 inhabitants	720	680	615
4.	Number of owners of radio sets per 10,000 inhabitants	2228	2359	2465
5.	Number of owners of television sets per 10,000 inhabitants	104	818	1365
6.	Number of public libraries per 10,000 inhabitants	11.0	10.9	10.7
VI.	*Housing Services*			
1.	Average surface per urban inhabitant in towns with more than 1 million inhabitants	...	49.5	...
2.	Average surface for inhabitants in the whole country	...	51.5	...
3.	Total rent as percentage of the wage fund of workers and employees	1.20	1.14	1.11[b]
4.	Percentage of population with:			
	−current water	23.5	32.9	36.8
	−electricity	73.8	82.2	85.4

[a] 1966/1967.

[b] 1970.

Basic Table B1. Enlarged consumption of households financed from individual and collective resources
(In millions of zlotys)
Poland

Goods and services by categories of needs of the population	1960			1965			1969		
	Direct household purchases	Consumption in kind financed from: collective funds	Total household consumption	Direct household purchases	Consumption in kind financed from: collective funds	Total household consumption	Direct household purchases	Consumption in kind financed from: collective funds	Total household consumption
	1	2	3	4	5	6	7	8	9
1.00 *Food*	132,232	3500	135,732	16,318	4920	168,238	201,917	5883	207,800
1.01 Bread and cereals	20,705	–	20,705	24,080	–	24,080	27,110	–	27,110
1.02 Meat and poultry	31,549	–	31,549	40,331	–	40,331	54,812	–	54,812
1.03 Sea food	2169	–	2169	3135	–	3135	4237	–	4237
1.04 Milk, cheese, eggs, butter	32,034	–	32,034	38,383	–	38,383	46,416	–	46,416
1.05 Oils and fats	9108	–	9108	10,992	–	10,992	10,733	–	10,733
1.06 Potatoes and vegetables	18,560	–	18,560	24,230	–	24,230	31,021	–	31,021
1.07 Fresh and dried fruit									
1.08 Sugar, chocolate, confectionery	12,166	–	12,166	14,277	–	14,277	16,309	–	16,309
1.09 Other food products	5941	–	5941	7930	–	7930	11,279	–	11,279
1.10 Food consumption outside the home	–	3500	3500	–	4920	4920	–	5883	5883

Basic Table B1. *Poland* (cont.)

		1960			1965			1968		
		1	2	3	4	5	6	7	8	9
2.00	*Beverages*	22,096	–	22,096	32,803	–	32,803	48,171	–	48,171
2.01	Non-alcoholic	905	–	905	1717	–	1717	2597	–	2597
2.02	Alcoholic	21,191	–	21,191	31,086	–	31,086	45,574	–	45,574
3.00	*Tobacco and matches*	8702	–	8702	10,851	–	10,851	13,410	–	13,410
4.00	*Clothing and footwear*	44,004	–	44,004	55,443	–	55,443	71,665	–	71,665
4.01	Clothing ⎤	39,600	–	39,600	51,295	–	51,295	67,208	–	67,208
4.02	Footwear ⎦									
4.03	Repairs of clothing and footwear	4404	–	4404	4148	–	4148	4457	–	4457
5.00	*Personal care*	4203	–	4203	6618	–	6618	8712	–	8712
5.01	Toilet articles, cosmetics and perfume	3381	–	3381	5144	–	5144	6853	–	6853
5.02	Hairdresser and other aesthetic care services	822	–	822	1474	–	1474	1859	–	1859
6.00	*Housing*	22,796	1700	24,496	37,361	2781	40,142	51,950	2168	54,118
6.01	Real rent	1793	1700	3493	3176	2781	5957	6332	2168	8500
6.02	Imputed rents of owners	2400	–	2400	2650	–	2650	3120	–	3120
6.03	Energy, water and urban heating	5767	–	5767	13,727	–	13,727	19,019	–	19,019
6.04	Furniture and other household equipment	12,636	–	12,636	17,248	–	17,248	22,643	–	22,643

Basic Table B1. *Poland* *(cont.)*

6.05	Services connected with housing	200	–	200	560	–	560	836	–	836
7.00	*Transport*	10,702	–	10,702	15,785	–	15,785	22,411	–	22,411
7.01	Purchase and repairs of vehicles	4211	–	4211	6885	–	6885	9149	–	9149
7.02	Services of public transport and repairs	6491	–	6491	8900	–	8900	13,262	–	13,262
8.00	*Telecommunications* (excluding radios and television sets)	1193	–	1193	1804	–	1804	2318	–	2318
9.00	*Medical goods and services*	3039	11,200	14,239	4021	16,191	20,212	4525	22,768	27,293
9.01–9.02	Pharmaceuticals (including medical apparatus)	2196	4526	6722	2960	5446	8406	3379	8229	11,608
9.03–9.06	Establishments for prophylactic treatment (hospitals, clinics, sanatoria)	477	3370	3847	603	4631	5234	661	6921	7582
9.07–9.12	Establishments without patients[a] Ambulatories, preventive medicine	366	2364	2730	458	3659	4114	484	5077	5561
	Other services	–	940	940	–	2454	2454	–	2541	2541
10.00	*Social services*	313	1656	1969	460	2115	2575	700	3020	3720
10.01–10.03	Pre-school establishments, children's homes, holiday colonies	313	1158	...	460	1425	...	700	1981	...
10.04	Establishments for handicapped people		164	...		250	...		432	...
	Other services		334	...		440	...		607	...

Basic Table B1. *Poland* (cont.)

		1960			1965			1968		
		1	2	3	4	5	6	7	8	9
11.00	*Education and research*	400	10,654	11,054	517	15,631	16,148	523	22,526	23,049
11.01	School books and school equipment	-	544	544	-	610	610	-	1780	1780
11.02	Primary schools		4634	...		6018	...		7885	...
11.03	Secondary and specialized schools		469	...		782	...		875	...
11.04-11.07	Technical, professional and specialized schools and evening classes for adults	400	1875	...	517	3392	...	523	4506	...
11.05	Higher education and university and post-university research		1332	...		2016	...		3155	...
11.08	Other		1800	...		2813	...		4326	...
12.00	*Culture and information*	2332	497	2829	3827	734	4561	5302	1084	6386
12.01	Books, newspapers, periodicals	1602	-	1602	2294	-	2294	3029	-	3029
12.02	Cultural services	730	497	1227	1588	784	2267	2278	1084	3357
13.00	*Sports, leisure and entertainment*	7966	1000	8966	14,550	2100	16,650	19,114	3294	22,408
13.01	Articles for leisure and recreation (radio sets, records, musical instruments, toys, etc.)	5546	-	5546	9886	-	9886	12,609	-	12,609
13.02	Sport equipment	140	-	140	524	-	524	675	-	675
13.03-13.08	Services	2280	1000	3280	4140	2100	6240	5830	3294	9124
14.00	*Other goods and services*	2352	272	2624	6377	24	6401	6239	160	6399
15.00	*Enlarged consumption*	262,330	30,479	292,809	353,735	44,496	398,231	456,957	60,903	517,860

[a] Including prophylactic sanitary establishments.

Basic Table B2. Gross social benefits
(In millions of zlotys)
Poland

Social benefits	From all sources		
	1960	1965	1969
A. Social benefits in kind or in the form of services	30,479	44,496	60,903
B. Social cash transfers	23,119	32,899	47,680
1. Old-age pensions	11,067	11,383	20,010
2. Invalidity pensions	...	6164	9304
3. Allowances (of which)	10,534	12,617	14,321
Family allowances	7744	8848	8478
Maternity allowances	418	340	438
Allowances for newborn children	146	105	103
Sickness allowances	2226	3324	5302
4. Scholarships	844	1271	1600
5. Other social transfers	674	1464	2445
C. Total expenditure for social benefits and transfers (A + B)	53,598	77,395	108,583

Basic Table B3.   Indicators of the development of public services
Poland

		1960	1965	1969
	1	2	3	4
I.	*Public concern with children up to 7 years*			
	1. Children up to 7 years benefiting from free medical services as percentage of all children of this age group	100.0	100.0	100.0
	2. Children in pre-school establishments as percentage of children up to 3 years	2.6	3.7	4.5
	3. Number of children up to 1 year per 1000 newborn children	945	959	966
II.	*Education*			
	1. Number of children aged 7 to 13 attending primary and secondary schools as percentage of all children in this age group	99.6	99.7	99.7
	2. Number of adolescents aged 14 to 17 in secondary and professional schools as percentage of all adolescents in this age group	64.8	73.1	67.2
	3. Number of young men aged 19 to 23 attending establishments for higher education as percentage of all young men in this age group	...	...	8.1
	4. Number of students in establishments for higher education per 10,000 inhabitants	55.4	79.8	98.7
III.	*Public Health*			
	1. Number of persons benefiting from free medical services in hospitals as percentage of total population	60.4	70.9	77.5
	2. Medical personnel per 10,000 inhabitants	40.5	48.3	54.9
	(a) of which doctors and specialists	12.7	16.2	18.5
	3. Number of beds in hospitals and clinics per 10,000 inhabitants	70.3	73.8	73.6
	4. Number of beds per doctor employed in hospitals and polyclinics	9.8	7.8	7.5
IV.	*Social Security and Insurance*			
	1. Number of old persons in old-age homes as percentage of the population in this age group	1.9	1.9	1.7
	2. Number of persons (including children) benefiting from organized free holidays	...	7.7	...
	3. Number of children placed free of charge (totally or partially) in holiday camps, sanatoria, etc., as percentage of the age group 7 to 14	...	25.3	...
	4. Average amount of old-age pensions as percentage of the average wage of workers and employees	40.0	41.8	48.6

Basic Table B3. *Poland (cont.)*

		1960	1965	1969
	1	2	3	4
V.	***Cultural Services and Leisure***			
1.	Number of persons benefiting from organized holidays (sanatoria, boarding houses, health establishments, in per cent)	...	7.7	...
2.	Average number of theatre and concert entries per 10,000 inhabitants	5946	5801	5600
3.	Average number of museum entries per 10,000 inhabitants	2698	4528	5524
4.	Average number of cinema seats per 10,000 inhabitants	221	232	199
5.	Average number of cinema visitors per 10,000 inhabitants	68,204	55,016	43,418
6.	Number of owners of radio sets per 10,000 inhabitants	1762	1789	1729
7.	Number of owners of television sets per 10,000 inhabitants	142	659	1172
8.	Number of public libraries per 10,000 inhabitants	2.4	2.6	2.6
VI.	***Housing Services***			
1.	Average surface per urban inhabitants in towns with more than 1 million inhabitants	...	...	13.6[a]
2.	Average surface per inhabitant in the whole country	...	...	13.2[a]
3.	Total rent as percentage of the wage fund of workers and employees	...	1.4	2.0
4.	Percentage of dwellings with:			
	−current water			
	(a) in towns	55.4	...	74.6[a]
	(b) in villages	3.6	...	11.7[a]
	−electricity			
	(a) in towns	100.0	...	100.0
	(b) in villages	61.8	...	95.0[a]
5.	Number of inhabitants per room	1.66	...	1.53

[a] 1970.

Basic Table B1a. Enlarged consumption of households financed from individual and collective sources, 1960
(In millions of current roubles)
U.S.S.R.

Goods and services by categories of needs	Personal expenditure for goods and services	Collective consumption					Total household consumption (1+6)
		Expenditure partially covered from social funds	Financed from the State budget	Financed from other sources	Total (3+4)	Consumption from all collective sources (2+5)	
	1	2	3	4	5	6	7
1.00–2.00 *Food and beverages*	45,012	–	1114	109	1223	1223	46,235
1.01 Bread and cereals	6784	–	–	–	–	–	6784
1.02 Meat and poultry	4002	–	–	–	–	–	4002
1.03 Sea food	1520	–	–	–	–	–	1520
1.04 Milk, cheese, eggs, butter	2075	–	–	–	–	–	2075
1.05 Oils and fats	2580	–	–	–	–	–	2580
1.06 Potatoes and vegetables	875	–	–	–	–	–	875
1.07 Fresh and dried fruit	850	–	–	–	–	–	850
1.08 Canned vegetables and fruit	487	–	–	–	–	–	487
1.09 Sugar, chocolate and confectionery	6042	–	–	–	–	–	6042
1.10 Other food products	10,829	–	–	–	–	–	10,829
1.11 Products bought in collective farms	3163	–	–	–	–	–	3163

Basic Table B1a. U.S.S.R. (cont.)

	1	2	3	4	5	6	7
1.12 Food consumption outside the home	5805	-	1114	109	1223	1223	7028
3.00 Tobacco and matches	1479	-	-	-	-	-	1479
4.00 Clothing and footwear	22,342	-	-	-	-	-	22,342
4.01 Clothing (and repairs)	16,645	-	-	-	-	-	16,645
4.02 Footwear (and repairs)	3963	-	-	-	-	-	3963
4.03 Accessories	1724	-	-	-	-	-	1724
5.00 Personal care	1146	-	-	-	-	-	1146
5.01 Toilet articles, cosmetics and perfume	886	-	-	-	-	-	886
5.02 Hairdressers and other aesthetic care services	260	-	-	-	-	-	260
6.00 Housing	9480	1230	-	-	-	1230	10,710
6.01 Real rent	612	1230	-	-	-	1230	1842
6.02 Imputed rent of owners	2672	-	-	-	-	-	2672
6.03 Energy, water and urban heating	1912	-	-	-	-	-	1912
6.04 Furniture and other household equipment (including repairs)	3608	-	-	-	-	-	3608
of which: electrical equipment	398	-	-	-	-	-	398
6.05 Products and services for building and repairs of dwellings	726	-	-	-	-	-	726

Basic Table B1a. *U.S.S.R.* (*cont.*)

7.00	*Transport*	4274	200	–	–	–	200	4474
7.01	Purchase of vehicles and repairs	727	–	–	–	–	–	727
7.02	Public transport services	3547	200	–	–	–	200	3747
8.00	*Telecommunications* (excluding radios and television sets)	510	–	–	–	–	–	510
9.00	*Medical goods and services*	883	353	3638	694	4332	4685	5568
9.01	Pharmaceuticals (including medical apparatus)	433	...	331	30	361	361	794
9.02	Establishments for prophylactic treatment (hospitals, clinics, ambulatories)	–	–	2718	509	3222	3222	3222
9.03	Sanitary-prophylactic establishments (anti-epidemic and disinfection stations, institutions for sanitary education)	–	–	160	2	162	162	162
9.04	Sanatoria, health institutions, dietectic feeding	450	353	–	–	–	353	803
10.00	*Social services*	256	751	199	20	219	970	1226
10.01	Pre-school establishments	211	644	–	–	–	644	855
10.02	Children's homes	–	–	199	20	219	219	219
10.03	Holiday colonies (holiday camps, extra-school establishments, etc.)	45	107	–	–	–	107	152
11.00	*Education and research*	27	248	4855	484	5339	5587	5614
11.01	Primary and secondary schools of	–	–	2674	...	...	...	...
	which schools for adults	–	–	168	...	...	...	...
11.02	Boarding schools	27	248	–	–	–	248	275

Basic Table B1a. *U.S.S.R.*   *(cont.)*

	1	2	3	4	5	6	7
11.03 Specialized secondary schools (technicums, schools for technical and professional training)	–	–	325	...	...	...	...
11.04 Higher education and university research	–	–	804	...	...	...	...
11.05 Technical professional schools (crafts, apprenticeships, schools for the mechanization of agriculture)	–	–	563	...	...	...	...
12.00 *Culture and information*	1500	–	411	153	564	564	2064
12.01 Books, newspapers, periodicals, including manuals, copybooks, school and office supplies	1500	–	–	–	–	–	1500
12.02 Activities for cultural education (cultural universities, clubs, cultural centres, libraries)	–	–	328	153	564	564	564
12.03 Services of art, radio and television	...	...	83	–	–	–	–
13.00 *Sports, leisure and entertainment*	3695	–	52	8	60	60	3755
13.01 Articles for leisure and entertainment (radio apparatus, records, musical instruments, toys, etc.)	1460	–	–	–	–	–	1460
13.02 Sport articles and services	235	–	52	8	60	60	295
13.03 Theatres, cinemas, concert halls and other spectacles of entertainment	1094	–	–	–	–	–	1094
13.04 Restaurant, bar and café services	906	–	–	–	–	–	906
14.00 *Other goods and services*	11,277	...	...	600	600	600	11,877
15.00 *Enlarged consumption*	101,881	2782	10,269	2068	12,337	15,119	117,000

Basic Table B1b. Enlarged consumption of households financed from individual and collective sources, 1965

U.S.S.R.

Goods and services by categories of needs

| | Personal expenditure for goods and services | Expenditure partially covered from social funds | Collective consumption | | | Consumption from all collective sources (2+5) | Total household consumption (1+6) |
| | | | Financed from the State budget | Financed from other sources | Total (3+4) | | |
	1	2	3	4	5	6	7
1.00–2.00 *Food and beverages*	62,451	–	1935	160	2095	2095	64,546
1.01 Bread and cereals	8903	–	–	–	–	–	8903
1.02 Meat and poultry	8373	–	–	–	–	–	8373
1.03 Sea food	2318	–	–	–	–	–	2318
1.04 Milk, cheese, eggs, butter	6986	–	–	–	–	–	6986
1.05 Oils and fats	1794	–	–	–	–	–	1794
1.06 Potatoes and vegetables	1767	–	–	–	–	–	1767
1.07 Fresh and dried fruit	1521	–	–	–	–	–	1521
1.08 Canned vegetables and fruit	902	–	–	–	–	–	902
1.09 Sugar, chocolate and confectionery	8740	–	–	–	–	–	8740
1.10 Other food products	17,823	–	–	–	–	–	17,823
1.11 Products bought in collective farms	3324	–	–	–	–	–	3324

Basic Table B1b. U.S.S.R. (cont.)

1.12	Food consumption outside the home	8740	–	1935	160	2095	2095	2095	(10,428)
3.00	*Tobacco and matches*	1909	–	–	–	–	–	–	1909
4.00	*Clothing and footwear*	26,834	–	–	–	–	–	–	26,834
4.01	Clothing (and repairs)	19,158	–	–	–	–	–	–	19,158
4.02	Footwear (and repairs)	5395	–	–	–	–	–	–	5395
4.03	Accessories	2281	–	–	–	–	–	–	2281
5.00	*Personal care*	1607	–	–	–	–	–	–	1607
5.01	Toilet articles, cosmetics and perfume	1203	–	–	–	–	–	–	1203
5.02	Hairdressers and other aesthetic care services	404	–	–	–	–	–	–	404
6.00	*Housing*	13,498	–	–	–	–	2300	2300	15,798
6.01	Real rent	896	–	–	–	–	2300	2300	3190
6.02	Imputed rent of owners	3727	–	–	–	–	–	–	3727
6.03	Energy, water and urban heating	3008	–	–	–	–	–	–	3008
6.04	Furniture and other household equipment (including repairs)	5312	–	–	–	–	–	–	5312
	of which: electrical equipment	981	–	–	–	–	–	–	981
6.05	Products and services for building and repairs of dwellings	555	–	–	–	–	–	–	555
7.00	*Transport*	5883	–	–	–	–	230	230	6113
7.01	Purchase of vehicles and repairs	1016	–	–	–	–	–	–	1016
7.02	Public transport services	4867	–	–	–	–	230	230	5097

Basic Table B1a. *U.S.S.R.* (cont.)

	1	2	3	4	5	6	7
8.00 *Telecommunications* (excluding radios and television sets)	760	-	-	-	-	-	760
9.00 *Medical goods and services*	1138	499	5041	1015	6056	6555	7693
9.01 Pharmaceuticals (including medical apparatus)	503	...	459	91	550	550	1053
9.02 Establishments for prophylactic treatment (hospitals, clinics, ambulatories)	-	-	4304	878	5182	5182	5182
9.03 Sanitary-prophylactic establishments (anti-epidemics and disinfection stations, institutions for sanitary education)	-	-	256	46	302	302	302
9.04 Sanatoria, health institutions, dietectic feeding	635	499	-	-	-	499	1134
10.00 *Social services*	471	1607	257	27	284	1891	2362
10.01 Pre-school establishments	399	1436	-	-	-	-	1835
10.02 Children's homes	-	-	257	27	284	1720	284
10.03 Holiday colonies (holiday camps, extra-school establishments, etc.)	72	171	-	-	-	171	243
11.00 *Education and research*	51	456	7721	951	8672	9128	9179
11.01 Primary and secondary schools of which schools for adults	-	-	4476	...	...	...	...
	-	-	317				
11.02 Boarding schools	51	456	-	-	-	456	507
11.03 Specialized secondary schools (technicums, schools for technical and professional training)	-	-	554	...	...	...	...

Basic Table Blb. U.S.S.R. *(cont.)*

11.04 Higher education and university research	–	...	1033	...	...	...	...
11.05 Technical professional schools (crafts, apprenticeships, schools for the mechanization of agriculture)	–	...	834	...	...	...	...
12.00 *Culture and information*	2117	–	728	732	1460	1460	3577
12.01 Books, newspapers, periodicals, including manuals, copybooks, school and office supplies	2117	–	–	–	–	–	2117
12.02 Activities for cultural education (cultural universities, clubs, cultural centres, libraries)	–	–	728	732	1460	1460	1460
12.03 Fine arts, radio and television	...	...					
13.00 *Sports, leisure and entertainment*	5457	–	38	8	46	46	5503
13.01 Articles for leisure and entertainment (radio apparatus, records, musical instruments, toys, etc.)	2577	–	–	–	–	–	2577
13.02 Sport articles and services	338	–	38	8	46	46	384
13.03 Theatres, cinemas, concert halls and other spectacles of entertainment	1217	–	–	–	–	–	1217
13.04 Restaurant, bar and café services	1325	–	–	–	–	–	1325
14.00 *Other goods and services*	11,229	...	–	890	890	890	12,119
15.00 *Enlarged consumption*	133,405	5092	15,720	3783	19,503	24,595	158,000

Basic Table B1c. Enlarged consumption of households financed from individual and collective sources, 1969
(In millions of current roubles)
U.S.S.R.

Goods and services by categories of needs	Personal expenditure for goods and services	Expenditure partially covered from social funds	Collective consumption			Consumption from all collective sources (2+5)	Total household consumption (1+6)
			Financed from the State budget	Financed from other sources	Total (3+4)		
	1	2	3	4	5	6	7
1.00–2.00 *Food and beverages*	82,356	–	2282	173	2455	2455	84,811
1.01 Bread and cereals	10,311	–	–	–	–	–	10,311
1.02 Meat and poultry	11,413	–	–	–	–	–	11,413
1.03 Sea food	2929	–	–	–	–	–	2929
1.04 Milk, cheese, eggs, butter	9822	–	–	–	–	–	9822
1.05 Oils and fats	1890	–	–	–	–	–	1890
1.06 Potatoes and vegetables	2360	–	–	–	–	–	2360
1.07 Fresh and dried fruit	2270	–	–	–	–	–	2270
1.08 Canned vegetables and fruit	1431	–	–	–	–	–	1431
1.09 Sugar, chocolate and confectionery	10,815	–	–	–	–	–	10,815
1.10 Other food products	25,485	–	–	–	–	–	25,485
1.11 Products bought in collective farms	3630	–	–	–	–	–	3630

Basic Table B1c. U.S.S.R. (cont.)

1.12	Food consumption outside the home	(12,086)	—	2282	173	2455	2455	(14,541)
3.00	*Tobacco and matches*	2627	—	—	—	—	—	2627
4.00	*Clothing and footwear*	39,102	—	—	—	—	—	39,102
4.01	Clothing (and repairs)	28,267	—	—	—	—	—	28,267
4.02	Footwear (and repairs)	7551	—	—	—	—	—	7551
4.03	Accessories	3284	—	—	—	—	—	3284
5.00	*Personal care*	2271	—	—	—	—	—	2271
5.01	Toilet articles, cosmetics and perfume	1743	—	—	—	—	—	1743
5.02	Hairdressers and other aesthetic care services	528	—	—	—	—	—	528
6.00	*Housing*	18,184	3244	—	—	—	3244	29,428
6.01	Real rent	1103	3244	—	—	—	3244	4347
6.02	Imputed rent of owners	4375	—	—	—	—	—	4374
6.03	Energy, water and urban heating	4320	—	—	—	—	—	4320
6.04	Furniture and other household equipment (including repairs)	7549	—	—	—	—	—	7549
	of which: electrical equipment	1829	—	—	—	—	—	1829
6.05	Products and services for building and repairs of dwellings	837	—	—	—	—	—	837
7.00	*Transport*	8074	250	—	—	—	250	8324
7.01	Purchase of vehicles and repairs	1389	—	—	—	—	—	1389

Basic Table B1c. *U.S.S.R.* (*cont.*)

	1	2	3	4	5	6	7
7.02 Public transport services	6685	250	-	-	-	250	6935
8.00 *Telecommunications* (excluding radios and television sets)	1160	-	-	-	-	-	1160
9.00 *Medical goods and services*	1642	701	6666	2052	8718	9419	11,061
9.01 Pharmaceuticals (including medical apparatus)	750	...	636	190	826	826	1576
9.02 Establishments for prophylactic treatment (hospitals, clinics, ambulatories)	-	-	5868	1838	7706	7706	7706
9.03 Sanitary-prophylactic establishments (anti-epidemic and disinfection stations, institutions for sanitary education)	-	-	333	87	420	420	420
9.04 Sanatoria, health institutions, dietectic feeding	892	701	-	-	-	701	1593
10.00 *Social services*	631	2115	295	65	360	2475	3106
10.01 Pre-school establishments	543	1905	-	-	-	1905	2448
10.02 Children's homes	-	-	295	65	360	360	360
10.03 Holiday colonies (holiday camps, extra-school establishments, etc.)	88	210	-	-	-	210	298
11.00 *Education and research* of which:	52	478	9921	1749	11,670	12,148	12,200
11.01 Primary and secondary schools	-	-	5413	...	...	...	...
of which for adults	-	-	277	...	...	...	...

Basic Table B1c. U.S.S.R. (cont.)

11.02	Boarding schools	52	478	478	...	...	478	530
11.03	Specialized secondary schools (technicums, schools for technical and professional training)	-	-	783	...	...	...	...
11.04	Higher education and university research	-	-	1375	...	...	...	...
11.05	Technical professional schools (crafts, apprenticeships, schools for the mechanization of agriculture)	-	-	1226	...	...	...	...
12.00	*Culture and information*	3122	-	1404	1224	2628	2628	5750
12.01	Books, newspapers, periodicals, including manuals, copybooks, school and office supplies	3122	-	-	-	-	-	3122
12.02	Activities for cultural education (cultural universities, clubs, cultural centres, libraries)	-	-	1404	1224	2628	2628	2628
12.03	Fine arts, radio and television	...	...	...	...	...	...	...
13.00	*Sports, leisure and entertainment*	7692	-	41	12	53	53	7745
13.01	Articles for leisure and entertainment (radio apparatus, records, musical instruments, toys, etc.)	3855	-	-	-	-	-	3855
13.02	Sport articles and services	490	-	41	12	53	53	543
13.03	Theatres, cinemas, concert halls and other spectacles of entertainment	1416	-	-	-	-	-	1416
13.04	Restaurant, bar and café services	1931	-	-	-	-	-	1931
14.00	*Other goods and services*	16,265	-	-	1250	1250	1250	17,515
15.00	*Enlarged consumption*	183,078	6788	20,609	6525	27,134	33,922	217,100

Basic Table B2. Gross social benefits
(In millions of current roubles)
U.S.S.R.

Social benefits	1960		1965		1968	
	from all sources	from the State budget	from all sources	from the State budget	from all sources	from the State budget
A. Social benefits in kind or in the form of services	15,119	...	24,595	...	33,922	...
B. Social cash transfers	10,400	7790	14,920	11,106	21,600	15,982
1. Old-age pensions	7200	4946	10,600	7407	15,000	10,430
2. Invalidity pensions						
3. Allocations (of which)	2600	2334	3500	3041	5300	4564
Family allowances						
Maternity allowances	...	1005	...	1078	...	1226
Allowances for newborn children						
Sickness allowances	...	1329	...	1963	...	3338
4. Scholarships	600	501	820	650	1300	980
5. Other social transfers	...	...	...	...	...	...
C. Total expenditure on social benefits and transfers (A + B)	25,519	...	39,515	...	55,522	...

Basic Table B3. Indicators of the development of public services
U.S.S.R.

		1960	1965	1969
	1	2	3	4
I.	*Public concern with children up to 7 years*			
1.	Children up to 7 years benefiting from free medical services as percentage of all children of this age group	100	100	100
2.	Children in pre-school establishments as percentage of the number of children up to 7 years	12.5	23.0	31.0
3.	Number of children up to 1 year per 1000 newborn children	965	973	974
II.	*Education*			
1.	Number of children aged 7 to 15 attending primary and secondary schools as percentage of all children in this age group	...	~100	~100
2.	Number of adolescents aged 16 to 18 attending secondary schools as percentage of all adolescents in this age group	...	...	~80
3.	Number of adolescents aged 14 to 19 in technical professional schools as percentage of all adolescents in this age group	...	...	~11
4.	Number of pupils attending specialized secondary schools per 10,000 inhabitants	95	158	178
5.	Number of students in establishments for higher education per 10,000 inhabitants	111	166	189
III.	*Public Health*			
1.	Number of persons benefiting from free medical services as percentage of total population	100	100	100
2.	Medical personnel per 10,000 inhabitants	84.9	97.3	110.8
	(a) of which doctors and specialists	20.1	24.0	26.7
3.	Number of beds in hospitals and clinics per 10,000 inhabitants	80.4	95.8	106.2
4.	Number of beds per doctor employed in hospitals and polyclinics	~4.0	~4.0	~4.0
IV.	*Social Security and Insurance*			
1.	Number of children placed free of charge (totally or partially) in holiday camps as percentage of the number of pupils in classes 1 to 8	14.1	18.1	21.0
2.	Average duration of paid leave of adult workers and employees in working days	18.5[a]	19.3[b]	20.9[c]
3.	Average amount of old-age pensions as percentage of the average wage of workers and employees	...	50	...

Basic Table B3. *U.S.S.R.* *(cont.)*

	1960	1965	1969
1	2	3	4

V. *Cultural Services and Leisure*

1. Number of persons benefiting from organized leisure (sanatoria, boarding houses, health establishments, in per cent)	2.9	3.6	4.1
2. Average number of theatre entries per 10,000 inhabitants	4299	4400	4630
3. Average number of cinema entries per 10 inhabitants	17	18	19
4. Number of owners of radio sets per 10,000 inhabitants	1290	1650	1930
5. Number of owners of television sets per 10,000 inhabitants	220	680	1270
6. Average number of readers per library	0.8	0.9	0.9
7. Number of libraries per 10,000 inhabitants	6.4	5.5	5.2

VI. *Housing Services*

1. Average surface per urban inhabitant in towns with more than 1 million inhabitants	9.1	10.9	11.6
2. Average surface per inhabitant in the whole country	8.8	9.9	10.8
3. Total rent as percentage of the wage-fund of workers and employees	1.0	1.0	0.9
4. Percentage of dwellings with:			
−running water	...	...	68.6
−electricity	...	...	99.2

[a] At 1 April 1958.

[b] At 31 March 1964.

[c] At 30 April 1968.

CHAPTER 3
A Comparative Analysis of the Structure and Development of Enlarged Consumption in France, Italy and Switzerland*

For some decades already, State intervention in capitalist economies has gone far beyond the scope of conjunctural policies and short-term government action for redressing temporary disequilibria. By now the public authorities have a decisive role in shaping and developing the basic structure of the economy and its social relations.

It is true that liberalism at its most classic stage exercised a certain degree of interventionism, especially in the sectors of health (hospitals and hospices), education (primary schools, etc.) and roads (national or provincial network). But at present the range and extension of government measures have changed the character of public action both in quantitative and qualitative terms. The inadequacy or even failure of liberal systems to bring about a satisfactory allocation of resources in several fields (income distribution, access to education, medical treatment, housing, the protection of the environment, etc.) as well as the tendency of the market economy to create and perpetuate inequalities have demonstrated the need of at least a partial collective control of market mechanisms. Moreover, the growth and spread of technical innovatiions at various levels tends to perpetuate and amplify inequalities inherited from the past and to create new ones which manifest themselves in income and consumption differentials and unequal opportunities among social classes. Finally, the growing awareness of a frequently close interdependence of individual and collective preferences (or utilities) make it necessary for the State to act increasingly as arbiter between different possible choices.

In this connection, it is legitimate to question the respective functions of the market and State in a capitalist system. Do the public authorities aim at reconciling the conflicting interests of various social groups and thus to orient the economic system towards more collective and solidary types of control? Or, if used as an instrument by the ruling classes, is it intended to preserve the essential features of the liberal system? No simple and direct answer to these questions can be obtained from an observation and analysis of reality in so far as the State is itself the focal point of the clash of interests among social groups; furthermore, the complexity of instruments at the disposal of the public authorities makes for a certain ambiguity in the objectives they aim at and the effective role they claim to play.

----

* This chapter has been prepared by V. Cao-Pinna and A.Foulon assisted by J.Benard, J.N. Du Pasquier and L. Solari who supplied critical comments to ealier drafts.

Although the subsequent comparisons do not pretend to go into the processes of public decision-making whether planned or not-or into the whole range of economic government interventions which have characterized the French, Italien and Swiss economies during the 1960s, it must be stressed that the questions dealt with have to be viewed as part of a considerable broader set of problems.

The choices of the forms of public intervention on behalf of households, especially those concerning their incomes and consumption in a wider sense, are made in three major fields:

(i) The share of total resources allocated to collective funds (Central Government, local authorities, Social Security): this share can be assessed in a first approximation as the ratio of taxation or "para-taxation" to National Product. The system of collective taxation is an important instrument of economic and social policy; the nature of the tax and its incidence on disposable incomes and prices should not be viewed independently but as a complement to the choices concerning social transfers and collective consumption.

(ii) The allocation of collective funds to various types of uses and different classes of the population raises both quantitative and qualitative problems which are at the centre of budgetary policy. If interest is focused on interventions on behalf of households, the following can be briefly stated:

-What are the desirable-if not optimal-proportions between "divisible non-market" production (education, health, roads, etc.)[1] and transfers allocated to household incomes or consumption? The methods of management as well as the economic and social impact of the two categories are very different, if only because in the former the public authorities compete with, or eliminate, the market whereas in the latter they aim at correcting certain distributive disequilibria, as and when the need arises, by regulating certain mechanisms with the help of legislation.

-What are the proportions of collective funds allocated directly to households in the form of transfers in kind (that is at the free disposal of households)? Apart from the fact that the two forms or redistribution have neither the same significance nor the same economic impact, their efficiency in reducing inequalities varies considerably according to their origin and to the fields in which they are applied.

-Finally, what is the reciprocal influence between economic growth and the volume of public and private funds? That is, what division between public and private financing is compatible with a "desired" rate of growth or, conversely, what rate of growth results from a given division between public and private financing, notably in the sphere of consumption?

(iii) There is finally the adaptation of these various mechanisms to the objectives aimed at. This presupposes, on the one hand, the establishment of priorities, that is, of norms which render social inequalities inacceptable;[3] and on the other, an identification of the various types of disparities, of their size and their possible cumulative effects. It must be

---

[1] Granted that allocations to "indivisible" public services (justice, armies, etc.) are governed by other preoccupations which have little in common with the formulation of social policy.
[2] Such as, for example, reimbursement of medical expenses.
[3] Reference to an income distribution which is supposed to be identical to marginal productivities remains largely theoretical, hardly operational and highly questionable from a social point of view.

stated in this connection that the options chosen for the incidence and structure of taxation as well as for the different modalities of the re-allocation of collective services are largely interdependent, if only because they have a positive or negative influence on the incomes and consumption of each social group.

The comparison between France, Italy and Switzerland, which is the scope of this chapter, will deal only with some aspects of points (i) and (ii). As has been stressed earlier, none of the three countries disposes of instruments for analysing social inequalities and for estimating the extent to which the policies adopted have contributed towards reducing them. Moreover, the gaps and disparities of the statistical apparatus as well as the need for harmonizing the methods used have often necessitated a presentation of the information in global terms, thus limiting its explanatory and interpretative value. In the following, five points will be examined:

(i) The share of enlarged consumption in national resources. The share of market consumption in national income is in steady decline, it will be seen how the inclusion of collective consumption modifies this tendency and with the help of what forms of financing and institutions collective funds take care of enlarged consumption;

(ii) The development of collective consumption by categories of needs. The behaviour of the consumption of goods and services and that of traditional consumption categories compared to consumption linked to innovations reflects, to a large extent, the modifications which have occurred in the population's way of life during the period 1959 to 1969;

(iii) Changes in the allocation of consumption between market and non-market forms of the acquisition of goods and services reveal that such a distinction is highly conventional; this is because public intervention varies in intensity and between needs, thus creating sectors which lie half-way between market and non-market consumption.

(iv) Developments in the methods of financing enlarged consumption play a relatively important role. It seems that in a liberal system the mechanisms and institutions for financing the various components of enlarged consumption are much more significant for certain orientations of public intervention than is the division into market and non-market types of consumption, and that they partly reveal the economic and social functions of the State.

(v) Finally, the relationship between the direct participation of households in the financing of collective funds and the benefits they derive from them makes it possible to evaluate, at least in global terms, the extent to which they gain (or lose) in the process of taxation-reallocation compared to other economic agents.

3.1   SOURCES OF INFORMATION AND DIFFICULTIES OF COMPARISON

Before embarking on an analysis of results, it must be pointed out that, in spite of efforts made to arrive at a common methodology which takes account of the methodological differences of data collection in each country, certain distortions could not be avoided. In comparing the three West European countries, the most important differences in method were:

(i) The nomenclature of goods and services. Whereas for France and Italy harmonization could be achieved at the level of eighty-two categories of goods and services, the more aggregate nature of Swiss statistical information made a more detailed breakdown impossible, for the following reasons: there is no distinction between real and imputed rents; medical services are aggregated while school

school canteens, university hostels and restaurants are not included anywhere. In general it will be noted that the nomenclature used within each of the fourteen categories of needs is much more simplified in Switzerland than in France and Italy.

(ii) The content of certain items of nomenclature. In particular, "Social services" (10.00) cover only establishments for children in Switzerland whereas in France and Italy they also include (albeit partial) estimates for orphanages and institutions for incapacitated and old persons. The category "Other goods and services" (14.00) covers a very heterogeneous collection of products in all three countries and these are often only very approximate estimates.

(iii) Statistical information on local authorities, private administrations and enterprises. Little is known in any of the three countries about the amount and nature of expenditure incurred by these sectors on behalf of households. The highly fragmentary data which have been used always involve an under-estimation of these collective funds.

(iv) The special institutional framework of Switzerland. Since there is no generalized and public system of Social Security in this country, it was necessary to adapt the institutional breakdown for France and Italy. In France and Italy collective financing of certain types of consumption, notably in the medical field (9.00) and in social services (10.00) covers only financing by the State, local authorities and above all Social Security, at the exclusion of mutual and private insurance. Collective financing in Switzerland however, is provided by public organizations and insurances, but mainly by private insurance companies where affiliation is sometimes compulsory and sometimes optional. Thus, to ensure a minimum of comparability, Social Security institutions in the Swiss·tables have been substituted by private insurance companies.

(v) The content of subsidies and social benefits in kind. Certain current subsidies can be interpreted as social benefits and vice versa, in particular for public transfers, housing, medical services, social services and leisure.[4] Thus Swiss estimates include in "social benefits" payments by public administrations to private assistance institutions which could be recorded as subsidies to production. Conversely, subsidies to production granted to social housing in France could be incorporated in social benefits aiming to reduce the rents of this category of housing. To the extent that these ambiguities could not be systematically eliminated, each participant was left free to interpret the harmonized definitions according to the mechanisms and conventions applying in his own country; there are, therefore, certain anomalies between the three countries but they affect only small amounts and do not result in a strong bias.

(vi) Statistical difficulties prevented a presentation of Swiss tables for 1965. In general, Switzerland could not be included in the comparisons at all levels or in all details, and the analysis and interpretation of the results for this country must therefore remain more general than for the other two.

Fianally, let us recall that the comparison between the three countries of Western Europe in this chapter is based on enlarged consumption at factor cost; any confrontation with the results of the socialist countries in Chapter 2 can only be attempted after harmonizing the methods of assessment; this is done in Chapter 4.

3.2   ENLARGED CONSUMPTION AND NATIONAL RESOURCES

During the period reviewed, none of the three countries has experienced particular economic difficulties in the form of either a recession or hyper-inflation. The

---

[4]See Chapter 1, Section 1.2.

annual rates of growth of Gross Domestic Product (GNP)[5] and of Disposable National Income (DNI) ranged in value between 9 and 11 per cent and those of Gross Domestic Product in volume between approximately 4.5 and 6 per cent, and they remained fairly steady.

It will be noted that at the aggregate level the French and Italian rates of expansion were more or less identical (GNP) in value 10.5 per cent and in volume 5.8 per cent, DNI 10.4 per cent and the price index for private consumption 4 per cent while the corresponding rates in Switzerland were slightly lower (9.0, 4.5, 9 and 3.4 per cent respectively).

When the size of the population and its development in the three countries is taken into account, a comparison of these indicators per head of the production brings out the following differences in level and changes (see Tables 3.1 and 3.2 and Chart 3.4):

(i)   firstly, different rates of increase of the population—more rapid in Switzerland than in France, and more rapid in France than in Italy—were reflected in smaller annual rates of income increases in Switzerland (7.1 per cent) than in France (9.1 per cent) and in Italy (9.8 per cent);

(ii) secondly, when expressed in Swiss francs (bearing in mind the pitfalls of using an official rate of exchange), the levels of income and private consumption per head were very close to each other in 1969 in absolute terms in Switzerland and in France, but some 40 to 45 per cent lower in Italy.

An analysis of the two major components of enlarged consumption evaluated at factor cost reveals the predominant but diminishing role played by private consumption in all three countries and, correspondingly, the relatively moderate but growing importance of collective consumption which rose from about 6 to 8 or 9 per cent of the total in value and from 5 to about 6 or 7 per cent in volume between 1959 and 1969.

The rate of growth of enlarged consumption in value was of the order 10 per cent per annum in France and Italy and of 8.4 per cent in Switzerland, that is slightly faster than that of private consumption alone, whether measured at market prices or factor costs, but less rapid than that of National Product or Income (which amounted to about 58 and 65 per cent in France and Switzerland and to 67 and 72 per cent in Italy in 1969) declined more slowly than that of private consumption, on account of the increase in collective consumption which will be examined below.

---

[5]Sources: <u>Yearbook of National Accounts Statistics, 1968 and 1971,</u> United Nations.

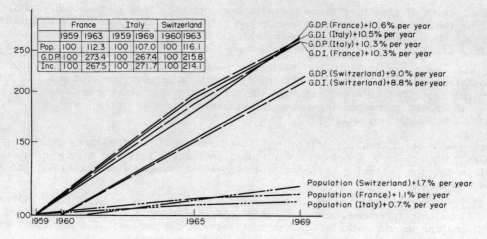

	France		Italy		Switzerland	
	1959	1963	1959	1969	1960	1963
Pop.	100	112.3	100	107.0	100	116.1
G.D.P.	100	273.4	100	267.4	100	215.8
Inc.	100	267.5	100	271.7	100	214.1

G.D.P.(France)+10.6% per year
G.D.I.(Italy)+10.5% per year
G.D.P.(Italy)+10.3% per year
G.D.I.(France)+10.3% per year

G.D.P.(Switzerland)+9.0% per year
G.D.I.(Switzerland)+8.8% per year

Population (Switzerland)+1.7% per year
Population (France)+1.1% per year
Population (Italy)+0.7% per year

Chart 3.1.　Implicit price indices of enlarged consumption.

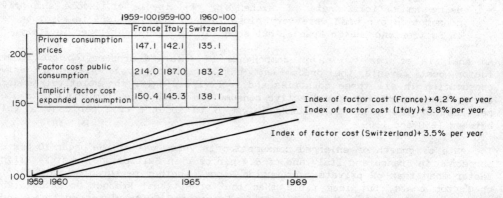

	1959-100	1959-100	1960-100
	France	Italy	Switzerland
Private consumption prices	147.1	142.1	135.1
Factor cost public consumption	214.0	187.0	183.2
Implicit factor cost expanded consumption	150.4	145.3	138.1

Index of factor cost (France)+4.2% per year
Index of factor cost (Italy)+3.8% per year
Index of factor cost (Switzerland)+3.5% per year

Chart 3.2.　Gross domestic product, disposable income,
　　　　　　　population.

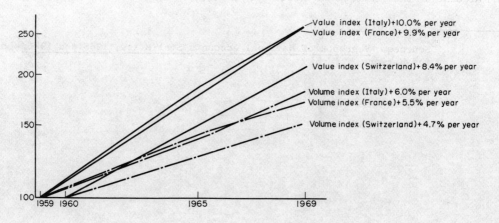

Value index (Italy)+10.0% per year
Value index (France)+9.9% per year

Value index (Switzerland)+8.4% per year

Volume index (Italy)+6.0% per year
Volume index (France)+5.5% per year
Volume index (Switzerland)+4.7% per year

Chart 3.3.　Enlarged consumption

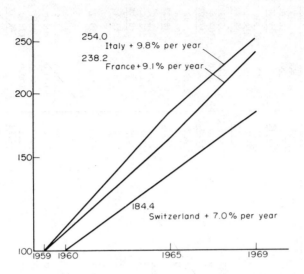

Chart 3.4. Disposable income per resident inhabitant.

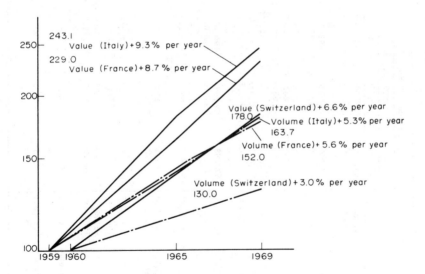

Chart 3.5. Enlarged consumption per resident inhabitant.

Table 3.1
Values at current prices and indices

		France (10^6 FF)			Italy (10^9 LI)			Switzerland (10^6 FS)	
		1959	1965	1969	1959	1965	1969	1960	1969
Population (10^3)		44,730	48,794	50,225	49,356	51,575	52,800	5362	6224
(a) Gross Domestic Product	Value	267,400	489,000	731,000	19,353	36,610	51,758	36,565	79,205
	Indices	100	182.9	273.4 +10.6%	100	189.2	267.4 +10.3%	100	216.6 +9.0%
(b) Disposable National Income	Value	243,500	434,100	651,300	17,732	33,922	48,175	33,125	70,910
	Indices	100	178.3	267.5 +10.3%	100	191.3	271.7 +10.5%	100	214.1 +8.8%
(c) Disposable National Income per head	Value	5444 FF	8897 FF	12,968 FF	359,267 LI	657,722 LI	912,405 LI	6178 FS	11,393 FS
	Indices	100	163.4	238.2 +9.1%	100.0	183.1	254.0 +9.8%	100.0	184.4 +7.0%
(d) *Private household consumption* (at market prices)	Value	171,432	298,017	437,490	13,362	24,053	33,802	22,714	46,192
	Indices	100.0	173.8	255.2 +9.8%	100.0	180.0	253.0 +9.7%	100.0	203.4 +8.2%
(e) *Private household consumption* (at factor cost)	Value	157,088	274,964	394,053	12,398	22,344	31,327	20,895	42,299
	Indices	100.0	175.0	250.8 +9.6%	100.0	180.2	252.7 +9.7%	100.0	202.4 +8.1%
(f) (e/a) Share of private consumption in GDP	Per cent	58.7	56.2	53.9	64.1	61.0	60.5	57.1	53.4
(g) e/b Share of private consumption in Disposable National Income	Per cent	64.5	63.3	60.5	69.9	65.9	65.0	63.1	59.7
(h) *Enlarged consumption* (at factor cost)	Value	166,225	295,527	427,346	13,267	24,536	34,500	22,143	45,754
	Indices	100.0	177.8	257.1	100.0	184.9	260.0	100.0	206.6
(i) Enlarged consumption per head	Value	3717 FF	6057 FF	8509 FF	268,802 LI	475,734 LI	653,409 LI	4130 FS	7351 FS
	Indices	100.0	163.0	229.0 +8.7%	100.0	177.0	243.1 +9.2%	100.0	178.0 +6.7%
(j) h/a Share of enlarged consumption in GDP	Per cent	62.2	60.4	58.5	68.6	67.0	66.7	60.6	57.8
(k) h/b Share of enlarged consumption in Disposable National Income	Per cent	68.3	68.1	65.6	74.8	72.3	71.6	66.8	64.5

Source: *Statistical Yearbooks of National Accounts, 1968–1971*, U.N., 1969–1973.

Table 3.2
Comparison of values per head in Swiss francs in 1969[a]

	France	Italy	Switzerland
Disposable national income per head			
Values	10,754	6272	11,393
Relative indices[b]	94.4	55.1	1.0
Private household consumption per head			
(at market prices)			
Values	7224	4400	7422
Relative indices[b]	97.3	59.3	1.0
Enlarged consumption per head			
(at factor cost)			
Values	7057	4492	7351
Relative indices[b]	96.0	61.1	1.0

[a] Average annual exchange rates: 1 Swiss franc = 1.2058 French francs,
1 Swiss franc = 145.47 lire.

[b] Value per head of Switzerland = 1.

The implicit costs[6] of enlarged consumption increased by about 4 per cent in France and Italy and by 3.5 per cent in Switzerland during the period–that is more rapidly than the prices of private consumption; this was due to the rather rapid average annual increase in the prices of collective consumption (in Switzerland by 5.6 per cent, France 7.9 per cent and Italy 6.5 per cent) caused by a relatively rapid rise in the wages and salaries of public employees which constitute a major

---

[6] Although none of the participants was in a position to estimate factor costs for the different components of enlarged consumption (see Section 1.5), a limitation of comparisons in current values without an attempt to estimate the development of prices and volume, if only at the aggregate level, would have been to rough a procedure. The following hypotheses were therefore made: (i) As a first approximation it was assumed that, for private consumption, indices at factor cost moved in step with those of the implied prices of national accounts (that is that the rates of taxation on consumption and net subsidies remained stable during the period); this was in fact almost the case for Switzerland (at about 8 per cent) and Italy (at about 7.2 per cent) but not for France, where this rate rose from 8.4 per cent in 1959 to 9.9 per cent in 1969. (ii) The index of public consumption at factor cost can be calculated by assuming that it behaved as the composite index of the average pay in public employment (coefficient 0.8) and the implied index of the consumption of goods and services by the administration in the U.N. national accounts (coefficient 0.2). The price index for private consumption was used to deflate the value figures of private consumption at factor cost, and that of the factor cost of public consumption to deflate the data on the value of divisible public consumption, thus arriving at an implied index of the factor costs of enlarged consumption. The results are presented in Charts 3.2 and 3.3.

element in these prices.[7]

If these disparities in the development of values as well as costs are taken into account, the relative average annual growth in the volume (value at constant prices) of enlarged consumption has been more rapid in Italy (6.0 per cent) and in France (5.5 per cent) than in Switzerland (4.7 per cent).

A comparison of enlarged consumption per head (see Tables 3.1 and 3.2 and Chart 3.5) gives a roughly similar picture to that of income and private consumption per head; in view of the differences in population increases, the average annual growth of enlarged consumption per head, in value as well as in volume, was slightly more rapid in Italy (9.3 and 5.3 per cent respectively) than in France (8.7 and 4.3 per cent) and in Switzerland (6.6 and 3 per cent). However, since the southern regions still remain considerably under-developed in spite of their growth being more rapid than that of other regions, the absolute level of enlarged consumption per head in Italy (estimated in Swiss francs) was still some 40 per cent lower than in the other two countries in 1969.

This is not the place for a detailed analysis of the factors which explain these disparities in levels of development and rates of growth between the three countries in the 1960s. The few general observations made so far place the comparison of the structure and development of the consumption in the global context of the respective economies in only a schematic form. Of much smaller size than the other two, Switzerland had the highest economic standard but the lowest rate of growth so that, by 1969, national product and private and enlarged consumption per head were very close to those of France. Conversely, in Italy where the population was much larger but where its increase was least rapid, per capita rates of growth were substantially higher than in the other two countries; even so, the levels of per capita income and consumption still lagged behind those in France and Switzerland in 1969. At the same time the growth rate of the national product and income of the three economies was, on the whole, steady during the period: this means that political, economic and social events, notably the end of the war in Algeria, the inflow of repatriated persons and the crisis of 1968 in France, were absorbed and digested without causing serious setbacks.

In Switzerland there has been a very large increase in the foreign segment of the population[8] which largely accounted for the demographic increase of the population

---

[7] The index of average pay of the public administration sector was: in France with 1959 = 186.8 in 1968, that is in an average annual increase of 7.2 per cent; in Italy the index rose to 186 from 1959 to 1969, implying an annual increase of 6.4 per cent: in Switzerland, with 1960 = 100, the index rose to 163.5 in 1969 and the annual increase was 5.6 per cent. The significance of these indices in the calculations of footnote 6 is limited; they assume, notably, that labour productivity remained constant in these sectors during the period, a quesstionable assumption, particularly in sectors whose production function has been modified (health, social services).

[8] Composition of the Swiss population (per cent)

	1960	1970
Swiss population	89	83
Foreign population	11	17

and the relatively slow advance of national income per head. But since immigrants belong essentially to the active part of the population with low or average incomes, these tendencies have not substantially affected the share of private household consumption in Gross Domestic Product (it amounted to 65 per cent in 1960 and 67 per cent in 1969).

Finally it will be noted that, at the aggregate level, the relative position of the three countries with regard to levels and development does not change much if enlarged consumption rather than private household consumption is considered. This is due in part to the method used in national accounts which evaluates the latter at market prices and the former at factor cost while the net tax rates on market consumption are very close to each other. But, more fundamentally, such a result brings out the similarity of the economic systems of the three countries, that is the predominance of market consumption and the apparently marginal weight, at least at the global level, of non-market collective consumption which is common to them. In other words, this means that the concept of enlarged consumption applied to liberal economies, useful as it might be for purposes of international comparison, has an analytical and theoretical value only if its structure is examined in detail, that is by categories of needs, the forms of acquisition of goods and services and the methods of financing.

3.3   THE STRUCTURE AND DEVELOPMENT OF ENLARGED CONSUMPTION BY CATEGORIES OF
        NEEDS

One of the important consequences of a simultaneous consideration of private and public consumption is that the considerably more rapid increase of public consumption (at average annual rates of 13.8 per cent in France, 13.8 per cent in Italy and 12.0 per cent in Switzerland) has accentuated the general tendency of the share of private consumption of goods to decline while that of services in the frame of enlarged consumption increased.

Table 3.3
Breakdown of enlarged consumption into goods and services
(in per cent)

	France		Italy		Switzerland
	1959	1969	1959	1969	1969[a]
Goods	67.0	60.9	68.8	65.3	(61.0)
Services	33.0	39.1	31.2	34.7	(39.0)
Total	100.0	100.0	100.0	100.0	100.0

[a] Estimates.

Even though the comparison is limited to values, thus ignoring the development of prices and costs (notably of relative prices and costs), the changes in the composition of enlarged consumption by categories of needs have been very similar in the three countries.

In the first place (see Table 3.4 and Chart 3.6), there has been a decline in the share of food and beverages which accounted for no more than about 30 per cent of consumption in France and Switzerland and 38 per cent in Italy. This by now classical tendency was accompanied by clear modifications in the composition of

Table 3.4

Composition of private and collective consumption by categories of needs (Values in per cent)

	France 1959			France 1965		France 1969			Italy 1959			Italy 1965		Italy 1969			Switzerland 1960			Switzerland 1969		
	Private consump-tion[a]	Divisible public consumption[a]	Enlarged consump-tion[a]	Private consump-tion[a]	Enlarged consump-tion	Private consump-tion[a]	Divisible public consumption[a]	Enlarged consump-tion	Private consump-tion[a]	Divisible public consumption	Enlarged consump-tion	Private consump-tion[a]	Enlarged consump-tion	Private consump-tion[a]	Divisible public consumption[a]	Enlarged consump-tion	Private consump-tion[a]	Divisible public consumption[a]	Enlarged consump-tion[a]	Private consump-tion[a]	Divisible public consumption[a]	Enlarged consump-tion[a]
1. Food	34	–	32	28	28	28	–	25	40	–	38	36	36	37	–	34	28	–	26	26	–	24
2. Beverages	8	–	7	5	6	5	–	5	5	–	4	4	4	4	–	4	7	–	7	8	–	7
3. Tobacco, matches	1	–	1	1	1	1	–	1	1	–	1	1	1	1	–	1	2	–	2	1	–	1
4. Clothing, footwear	11	–	10	9	9	9	–	8	10	–	9	9	9	9	–	9	9	–	9	8	–	7
5. Personal care	1	–	1	2	1	2	–	2	1	–	1	1	1	1	–	1	2	–	2	2	–	2
6. Housing	17	–	16	21	17	21	–	19	19	–	18	16	16	18	–	16	24	–	23	25	–	23
7. Transport	7	0[b]	7	8	8	8	0[b]	8	5	–	5	7	7	9	–	8	7	–	6	8	–	8
8. Telecommunications	1	1	1	1	1	1	–	1	1	–	1	1	1	1	–	1	1	–	1	1	–	1
9. Medical goods and services	6	8	6	9	8	9	9	9	5	16	6	7	7	7	16	8	6	35	9	7	27	8
10. Social services	1	16	2	1	2	1	14	2	1	17	2	2	2	1	15	2	1	5	1	1	5	1
11. Education	1	58	5	1	6	1	65	7	1	58	5	6	6	1	62	6	2	53	6	2	61	6
12. Culture, information	2	4	2	2	2	2	3	2	1	6	2	2	2	2	4	2	2	2	2	2	3	3
13. Sports, leisure, entertainment	6	3	6	8	7	8	4	7	7	1	7	6	6	6	1	6	2	1	3	2	1	3
14. Other goods and services	4	11	4	4	4	4	5	4	3	2	3	2	2	2	2	2	1	4	7	7	3	7
15. Total consumption	100	100	100	100	100	100	100	100	100	100	100	100	100	100	100	100	100	100	100	100	100	100

a At factor cost.   b Less than 0.5 per cent.

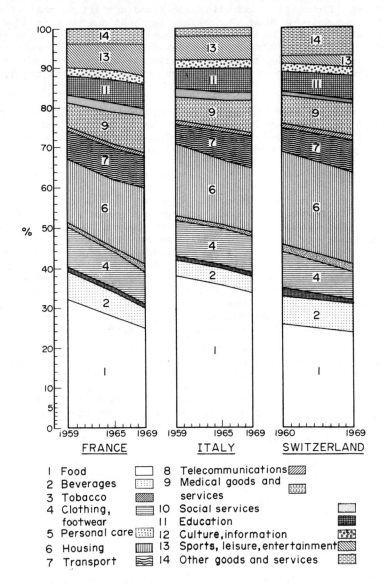

1	Food	8	Telecommunications
2	Beverages	9	Medical goods and services
3	Tobacco		
4	Clothing, footwear	10	Social services
5	Personal care	11	Education
6	Housing	12	Culture, information
7	Transport	13	Sports, leisure, entertainment
		14	Other goods and services

Chart 3.6.   The structure of enlarged consumption by categories of needs.

food expenditure: a decline in the share of beverages and traditional foodstuffs (bread, potatoes, flour, milk and oils, etc.) and a shift to meat, fruit, sugar and chocolate consumption. These changes are no doubt due to a combined price and income effect which cannot be analysed here but they suggest that, as far as food is concerned, the three countries have attained, if not to saturation point, at least a sufficiently high degree of satisfaction of population needs[9] to permit a considerable diversification of this consumption already at the beginning of the period.

The share of expenditure on <u>clothing</u> also declined in all three countries (in 1969 it was 8 per cent in France, 9 per cent in Italy and 7 per cent in Switzerland). The fall in relative prices, due largely to the wide diffusion of synthetic textiles, has certainly played a decisive role in this development.

Expenditure on <u>housing</u> is more difficult to analyse. From 1959 to 1969 its share in the total has slightly declined in Italy and Switzerland but increased in France; these divergencies can be explained mainly by the different behaviour of rent. The three countries registered more or less parallel tendencies in their expenditure on the utilization of dwellings (water, electricity, furniture, electrical equipment and products for maintenance); the proportion for consumption and for total expenditure on housing declined on account of the progressive increase in the stock of durables and of the marked drop in the prices of certain goods, notably electrical household equipment. By contrast, there has been an increase in the share of rent, notably in France and Switzerland, resulting from a series of factors connected with the complex functioning of the housing market. It is not possible to assess the weight of each of these factors in the three countries but the following four elements can be singled out:

(i) The progressive urbanization of the population: in France 61.1 per cent had their main residence in towns of more than 2000 inhabitants in 1962; in 1968 this proportion had increased to 71.4 per cent. In Switzerland the proportion of all residences in towns with more than 2000 inhabitants rose from 68.4 per cent in 1960 to 72.3 per cent in 1969. In Italy the proportion of people residing in communes of more than 10,000 inhabitants rose from 60 per cent in 1961 to 65 per cent in 1971.

(ii) The increase in the proportion of house-owners in France and Italy which was reflected in an increase in the share of "imputed" rent, due especially to the widespread use of mechanisms to facilitate access to ownership.

(iii) The improved average housing standards, with regard to the number of rooms per inhabitant[10] and the availability of running water, bathrooms electricity and household equipment.[11]

(iv) Finally, particularly evident in France during this period due to a progressive lifting of rent regulations, the speculatory character of real estate investment with regard to both land and construction has played quite a significant role in the rise in rents.

[9] Number of calories and quantity of proteins consumed per day: in France :1957-59; 2940 calories and 98 grams; 1967: 3180 calories and 100 grams; in Italy: 2630 calories and 77 grams and 2940 calories and 87 grams respectively; in Switzerland: 3120 calories and 90 grams and 2990 calories and 84 grams (<u>Statistical Yearbooks, 1964-1970, United Nations</u>).

[10] France: 1962-0.99, 1968-1.1; Italy: 1960-0.83, 1969-1.0; Switzerland: 1960-1.28, 1970-1.34.

[11] Percentage of households equipped with refrigerators: France, 1962-40.3 per cent, 1969-82.8 per cent; Italy, 1961-26.3 per cent, 1970-76.3 per cent; Switzerland, 1970-80 per cent. Washing machines: France, 1962-30.1 per cent, 1969-60.1 per cent; Italy, 1961-6 per cent, 1970-52.6 per cent; Switzerland, 1970-76 per cent. Vacuum cleaners: France, 1962-34.9 per cent, 1969-54.9 per cent.

Table 3.5
The development of enlarged consumption (Value indices and average annual growth rates)

	France		Italy		Switzerland	
	Indices 1959 = 100	Average annual growth rates %	Indices 1959 = 100	Average annual growth rates %	Indices 1960 = 100	Average annual growth rates %
1. Food	203.0	+ 7.3	234.5	+ 8.9	188.5	+ 7.3
2. Beverages	169.0	+ 5.4	226.3	+ 8.5	221.3	+ 9.2
3. Tobacco, matches	148.9	+ 4.1	221.1	+ 8.3	121.2	+ 2.2
4. Clothing and footwear	210.3	+ 7.7	233.3	+ 8.8	166.6	+ 5.8
5. Personal care	403.3	+ 15.0	268.3	+ 10.4	217.6	+ 9.0
6. Housing	298.5	+ 11.6	231.8	+ 8.8	207.4	+ 8.4
7. Transport	295.4	+ 11.4	395.9	+ 14.8	251.8	+ 10.8
8. Telecommunications	312.6	+ 12.1	391.4	+ 14.6	190.9	+ 7.4
9. Medical goods and services	372.7	+ 14.1	359.9	+ 13.7	236.4	+ 10.0
10. Social services	286.1	+ 11.1	288.5	+ 11.2	286.2	+ 12.4
11. Education and research	364.6	+ 13.8	361.6	+ 13.7	280.8	+ 12.2
12. Culture and information	272.5	+ 10.5	345.0	+ 13.2	218.3	+ 9.1
13. Sports, leisure, entertainment	341.4	+ 13.1	249.1	+ 9.6	207.7	+ 8.5
14. Other goods and services	253.7	+ 9.8	253.2	+ 9.7	190.2	+ 7.4
15. Enlarged consumption	257.1	+ 9.9	260.0	+ 10.0	206.6	+ 8.4

Between 1959 and 1969 the proportion devoted to transport has increased in France from 6.8 to 7.8 per cent, in Italy from 5.1 to 7.7 per cent and in Switzerland (1960 to 1969) from 6.3 to 7.7 per cent. These increases occurred despite the fall in relative prices for motor vehicles and fuel, largely because of an increase in car parks (the average number of passenger cars per inhabitant rose during the period from 0.14 to 0.24 in France, from 0.05 to 0.17 in Italy and from 0.11 to 0.21 in Switzerland) and the volume of connected expenditures such as repairs, petrol and oil.[12] By contrast it appears that the proportion of consumption of collective transport diminished slightly or remained virtually stable (in France the proportion of collective transport in enlarged consumption dropped from 2.9 to 2.7 per cent, and for Italy the corresponding figures were 2.1 and 2.3 per cent). However, this near stagnation was accompanied by a change in the composition of this category of transport:

(i) in spite of a considerable increase in railway traffic between the suburbs and the towns, which was due to urbanization, the total share of rail transport appears to have declined in the three countries;

(ii) although representing a modest share in the transport budget of households, air travel has registered a constant and rapid advance.

Table 3.6
Indicators of the utilization of collective transport

	France		Italy		Switzerland	
	1959	1969	1959	1969	1960	1969
Number of railway km per inhabitant	751	777	637	612	1572	1301
(of which suburban)	100[a]	121[a]				
Number of km by air per inhabitant[b]	100	233	21	135	180	616

[a] Paris suburbs.

[b] Number of km carried by internal and international transport by the air companies registered in each country. Source: Statistical Yearbook, UN, 1964, 1970, United Nations.

Expenditure on telecommunications amounted to about 1 per cent of expanded consumption throughout the period. It will be noted, however, that-limited as this category of expenditure has remained- there are marked differences in telephone equipment between the three countries; in spite of a rapid increase in investment, the number of telephones per inhabitant in France (0.09 in 1959 and 0.16 in 1969) and in Italy (0.07 and 0.16) remained very much below that in Switzerland (0.29 and 0.45) and in some other Western European countries.[13]

------

[12] It will be noted that the consumption of "roads" through motor vehicle utilization are not included in collective consumption. Its exclusion, which is due to lack of information, obviously involves an under-estimation not only of collective consumption but also of the share of expanded consumption devoted to individual transport.

[13] Number of telephones per inhabitant in 1969: United Kingdom-0.25, Federal Republic of Germany-0.21, Belgium-0.20.

The consumption of <u>medical goods and services</u> grew markedly in the three countries both in absolute value and as a proportion of enlarged consumption (during the period this proportion rose from 6.3 to 9.2 per cent in France, from 5.5 to 7.6 per cent in Italy and from 7.2 to 8.3 per cent in Switzerland). Hospital expenditure increased most rapidly (at annual averages of 16.4 and 14 per cent in France and Italy respectively) while expenditure on treatment in ambulatories and pharmacies and on running costs rose less rapidly. This was only partially due to demographic developments, notably to increases in the extreme age brackets of the population pyramid (which were particularly marked in Italy) since children and old people have the highest consumption of medical services. The essential factors responsible for this expansion have been the quantitative and qualitative increase in supply, in particular of hospital and specialized treatment, as well as the sometimes very rapid increases in the cost of these services, particularly in hospitals. Moreover, in France and Italy the progressive extension of social insurance covering the financial risks of sickness has involved an increase in the share of collective consumption connected with the general administration of health.

Table 3.7
Indicators for the medical sector

	France		Italy		Switzerland	
	1959	1969	1959	1969	1960	1969
Gross mortality rate (per 1000)	11.3	11.3	9.2	10.1	9.5	9.3
Infant mortality rate (per 1000)	29.5	16.4	45.4	30.3	22.2	15.4
Life expectancy: Men	68.0 (1968)		67.2 (1960–62)		68.7 (1958–63)	
Women		75.5 (1968)		72.3 (1968)		74.1
Share of children of less than 5 years in the population (per cent)	8.8	8.4	8.3	8.8	8.2	8.2
Share of persons of more than 60 years in the population (per cent)	16.6	18.8	13.2	15.2	15.0	16.5
Density of doctors per 1000 inhabitants	0.993	1.286 (1968)	1.773	(1968)	0.915	0.874 (1970)
	0.993	1.286	1.773		0.915	0.874
Density of dentists per 1000 inhabitants	0.326	0.392		nd	0.410	0.403
Number of hospital beds per 1000 inhabitants	9.8	10.3		10.3	12.63	11.16
Implicit prices of medical consumption (at market prices	100	163.3 (+5.0% per yr	1960:100	154.2 (+4.9% per yr	100	150.3 (+4.7% per yr

Sources: Statistical Year Books, 1964,1970: Demographic Year Book, 1970 and Year Book od National Accounts Statistics, 1971, U.N., and World Health Statistics, 1971, U.N., and World Health Statistics, W.H.P., 1968.

In the absence of more precise indicators of health standards, it appears from the usual mortality and life-expectancy rates that during the period the sanitary conditions in the three countries was no doubt rather similar; it can be assumed that alcoholism and the larger proportion of old people in the population have a significant bearing on the higher mortality rate in France, while the lower density of doctors in the South is partly responsible for a high infant mortality in Italy.

The development of expenditure on <u>education and research</u> was virtually parallel in the three countries: it increased at an average annual rate of 13.7 per cent in France and Italy and of 12.5 per cent in Switzerland, that is more rapidly than most other items; hence its share in enlarged consumption rose very markedly (in France from 4.6 to 6.6 per cent, in Italy from 4.6 to 6.4 per cent and in Switzerland from 4.6 to 6.3 per cent).

Table 3.8
Indicators for the educational sector

	France		Italy		Switzerland	
	1959	1969	1959	1969	1960	1969
Share of persons in the population:		(1968)		(1968)		
5 to 9 years per cent	8.9	8.4	8.0	8.0	7.8	7.8
10 to 14 years per cent	8.4	8.3	8.3	7.5	8.1	7.4
15 to 24 years per cent	12.5	16.1	15.9	14.9	14.0	16.9
Percentage of persons in the age group:			(1960)			
6 to 14 in primary schools	77.7	70.4	83.8	88.0	na	na
6 to 14 in secondary schools	18.4	28.8			na	na
15 to 18 in secondary schools	33.2	46.9	16.0[a]	32.9[a]	na	na
20 to 24 in higher education	3.3	11.5	4.7	11.2	na	na
Registered pupils:	(1962)	(1968)	(1962)	(1968)	(1961)	(1968)
Total (thousands)	10,525.9	11,879.1	8433.6	9994.5	887.7	965.9
Number per inhabitants	0.24	0.24	0.17	0.19	0.17	0.16
Percentage by degree of instruction[b]						
pre-primary and 1st degree	70.3	60.7	66.8	60.2	65.0	49.7
2nd degree	26.2	32.6	30.0	34.9	31.4	44.4
of which technical	(4.9)	(9.1)	(6.8)	(8.7)	(15.3)	(15.4)
3rd degree	3.5	5.2	2.7	4.2	3.6	4.0
special	c	1.5	0.5	0.7	c	1.9
Percentage of scholarships	(1965–66)					
	12.5%	13.7%	na	na	na	na
Number of teachers per 10 pupils registered	(1962)	(1968)	(1962)	(1968)	na	na
	0.32	0.42	0.57	0.57		

[a] 14 to 19 years,   [b] UNESCO definition,   [c] Included in instruction of 1st degree.

Sources: Annex I, Table 3, *Statistical Year Books, 1964–1971*, U.N., W.H.O.

The combination of the following factors explain this expansion:

(i) Demographic reasons. The increase in the proportion of school-going age groups in the population resulting from the post-war baby boom and the increase in school attendance within different age groups, rapidly raised the number of pupils and students, particularly at the beginning of the period. And, more important, the progressive shift of the most numerous cohorts of pupils towards higher age groups led to a gradual increase of expenditure on education in the secondary and then the higher education sectors at the expense of primary education in all three countries.

(ii) Institutional factors. For instance, the extension of compulsory schooling to 16 years since 1967 in France, the increase of establishments for secondary technical education (France and Italy) and the relatively wider access to universities (the creation of technological institutes and university diplomas accessible to students without secondary school diplomas in France) and the increase in the number and amount of scholarships and pre-salaries for students in France and Italy.

(iii) Economic factors. It seems that the average cost per pupil or student has risen rather rapidly during the period, especially in Switzerland where the population of school age has grown only a little. The increase in the relative importance of secondary and subsequently of higher education as well as that of technical and scientific departments, whose costs are generally higher than those for primary and classical education, largely account for this tendency.

Only limited significance can be attributed to the relative stability of the share of expenditure on social services in enlarged consumption. These are not only greatly under-valued in all three countries because of a sizeable under-estimation of local authority expenditure, but the items which make up the category are very heterogeneous. It seems that in France, at any rate, the increase of the higher age groups led to a corresponding increase in the expenditure of hospices and old-age homes. Moreover, the generalization of compulsory old-age pension systems

Table 3.9

Typical indicators for the sectors of culture, sports and entertainment

	France		Italy		Switzerland	
	(1961)	(1968)	(1961)	(1968)	(1963)	(1969)
Daily newspapers						
Number	136	109	91	70	137	121
Copies per 1000 inhabitants	257	243	101	127	365	368
	(1961)	(1968)	(1961)	(1969)	(1963)	(1969)
Annual cinema entries per inhabitants	7.5	4.0	15.1	10.0	8.6	5.0
	(1960)	(1969)	(1960)	(1969)	(1960)	(1969)
Number of sets per 1000 inhabitants						
Radio	241	314	162	213	270	289
Television	41	201	43	170	24	184

Sources: Statistical Year Books, 1964-1971, U.N.

in France and Italy resulted in an increase in expenditure on the general administration of the institutions in question.

The share of consumption linked with culture, sports and leisure, in total
enlarged consumption, has on the whole increased (in France from 7.7 to 9.7 per
cent, in Italy from 8.1 to 8.3 per cent and in Switzerland from 4.5 to 4.7 per
cent). This was accompanied by a fairly similar shift in composition in France and
Italy:

  (i) a decline in the share of certain traditional expenditure items-theatre,
      cinema, sport events; in France, books and newspapers; and in Italy, sport
      articles;
 (ii) an increase in the share of expenditure on television, museums, hotels and
      restaurants and, in Italy, on books.

As much as from divergent price developments in this category, these changes
result from modifications in socio-cultural preferences (increase in the number of
persons taking holidays, in the motor vehicles park,etc.) and from larger supplies
(extension of the hotel network, sports equipment, etc.).

For the same reasons as indicated for social services, it is difficult to analyse
the development of the categories other items. Their proportion of consumption has
not changed much during the period (in France from 6.7 to 6.9 per cent, in Italy
from 4.8 to 4.6 per cent and in Switzerland from 10.5 to 9.5 per cent). The only
notable shift consisted in the decline of the proportion of expenditure on tobacco
and matches in Italy and Switzerland and, in all three countries, in an increase
in the proportion of services, particularly those linked with personal care and,
to a lesser extent, with banking and insurance.

As a whole, the analysis of the developments in the structure of enlarged
consumption in the three countries during the 1960s-schematic as it is bound to
be-does not substantially modify the findings on private consumption at market
prices alone but only accentuates the tendencies of the latter in many ways.

The gaps between economic standards expressed in values per head and between rates
of population and national income increases have, in certain instances, produced
more pronounced changes in the structure of enlarged consumption in Italy than in
France, and more in France than in Switzerland.

These changes only confirm the by now classical shift of total consumption from
goods to services, on the one hand, and the fall in the share of expenditure for
the satisfaction of primary or traditional needs (food, beverages, clothing,
cinema, theatre, etc.) in favour of categories of goods and services influencing
the environment of the individual categories of consumption and the diffusion of
recent innovations (such as individual transport, television, health, education,
personal care, etc.), on the other. Such developments are to a large extent
typical of relatively high living standards. But in certain instances they also
reflect demographic changes, notably the ageing of the population, but most of all
changes in ways of life connected with urbanization, progress in education and
information, the frequently very rapid dissemination of technical progress and the
growing awareness of the collective nature of certain needs.

3.4   MARKET AND NON-MARKET FORMS OF ENLARGED CONSUMPTION

Strictly and narrowly defined, market consumption is identical with acquisitions of goods and services whose prices paid for by households cover costs of production;[14] in so far as social benefits in kind, or in the form of services, are included and if self-consumption of food by farmers and imputed rent is considered at least potentially "market" consumption,[15] then the concept is equivalent to "private consumption"[16] in this study. Conversely, non-market consumption covers free or virtually free consumption: it consists essentially of divisible services produced by the public administrations, that is of "divisible public consumption".

On the basis of these definitions and at a global level market consumption accounted for more than 90 per cent of enlarged consumption from 1959 to 1969 in the three countries, but it increased less rapidly than non-market consumption. Private consumption (at factor cost) in France progressively declined from 93.4 per cent of enlarged consumption in 1959 to 92.2 per cent in 1969, in Italy from 93.4 to 90.8 per cent and in Switzerland from 94.3 to 92.5 per cent (between 1960 and 1969). Thus the allocation of enlarged consumption between market and non-market during the period was very similar in the three countries at the aggregate level but with public consumption occupying a somewhat more important place in Italy than in France and Switzerland.

Throughout the period reviewed, and in all three countries, the distribution between divisible private and public consumption by categories of needs was along the following broad lines (see Tables 3.3 and 3.11):

(i) All goods (food, beverages, tobacco, clothing, personal care, household equipment, pharmaceuticals, private vehicles and goods linked to culture, leisure and other categories of needs) as well as numerous services (housing, transport, telecommunications, cultural, sports, financial, maintenance and domestic services) belong exclusively to the private sphere, that is market consumption.
(ii) Medical services, in particular hospital treatment, a large part of social services (hospices, orphanages, establishments of handicapped persons, etc.) and cultural services (libraries, cultural centres, radio and television) belong to private and public consumption in varying proportions.
(iii) By contrast, services of assistance, prophylactic and preventive medicine and education are almost entirely a part of public consumption and represent about 60 per cent of it. The services of the general administration are by definition, totally included in public consumption of Western countries.

As to the consumption categories which are considered as belonging entirely to the "market" sphere, it must be stressed that this does not mean that the markets in question are totally beyond the reach of public action. In fact, the State

---

[14]Following the criteria of European national accounts (E.S.A.), the price must cover at least 50 per cent of production costs.
[15]This definition does not mean that the corresponding expenditure is at the final charge to households since certain consumption categories can be totally or partially financed or reimbursed from collective funds, e.g. of the type of Social Security (see Section 3.5).
[16]It will be noted that this self-consumption is evaluated with reference to the market prices of corresponding goods and services.

Table 3.10

Aggregates of enlarged consumption. Values, percentages and average rates of growth

Main categories of total final consumption	Direct net household purchases at market prices (1)	Indirect taxes (2)	Subsidies to producers (3)	Direct net household purchases (at factor cost) 4=1-2+3	Social benefits in kind (5)	Private consumption (at factor cost) 6=4+5	Public consumption (at factor cost) (7)	Enlarged household consumption 8=6+7
France								
1959: 10^6 F	162,229	18,439	4095	147,885	9203	157,088	9137	166,225
per cent	97.6	11.1	2.5	89.0	5.5	94.5	5.5	100.0
1965: 10^6 F	275,793	33,783	10,730	252,740	22,224	274,964	20,563	295,527
per cent	93.3	11.4	3.6	85.5	7.5	93.0	7.0	100.0
1969: 10^6 F	400,719	61,752	18,315	357,282	36,771	394,053	33,293	427,346
per cent	93.8	14.4	4.3	83.6	8.6	92.2	7.8	100.0
Average annual growth (1959–1969): per cent	+9.5%	+11.7%	+16.2%	+9.2%	+14.8%	+9.6%	+12.8%	+9.9%
Italy								
1959: 10^9 Lire	12,689	1143	179	11,725	673	12,398	869	13,267
per cent	95.6	8.6	1.3	88.3	5.1	93.4	6.6	100.0
1965: 10^9 Lire	22,405	2191	482	20,696	1648	22,344	2192	24,536
per cent	91.3	8.9	2.0	84.4	6.7	91.1	8.9	100.0
1969: 10^9 Lire	31,276	3256	781	28,801	2526	31,327	3173	34,500
per cent	90.6	9.4	2.3	83.5	7.3	90.8	9.2	100.0
Average annual growth (1959–1969): per cent	+9.4%	+11.0%	+15.9%	+9.4%	+14.1%	+9.7%	+13.8%	+10.0%
Switzerland								
1960: 10^6 SF	22,115	2181	362	20,296	599	20,895	1248	22,143
per cent	99.9	9.9	1.6	91.6	2.7	94.3	5.7	100.0
1969: 10^6 SF	44,323	5020	1127	40,430	1869	42,299	3455	45,754
per cent	96.9	11.0	2.5	88.4	4.1	92.5	7.5	100.0
Average annual growth (1960–1969): per cent	+8.0%	+9.7%	+13.4%	+8.0%	+13.5%	+8.1%	+12.0%	+8.4%

Table 3.11

Breakdown of the value of enlarged consumption into private and divisible public consumption
(In percentage shares)

	France 1959			France 1969			Italy 1959			Italy 1969			Switzerland 1960			Switzerland 1969		
	Private consumption	Divisible public consumption	Enlarged consumption	Private consumption	Divisible public consumption	Enlarged consumption	Private consumption	Divisible public consumption	Enlarged consumption	Private consumption	Divisible public consumption	Enlarged consumption	Private consumption	Divisible public consumption	Enlarged consumption	Private consumption	Divisible public consumption	Enlarged consumption
1. Food	100	–	100	100	–	100	100	–	100	100	–	100	100	–	100	100	–	100
2. Beverages	100	–	100	100	–	100	100	–	100	100	–	100	100	–	100	100	–	100
3. Tobacco, matches	100	–	100	100	–	100	100	–	100	100	–	100	100	–	100	100	–	100
4. Clothing, footwaer	100	–	100	100	–	100	100	–	100	100	–	100	100	–	100	100	–	100
5. Personal care	100	–	100	100	–	100	100	–	100	100	–	100	100	–	100	100	–	100
6. Housing	100	–	100	100	–	100	100	–	100	100	–	100	100	–	100	100	–	100
7. Transport	99.6	0.4	100	99.6	0.4	100	80.7	19.3	100	81.1	18.9	100	100	–	100	100	–	100
8. Telecommunications	100	–	100	100	–	100	100	–	100	100	–	100	100	–	100	100	–	100
9. Medical goods and services	92.8	7.2	100	92.7	7.3	100	43.2	56.8	100	37.3	62.7	100	73.1	26.9	100	75.7	24.3	100
10. Social services	51.2	48.8	100	42.6	57.4	100	17.1	82.9	100	11.4	88.6	100	75.0	25.0	100	71.7	28.3	100
11. Education	31.6	68.4	100	23.1	76.9	100	78.9	21.1	100	81.7	18.3	100	35.0	65.0	100	26.5	73.5	100
12. Culture, information	86.8	13.2	100	87.8	12.2	100	98.7	1.3	100	97.9	2.1	100	95.1	4.9	100	91.4	8.6	100
13. Sports, leisure, entertainment	97.4	2.6	100	95.8	4.2	100	94.1	5.9	100	91.1	8.9	100	97.9	2.1	100	96.2	3.8	100
14. Other goods and services	87.3	12.7	100	92.3	7.7	100							96.6	3.4	100	96.9	3.1	100
15. Total consumption	94.5	5.5	100	92.2	7.8	100	93.4	6.6	100	90.8	9.2	100	94.4	5.6	100	92.4	7.6	100

exercises fairly close control[17] over the numerous market sectors of the economy through various channels and instruments.

Several forms of control can be singled out:

(i) <u>The control of the nature and quality of products</u> generally aims at prophylactic, sanitary and public safety objectives. In Switzerland this supervision is still embryonic and hence much less developed than in the two other countries; it concerns mainly dairy produce and pharmaceuticals. In France and Italy, the Ministry of Agriculture is charged with the application of legislation and regulation for some foods such as the slaughter of livestock, the quality, purity and content of tinned food, and the production, circulation and distribution of alcohol. Similarly, in the field of pharmaceuticals and cosmetics, the Ministries of Health impose upon producers a fairly strict regulation of production accompanied by technical and scientific controls by public laboratories. Finally, in France, the State has compelled manufacturers to install belts in motor cars. Such legislation certainly does not mean that the production and consumption of the goods in question cease to be of a market and often of a very highly competitive nature, but they do involve an interference by the public authorities for the purpose of maintaining collective order in the functioning of the market economy through rules which should ensure a minimum of safety for the community.

(ii) <u>Price control</u> has mostly been exercised over the whole of market and non-market sectors, particularly in periods of inflation for instance, the stabilization plan of 1963 in France. However, certain sectors are subject to a more constant regulation and supervision in the three countries:

The regulation of agricultural prices is often strict. Through highly selective taxes and subsidies, the three countries have influenced agricultural production and its orientation at different levels: cereals, animal husbandry, dairy products and some other food products.[18] The complex motives for such policies-economic (the structural transformation of farms, the harmonization of agricultural production within the framework of EEC in France and Italy,balanced trade) and social (an attempt to maintain or increase agricultural incomes, retirement of farmers, etc.)-render an assessment of the precise consequences of agricultural price policies difficult; but they suggest, at least, that even though these products fall under the category of market consumption, they are produced in conditions of a closely supervised market.

In the field of housing, the State and local authorities intervene fairly energetically, both at the investment and the rent-control level. In France-with the exception of the free market which, apart from building permits, is not subject to any regulation in this respect-the public authorities play a decisive although diminishing role in the financing of investment in social housing,notably of H.L.M. Similarly, through legislation the State influences the amounts and increases of rents for social dwellings and dwellings built before 1948. Thus in 1967 dwellings subject to regulation

---

[17]The term "control" or "supervision" should not be interpreted here in the sense of strict control often used in theory of the economics of the public sector ("tutelage", "merit goods") but rather in the juridical sense of French law comparable to controlled freedom.

[18]In Switzerland the only products subject to price control during the 1960s were cereals and dairy produce.

accounted for some 85 per cent of households and 31 per cent of rents paid.[19] In 1970 about 68 per cent of authorized dwellings benefited fairly significantly from public aid in the form of premia and subsidies. In Italy, State intervention in housing has been centred so far on the regulation of rent rather than of the financing of social housing. Rent control, whose origin goes back a long way (1932-34), has often been modified: since the Second World War it has been progressively relaxed and in spite of a new rent freeze in 1963, which partially ended in 1967 and was hardly re-established after 1960, the proportion of dwellings subject to controlled rents continuously declilned during the 1960s (from 40 per cent in 1960 to =7 per cent in 1962 and 17 per cent in 1965). State financing of construction uses various channels (subsidies, long-term credits, etc.). However, it appears that the social groups which benefited most from measures facilitating access to ownership were mainly the middle class in the public and private sectors rather than the workers and the low-income brackets. New dwelling construction financed wholly or partially by the public authorities represented 26 per cent of the total investment in this sector in 1959 but only 7 per cent in 1969.

In Switzerland public assistance to housing is traditionally in the hands of the cantons. It consists mainly of a stimulation of social housing by means of credits and mortgage loans, on the one hand, and subsidies to current costs, on the other. The scope of these measures varies greatly from one canton to the other, as does rent control, which has been progressively relaxed and now exists mainly in urban concentrations. Since 1965 the Confederation has intervened in the housing market mainly through direct aid (participation in the mortgage debt, guarantees granted for loans) and also through indirect assistance (subsidies to research for raising productivity in construction, subsidies for the drawing up of local and regional development plans).

The share of dwellings built with the help of public authorities, in total dwelling construction, was about 10 per cent at the beginning of the 1960s and 15 per cent at the end of the period.

It will be seen in the following paragraphs that price control was and continues to be exercised, mainly in France and Italy, in a virtually permanent fashion in other sectors (medical goods and services, transport, telecommunications and energy).

(iii) The study of the financing of enlarged consumption in the next section will show how far systems of collective financing of household expenditure introduce certain constraints into the functioning of certain market sectors of consumption so· that an overlapping of "private" and "public" sectors sometimes renders the distinction between the two types of consumption artificial and purely conventional.

(iv) Finally, it must be noted that, although certain consumption categories are of a purely market nature according to the definition used, they are entirely, or for a large proportion, produced by public enterprises owned by the State or local authorities. This is the case in France, Italy and Switzerland for collective transport (railways, urban transport and telecommunciations), and treatment in public hospitals, as well as for radio and television in France and for tobacco, matches, electricity, gas and water in Italy. Public control over such sectors, often exercised in the form of monopolies, originated historically from the pursuit of different objectives but a common concern with the supply of services

---

[19] In so far as the estimate of imputed rent for owner-occupied dwellings, notably of old dwellings, is not significantly biased.

of collective interest (transport, communications, information and health) appears to be better ensured and protected through public production than through private initiative.

Finally, it must be admitted that in the definition adopted the concept of market consumption has a limited and sometimes ambiguous significance. It may certainly be considered that between 1959 and 1969 the three countries had one feature in common, namely that all goods and a large number of services were acquired by households in a market form. But, in addition to general economic policies, the authorities intervened in the functioning of particular markets such as agricultural production, housing, collective transport, etc. Public intervention is less widespread in these fields in Switzerland than in France and Italy; nevertheless the different means of State intervention reflects the inability of the market economy to satisfy certain needs and the growing awareness of collective-economic as well as social-interests by the public authorities, as representatives of the community they attempt to protect.

This is particularly evident for mixed consumption categories supplied in both market and non-market forms and, of course, for those which are entirely non-market.

Some 25 per cent of medical consumption is covered from non-market sources in Switzerland, 19 per cent in Italy and 7 per cent in France. The relatively high proportion in Switzerland is due to the fact that non-market medical consumption includes funds allocated by the public authorities to cantonal or communal hospitals which often account for more than 50 per cent of total expenditure on hospitals, whereas in France and Italy this type of subsidy is pratically non-existent, the major part of hospital treatment being of a market character although largely financed through social security by way of benefits in kind.

The differences between France and Italy are partly explained by the fact that in Italy the current expenses of public organs (State and Social Security) were proportionately heavier and also that lower prices were charged for medical treatment although these treatments are of an entirely market nature, as they are also in France.

In the sector of social services it will be noted that the non-market share increased substantially during the period to reach 57 per cent in France, 63 per cent in Italy and 28 per cent in Switzerland in 1969. The heterogeneous composition of this group makes only a partial analysis possible. Thus, in France, services supplied to persons in distress (in the mountains and at sea, establishments for beggars), assistance to the unemployed and administrative services of pension institutions, belong to the non-market sector. In the absence of adequate statistics on social services provided by private administrations which play an important role, non-market consumption in this field in Italy covers solely the current expenses of the State and of pension funds.

As to education-a collective service par excellence-the non-market sector has played a predominant and growing role during the period (it accounted for 77 per cent in France, 89 per cent in Italy and 74 per cent in Switzerland in 1969). In Switzerland a part of educational services is paid for by the private market sector, but nearly all educational services are provided almost entirely free of charge in France and Italy. In these two countries a fairly significant part of education is entrusted to the private sector, lay or religious, but the latter is progressively incorporated into the public educational system by means of convention, notably in France, so that current expenses are now entirely covered from State and local authority budgets.[20] In 1969 market consumption of education consisted of no more than the purchase of books and school supplies,[21] private lessons and a tiny residual share of the financing of private instruction.

In the field of expenditure on culture, information and leisure, market consumption predominates in the three countries but its share declined during the period (in France and Italy from 94.8 to 94.1 and 94.7 to 93.7 per cent respectively and in Switzerland from 96.4 to 93.6 per cent). In fact, non-market consumption covers only the limited part of these services which is closely linked to collective interests, namely radio and television, services of the general administration for cultural affairs and, to a lesser extent, public libraries.

As a whole, market and non-market consumption assumed rather similar patterns in the three countries during the period reviewed. The shifts during the decade have also been similar and there has been no marked change in the respective roles of the market and the public authorities as producers.

In each of the three countries a major part of non-market consumption is concentrated on education and, in Italy and Switzerland, on medical care and to a lesser extent on social services and services for culture and information. This shows that the State, in a broad sense, typically plays a predominant role in consumption categories on which investments in human capital (education, information) and its preservation (health, social services) closely depend, leaving only a secondary and minor role to the market sector.

It must be stressed again, however, that there is no absolute dichotomy between "market" and "non-market" consumption. In each of the three countries the State has resorted to a wide range of instruments in varying combinations to influence the functioning of the market sectors: selective controls of products and prices, financing of investment and consumption, total or partial public appropriation of means of production, etc. Thus, although a given consumption category may be of a market character, notably in housing, collective transport, food and a variable part of medical goods and services, this merely means that households acquire these goods and services against payment and that their consumption depends on price-income effects and individual preferences. But these market relations, particularly the determination of price and quantities, cannot be considered as strictly belonging to the market sector of consumption where supply-demand relationships are the only determinant elements: fairly tight or precise government controls influence the mechanisms and major factors which otherwise operate in these markets. Such sectoral controls-which are more widespread in France and Italy than in Switzerland-sometimes stem from the necessity to control the global interdependence between the different branches of the economy. But they can also be attributed in many cases to the need of imposing constraints (social, economic or ethical) of a collective nature on the functioning of the sectors and the needs in question which purely liberal mechanisms of the market economy tend or intend to neglect.

---

[20] With the exception of registration fees at universities which are, however, only a very small proportion of total expenditure on education.

[21] Notably in France school books in primary schools and in the lower classes of secondary schools have been freely supplied by the State since 1968.

The choice between free market, protected market and non-market conditions depends, of course, on the nature and urgency of the problems raised. The instruments and structure of each of these sub-systems are highly diversified, in particular at the institutional and legislative level. But once planning, particularly if it is forward-looking and hence dynamic, takes account of the constraints and collective consequences of such choices, certain questions must be answered in advance:

Which economic and social objectives are assigned to each of these sub-systems?

Under what conditions can controls or non-market sectors function, notably regarding the fiscal burden imposed on production and income, the choice of public investments, access to consumption of various population categories and the social returns of the mechanisms applied?
Are these means compatible with the objectives pursued? In particular, do they contribute to the satisfaction of needs or of total demand?

To what extent, and up to what levels, are the mutual exchanges between market and non-market sectors stimulating or paralysing, complementary or contradictory?

Each of these questions crops up behind the highly schematic sketch of the preceding comparison which revealed rather similar developments in the three countries, notably the growing non-market share of certain sectors. It is, however, not certain that the three countries have responded in similar fashion.

3.5.   THE STRUCTURE AND DEVELOPMENT OF THE FINANCING OF ENLARGED CONSUMPTION

The analysis of how enlarged consumption was financed is complementary to the study of market and non-market forms of acquisition of goods and services, since it also raises the question of the use of private and public funds. At the same time these two aspects of the problem are distinct in the sense that, if non-market consumption is almost exclusively financed from public funds,[22] market consumption is paid either from household incomes, made up in part of redistributed collective funds (pensions, scholarships, etc.) or of contributions of public institutions (Social Security, the State, etc.) which more or less reimburse consumer expenditure in due course, or are directly allocated in form of services.

To simplify the analysis, it is necessary:

(i) to bear in mind that social benefits and transfers as well as subsidies are expenditures at factor cost, as is the case for public and enlarged consumption;

(ii) to assume that the considered subsidies to production are exclusively to the benefit of the consumer;[23]

(iii) to suppose that cash transfers to households are spent entirely on consumption.[24]

---

[22] As already stated, non-market consumption supplied in the three countries by private administrations is negligible compared to that by the public administration and it is, moreover, underestimated in the statistics presented.
[23] See Section 1.5
[24] See Section 1.6.

It appears from Table 3.12 that in France and Italy similar shares of enlarged consumption have been financed from total social benefits in kind and public consumption (11 per cent in 1959 and 16.5 per cent in 1969) but that these were decidedly lower in Switzerland (8.3 and 11.6 per cent respectively).

It can further be seen that reimbursements, mainly by Social Security, played a considerably more important role in France (they accounted for about 4 per cent of enlarged consumption in 1969) than in Switzerland and Italy (1.5 and 0.5 per cent). By contrast, public consumption accounted for a larger proportion in Italy (9.2 per cent in 1969) than in the other two countries (about 7.6 per cent).

The role of collective funds in this field appears to be more important if subsidies, on the one hand, and cash transfers, on the other, are taken into account. The share of subsidies was larger in France (2.5 per cent in 1959 and 4.3 per cent in 1969) than in Italy and Switzerland (about 1.3 and 2.3 per cent at the beginning and end of the period). Similarly the share of cash transfers attained about 22 per cent in France, 16 per cent in Italy and 13 per cent in Switzerland.

As a whole, it was found that total collective financing of enlarged consumption has increased at an average annual rate approaching 13 per cent, that is more rapidly than enlarged consumption; this means that the collective contribution to total expenditure has increased during the period. But it was unequal in the three countries: 42 per cent in France, 35 per cent in Italy and 27 per cent in Switzerland in 1969.

Seen from the viewpoint of forms of financing, the following characteristics are brought out by the study:

(i) Social benefits in kind represent essentially the total or partial coverage of expenditure on market consumption by the State and Social Security, or private insurance institutions in Switzerland (see Table 3.13) which is considered to be of a market nature in Western national accounts. Their increased role in the financing of enlarged consumption is mainly due to medical consumption[25] which has risen more rapidly than total consumption[26] and has been covered increasingly by collective insurance schemes. In France the growing role since 1945 of Social Security compared to that of the State has manifested itself primarily in an extension of sickness insurance to new sectors of the population (extension of the regime to farmers in 1962 and to the self-employed in 1969, increase of the number of active persons in dependent employment affiliated to the general system) and, in the second place, through the introduction in 1960 of a system of conventions between Social Security organs and private health institutions which ensured a progressive adaptation of insurance schemes to the general regime and better conditions for taking over the costs of treatment, notably for reimbursements (between 70 and 100 per cent according to the type of treatment, doctors and hospitals). In 1969 about 95 per cent of the population was covered by one or other of the health insurance schemes and all these systems financed some 70 per cent of total medical expenditure. The State came to play a secondary role, mainly in hospital treatment for the poorest classes of the population and mostly to complement expenditure not covered by Social Security.

---

[25] And, incidentally, to expenditure on food linked with hospital treatment.
[26] See Section 3.3 above.

Table 3.12

Share of enlarged consumption financed directly from collective funds

| | France (10^6 FF) | | | | | | Italy (10^9 LI) | | | | | | Switzerland (10^6 FS) | | | |
| | 1959 | | 1965 | | 1969 | | 1959 | | 1965 | | 1969 | | 1960 | | 1969 | |
	Value	%[a]	Value	%[a]	Value	%[a]	Value	%[a]	Value	%[a]	Value	%[a]	Value	%[a]	Value	%[a]
(1) Social benefits in kind of which:	9203	5.6	22,224	7.5	36.771	8.6	673	5.0	1648	6.7	2526	7.3	599	2.7	1869	4.0
Reimbursements	(3381)	(2.0)	(9555)	(3.2)	(16,730)	(3.9)	(36)	(0.3)	(80)	(0.3)	(166)	(0.5)	(205)	(0.9)	(682)	(1.5)
(2) Divisible public consumption	9137	5.5	20,563	6.9	33,293	7.8	869	6.6	2192	8.9	3173	9.2	1248	5.6	3455	7.6
(3) Subsidies to production	4095	2.5	10,730	3.6	18,315	4.3	179	1.3	482	2.0	781	2.3	362	1.6	1127	2.4
(4) Social cash transfers	28,598	17.2	62,797	21.2	92,676	21.7	1869	14.1	3759	15.3	5661	16.4	1828	8.3	5969	13.0
(5) = 1 + 2 + 3 + 4 Total	51,033	30.8	116,314	39.2	181,055	42.4	3590	27.0	8081	32.9	12,141	35.2	4037	18.2	12,420	27.0
Index	100		227.9		354.8		100		25.1		338.2		100		307.7	
					+13.5% per year						+13.0% per year				+13.3% per year	

a Percentage of enlarged consumption.

Table 3.13
The collective financing of enlarged consumption by categories of needs[a]

		France					Italy					Switzerland [b]				
		Social benefits in kind		Sub-sidies	Non-market con.	Total[c] col. fin.	Social benefits in kind		Sub-sidies	Non-market con.	Total[c] col. fin.	Social benefits in kind		Sub-Inst.	Non-market con.	Total[c] col. fin.
		Total	of which S. Sec				Total	of which S. Sec.				Total	of which Priv.			
		1	2	3	4	5=1+3+4	6	7	8	9	10=6+8+9	11	12	13	14	15=11+13+14
Food	1959	2.8	1.0	1.2	-	4.0	1.9	0.4		-	1.9	1.4	-	4.5	-	5.9
	1965	2.4	1.0	2.7	-	5.1	1.9	0.7	na	-	1.9	na	na	na	na	na
	1969	2.2	1.1	4.5	-	6.7	1.8	0.7		-	1.8	1.1	-	5.9	-	7.0
Beverages	1959	1.2	0.4	-	-	1.2	-	-		-	0.0	-	-	-	-	0.0
	1965	1.2	0.4	-	-	1.2	'-	-	na	-	0.0	na	na	na	na	na
	1969	1.2	0.5	-	-	1.2	-	-		-	0.0	-	-	-	-	0.0
Tobacco, matches	1959	-	-	-	-	0.0	-	-		-	0.0	-	-	-	-	0.0
	1965	-	-	-	-	0.0	-	-	na	-	0.0	na	na	na	na	na
	1969	-	-	-	-	0.0	-	-		-	0.0	-	-	-	-	0.0
Clothing, footwear	1959	1.6	-	-	-	1.6	-	-		-	0.0	-	-	-	-	0.0
	1965	1.2	-	-	-	1.2	-	-	na	-	0.0	na	na	na	na	na
	1969	1.4	-	-	-	1.4	-	-		-	0.0	-	-	-	-	0.0
Personal care	1959	-	-	-	-	0.0	-	-		-	0.0	-	-	-	-	0.0
	1965	-	-	-	-	0.0	-	-	na	-	0.0	na	na	na	na	na
	1969	-	-	-	-	0.0	-	-		-	0.0	-	-	-	-	0.0
Housing	1959	1.7	1.0	1.5	-	3.2	0^d	-		-	ϵ	-	-	0.2	-	0.2
	1965	2.2	1.8	2.1	-	4.3	0^d	-	na	-	ϵ	na	na	na	na	na
	1969	2.6	2.2	3.3	-	5.9	0^d	-		-	ϵ	-	-	0.9	-	0.9
Transport	1959	0.1	0.1	14.2	0.4	14.7	0^d	-		-	ϵ	-	-	2.2	-	2.2
	1965	0.1	0.1	16.1	0.3	16.5	0.2	-	na	-	0.2	na	na	na	na	na
	1969	0.1	0.1	14.0	0.2	14.5	0.2	-		-	0.2	-	-	2.6	-	2.6
Telecommunications	1959	-	-	1.1	-	1.1	-	-		-	-	-	-	-	-	0.0
	1965	-	-	1.8	-	1.8	-	-	na	-	-	na	na	na	na	na
	1969	-	-	1.6	-	1.6	0.3	-		-	0.3	-	-	-	-	0.0
Medical goods, services	1959	58.7	50.6	4.6	7.1	70.4	62.3	48.9		19.3	81.6	21.3	10.6	3.4	26.9	51.6
	1965	73.5	66.5	3.2	7.7	84.4	74.6	63.7	na	17.8	92.4	na	na	na	na	na
	1969	75.6	70.0	3.3	7.3	86.2	74.8	66.7		18.9	93.7	33.4	16.7	7.1	24.3	64.8
Social services	1959	19.6	1.4	6.3	48.8	74.7	43.2	1.6		56.8	100.0	75.0	-	-	25.0	100.0
	1965	22.0	1.3	7.6	52.7	82.3	37.1	2.2	na	63.9	100.0	na	na	na	na	na
	1969	20.4	1.4	6.1	57.4	83.9	37.3	2.0		62.7	100.0	71.7	-	-	28.3	100.0
Education, research	1959	-	-	8.3	68.4	76.7	0^d	-		82.9	82.9	-	-	-	65.0	65.0
	1965	-	-	12.5	76.0	88.5	0.6	-	na	88.2	88.8	na	na	na	na	na
	1969	-	-	12.6	76.9	89.5	0.7	-		88.6	89.3	-	-	-	73.5	73.5
Culture, information	1959	1.7	-	1.9	13.2	16.8	0^d	-		24.1	21.1	-	-	-	4.9	4.9
	1965	0.5	-	3.2	12.1	15.8	0^d	-	na	18.7	18.7	na	na	na	na	na
	1969	0.5	-	2.5	12.2	15.2	0^d	-		18.3	18.3	-	-	-	8.6	8.6
Sports, leisure, entertainment	1959	0.1	-	0.8	2.6	3.5	1.0			1.3	2.3	-	-	-	2.1	2.1
	1965	0^d	-	0.9	2.9	3.8	1.7		na	2.3	4.0	na	na	na	na	na
	1969	0^d	-	1.4	4.2	5.6	2.0			2.1	4.1	-	-	-	3.8	3.8
Other goods, services	1959	-	-	-	12.7	12.7	0.3	-		5.9	6.2	-	-	-	3.4	3.4
	1965	0.4	-	-	12.3	12.7	0^d	-	na	6.5	6.5	na	na	na	nd	na
	1969	0.1	-	-	7.7	8.1	0.1	-		8.9	9.0	-	-	-	3.1	3.1
Enlarged consumption	1959	5.6	3.8	2.5	5.5	13.6	5.0	2.9	1.3	6.6	12.9	2.7	0.7	1.6	5.6	9.9
	1965	7.5	5.9	3.5	6.9	18.0	6.7	4.7	2.0	8.9	17.6	na	na	na	na	na
	1969	8.6	7.2	4.3	7.8	20.7	7.3	5.4	2.3	9.2	18.8	4.0	1.3	2.4	7.6	14.0

[a] The residual of total collective consumption (columns 5, 10 and 15) consist of the shares of direct household purchases by categories of needs.
[b] 1960 instead of 1959.
[c] Excluding cash transfers.
[d] Less than 0.1 per cent.
na: not available.

Similarly in Italy, Social Security,whose first law on compulsory insurance dates back to 1927, now ensures the protection of the whole wage-earning, retired, unemployed and child population, and of part of the self-employed for risks of sickness and maternity. In the majority of cases (general practitioners, specialists and dentists in dispensaries, hospitals, pharmaceuticals listed by INAM), Social Security takes over the cost of treatment fixed directly by national agreements; otherwise it reimburses, in part or by a lump sum, expenditures incurred by households. The State plays a more important role than in France, mainly in the financing of expenses for hospital treatment and for rural doctors paid by capitation by local authorities. The creation of a system comparable to a National Health Service and financed from taxation should increase the share of the State and local authorities in the financing of health expenditure in the 1970s. In 1969 about 75 per cent of medical treatment was covered by social services in kind.

In Switzerland, the health insurance system is based mainly on private insurance and only in a subsidiary fashion on the sickness funds of public authorities. When these institutions meet a minimum stipulated by a federal law on sickness and accident insurance, they receive a partial subsidy from the government, depending on the number of their members. However, it is at the cantonal level that the compulsory character of the insurance is decided upon. In the majority of cantons, adherence remains optional. Thus the rate of coverage of the population varies greatly from one canton to another, and the 80 to 90 per cent put forward in official statistics is a considerable over-estimation as each individual is free to belong to several health insurance institutions simultaneously to protect himself against the various risks of sickness, accident, loss of income, etc.Doctor's treatment, the cost of pharmaceuticals and hospitalization is covered at rates varying between 75 and 90 per cent. Dental treatment is generally not covered at all, or only minimally, by the insurance companies. Also, in contrast to France and Italy, certain insurances limit the period of their benefits, sometimes to only 180 days per year. It is estimated that in 1969 about one-third of medical consumption was covered, half of this being covered by public authorities and the other half by private insurance companies.

In the field of social services, the heterogeneous character of consumption makes a satisfactory comparison between the countries impossible. At best it may be noted that the State, the local authorities and, in France and Italy, to a minor extent Social Security have directly financed a varying but virtually constant share of services by means of deliveries in kind:[27] about 20 per cent in France, 37 to 40 per cent in Italy and 72 to 75 per cent in Switzerland. The bulk of this finance went to hospices, orphanages and establishments for handicapped people in each of the three countries.

With regard to the other items of enlarged consumption, social benefits in kind supplied solely by the State and local authorities did not exist at all in Switzerland and only to a very limited extent in Italy (public transport, the free supply of school books, leisure activities during paid leave of wage-earners). In France these supplies were of a very limited importance in the field of culture (free books and newspapers), transport (reimbursement of the costs of moving) and

---

[27]In certain cases, notably in Switzerland, the expenditure in question has been classified as social benefits by convention because it was not possible to determine exactly, from the financing mechanisms, whether social services or subsidies to production were involved.

clothing (for inhabitants of hospices) but Social Security played a certain role in housing expenditure; by means of allowances it took over 2 per cent of the total, that is about 13 per cent of the estimated expenditure on real rent at 1969 market prices.

On the whole-excluding cash transfers-social benefits in kind in 1969 covered about 9 per cent of enlarged consumption in France, 7 per cent in Italy and 4 per cent in Switzerland. They are determined by different mechanisms in each of the three countries but their bulk was used for medical consumption and social services. The less generalized system of collective coverage of medical expenditure in Switzerland accounts for the smaller share of this item in total consumption compared with the other two countries.

The role of the State in this field remained secondary in France and Italy (about 1.5 per cent of consumption) but was slightly more important in Switzerland (about 3 per cent). By contrast Social Security, which in France and Italy was the major distributor of benefits in kind, played a more or less identical role for medical consumption in the two countries but was more important in France for other expenditure items, notably housing.

Finally, the increase in the share of consumption financed by social benefits in kind was essentially due to the increase in medical expenditure and its coverage from social sources and, in France, to that of expenditure on rent.

(ii) No breakdown of subsidies by categories of needs[28] is available for Italy. In France and Switzerland there are marked differences, with regard to both their share in enlarged consumption (4.3 per cent in France and 2.4 per cent in Switzerland in 1969) and the range of consumption categories benefiting from them.

Expenditure on food covered by agricultural subsidies increased rapidly in France (from 1.2 per cent in 1959 to 4.5 per cent in 1969). In Switzerland this increase was less marked (4.5 to 5.9 per cent) but the level of coverage was higher,[29] reflecting the greater subsidization (or protection) of Swiss agriculture. In France these subsidies were granted mainly to cereal and fruit production and to animal breeding, but in Switzerland the dairy industry benefited primarily, with cereal and potato production and animal husbandry taking second place.

Expenditure on housing benefited from subsidies to production to the extent of 3 per cent in France and 1 per cent in Switzerland in 1969. In both countries this type of financing was intended[30] to reduce the cost of rent and charges of social housing such as HLM in France.

---

[28] Although for the period under review these amounts cannot be precisely evaluated, subsidies in Italy are concentrated on sectors with large deficits; in 1970 the breakdown was agriculture and food (29 per cent), transport and telecommunications (44 per cent), medical services (40 per cent), social and cultural services (40 per cent), as well as certain public enterprises, among which were oil, gas and electricity (3.0 per cent).

[29] In fact, if these subsidies were related to domestic agricultural production (excluding imports) only, the rate of the subsidies would certainly bu much higher in Switzerland and only slightly higher in France.

[30] In France public subsidies for equipment also contribute to lowering the cost of investment in social housing, and hence of rents, but in proportions which are difficult to estimate.

In the field of transport, mainly railways and, to a lesser extent, urban collective transport benefited from subsidies. They correspond, on the one hand, to financing of certain constraints of a public service imposed on the S.N.C.F. by the State in France and, on the other, to subsidies aiming in both France and Switzerland to compensate for preferential railway tariffs, particularly for large families, certain invalids and paid leave.[31]

Subsidies occupied a more important (and slightly rising) share in medical services in Switzerland (7 per cent in 1969) than in France (3.3 per cent). In both countries they were destined for hospitals but while they are essentially intended to help private clinics to lower their fees in Switzerland, in France they were granted solely to the public sector for covering part of the cost of instruction in university hospitals.

No subsidies to production are granted in Switzerland in other sectors of consumption. In France, the State and local authorities subsidize telecommunications, social services (hospices, orphanages and university hostels), education (private establishments under contract with the State) and, to a lesser extent, cultural services and leisure (library services, cultural centres, newspapers, sport clubs, national theatres, etc.). These subsidies aim mainly at lowering prices so as to permit larger dissemination (press, theatres) or wider access to certain collective services (university hostels, sport clubs).

Taken as a whole, the proportion of subsidies in enlarged consumption increased in all three countries, implying that selective public intervention in price determination has increased during the period. However, it was more important in France, where subsidies represented 4.3 per cent of consumption in 1969, than in Italy and Switzerland, where the corresponding ratios amounted to about 2.5 per cent.

(iii) Divisible public consumption is identical with non-market consumption examined under (ii). It is sufficient to recall in each of the three countries it relates mainly to education, where in 1969 it covered 77 per cent of expenditure in France, 89 per cent in Italy and 74 per cent in Switzerland. Its share in medical consumption was also relatively important in Italy (19 per cent) and in Switzerland (25 per cent). Public non-market social services accounted for 57 per cent of expenditure in France, 63 per cent in Italy and 28 per cent in Switzerland. Since they covered mainly the costs of general administration, they occupied a very minor place in other categories of needs.

As was shown in the preceding analysis, the increase in the proportion of non-market consumption in the financing of enlarged consumption is mainly attributable to increased expenditure on education in all three countries and of medical expenditure in Italy and Switzerland.

(iv) The share of cash transfers in national income[32] continued to grow during the period in all three countries: it rose from about 8 to 15 per cent in France, 10 to 12 per cent in Italy and 6 to 8 per cent in Switzerland. Assuming that all these payments are entirely used for consumption, they have contributed increasingly to the financing of enlarged consumption, of which they accounted for 22 per cent in France, 16 per cent in Italy and 13 per cent in Switzerland in 1969.

----

[31] It must be stressed, once again, that it is only because of a convention used for enterprise accounts that this financing is classified under subsidies; economically they could be included in social benefits.

[32] See Table 3.1.

Since cash transfers are not allocated a priori to any particular consumption, it is not possible to estimate, even at the global level,[33] the extent to which they have contributed to the financing of the different expenditure categories. But from the proportions indicated above it appears that there have been substantial differences in collective redistribution arising from this type of payment in all three countries. In Switzerland nearly 86 per cent of the transfers consisted of old-age pensions (76 per cent) and invalidity pensions. A major part of old-age pensions came from the obligatory federal system of old-age survivor insurance (AVS) and, for the remainder, from the pension funds of private enterprises which were optional during the period. AVS pensions are paid to persons more than 65 years old; the three-fold increase of their total amount is due mainly to the progressive raising of the average amount of allocations and, to a lesser extent, to the ageing of the population.

Invalidity pensions are paid entirely by the compulsory federal system of invalidity insurance (AI). The creation of this insurance as recently as 1960 explains the rapid growth of the amounts paid. 1960, the year the new insurance was instituted, cannot be considered a valid basis for comparison, but the 1969 data should be taken instead as representative of a more stabilized situation.

The sizeable share of pensions in the total transfers of social insurance is due less to the growth of that category-which lags far behind that in the neighbouring countries-than to the modest size of other transfers. Thus the extremely low level of family allowances will be noted, which reflects the traditional trend of the Swiss authorities to discourage any increase in the birth rate.

In the other two countries the scope of cash transfers has been much larger, with regard to both their nature and their amounts. In 1969 they consisted largely of old-age, war veteran and invalidity pensions (58 and 5 per cent in France and 69 and 5 per cent in Italy respectively). In France pensions are paid simultaneously by Social Security which adminsters the compulsory regimes of wage- and salary-earners and the multiple complementary regimes, notably for professionals and workers. These are granted in most cases from 65 years onwards, in certain professions from 55 (miners) or 60 years, and are raised by variable amounts if retirement occurs later. Their relatively rapid growth between 1959 and 1969 (by 14 per cent annually) was due to an extension of Social Security, in particular to farmers in 1962, the ageing of the population[34] and the progressive upward revision of allocations.

In Italy the National Institute of Social Security administers almost the entire system of compulsory pensions for wage- and salary-earners. Pensions are granted to men of over 60 and women over 55 years and supplements can be paid if the beneficiaries continue to work after the age limit. As in the other two countries, the increase of the total (15 per cent annually) was accounted for by the ageing of the population and also by successive changes in legislation which widened the provisions for supplementary pensions, for the cumulation of old-age pensions and reassignment to survivors.

---

[33]The situation would be different if data with a breakdown by categories of population were available, notably for groups whose income is largely made up of such transfers (retired persons, invalids, large families) and who save little.

[34]See Table 3.7.

Table 3.14

The structure of cash transfers (in values and percentages)

	France (10⁶ FF)								Italy (10⁹ LI)								Switzerland (10⁶ FS)					
	1959			1965		1969			1959			1965		1969			1960			1969		
	Social security	Total	%	Total	%	Social security	Total	%	Social security	Total	%	Value Total	%	Value Social security	Total	%	Private institutions	Value Total	%	Private institutions	Value Total	%
(1) Family allowances	7564	8819	30.9	15,225	24.3	16,123	19,475	21.0	429	549	29.4	946	25.2	786	1080	19.1	-	37	2.0	-	146	2.4
of which: (11) pre-natal allowances	-	-	-	-	-	-	-	-	(9)	(19)	(1.0)	(45)	(1.2)	(31)	(61)	(1.1)		na			na	
(2) Daily sickness pay[a]	1353	1353	4.7	4424	7.0	6102	6102	6.6	75	75	4.0	132	3.5	258	258	4.6	214	214	11.7	488	488	8.2
(3) Unemployment benefits	100	128	0.4	431	0.7	798	1210	1.3	41	41	2.2	125	3.3	107	107	1.9	-	1	0.1	-	2	ε
(4) Pensions	9775	15,439	54.0	37,257	59.3	40,428	58,230	62.8	698	1139	60.9	2538	67.5	3361	4182	73.8	730	1512	82.7	1460	5119	85.8
of which: (41) old age	(8873)	(14,537)	(50.8)	(34,295)	(54.6)	(36,009)	(53,811)	(58.1)	(652)	(876)	(46.9)	(2119)	(56.4)	(3098)	(3549)	(62.7)	(730)	(1461)	(79.9)	(1460)	(4554)	(76.3)
(42) war veterans									-	(217)	(11.6)	(276)	(7.3)	-	(730)	(6.5)						
(43) invalidity	(902)	(902)	(3.2)	(2962)	(4.7)	(4419)	(4419)	(4.7)	(46)	(46)	(2.4)	(143)	(3.8)	(263)	(263)	(4.6)	-	(51)	(2.8)	-	(565)	(9.5)
(5) Other	-	2859	10.0	5460	8.7		7659	8.3	8	65	3.5	18	0.5	20	34	0.6	-	64[b]	3.5	-	214[b]	3.6
of which: (61) studying, scholarships pre-salaries for studying	na			(790)	(1.3)		(1375)	(1.5)	-	(57)	(3.0)	na		-	(14)	(0.2)		na			na	
(62) allowances for repatriates	na			(600)	(1.0)		(51)	ε	-	-	-	-	-	-	-	-	-	-	-	-	-	-
(6) = 1+2+3+4+5	18792	28,598	100.0	62,797	100.0	63,751	92,676	100.0	1251	1859	100.0	3759	100.0	4352	5661	100.0	944	1828	100.0	1828	5967	100.0

a Caisses de Prévoyance, Caisses Maladie, C.N.A.

b Allocations to military personnel for loss of income.

na: not available

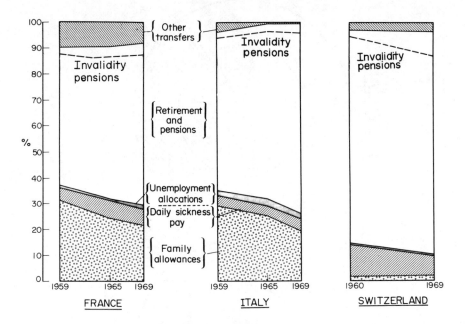

Chart 3.7.   Structure of cash transfers.

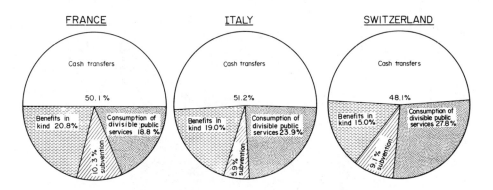

Chart 3.8.   Distribution of collective funds by type of
            allocation.

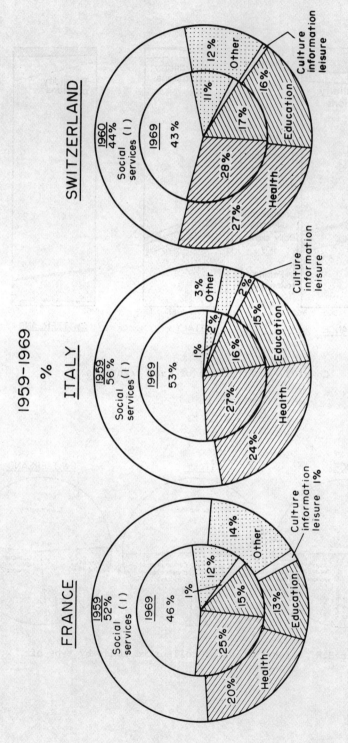

Chart 3.9 Functional distribution of collective funds
allocated to household consumption.

The increase in invalidity pensions is explained, mainly in France, by the extension of the regimes of Social Security to new categories of households and, in Italy, by an increase in benefits, particularly the raising of minimum allowances and the linking of pensions to the cost of living index.

The proportion of family allowances declined rather rapidly during the period in both France and Italy and accounted for no more than 20 per cent of cash transfers in 1969. They consisted in France of family allowances proper, which benefit all households with at least two children until their coming of age, whatever the household income; and of allocations to households with only one wage-earner who has less than a stipulated minimum income. In Italy family allowances are paid to households with at least one dependent child up to 8 years, up to 18 years if the children are apprenticed, or to 26 years for non-working students. In both countries close to 80 per cent of family allowances are paid by Social Security institutions. In both countries their global amount has also doubled between 1959 and 1969. The slower progression of family allowances than that of transfers in France can be explained partly by demographic developments (the coming of age of children born during the baby-boom after the Second World War and the slowing down of the birth rate during the 1960s) as well as by changes in the status of Algerian workers in 1965. Moreover, in both countries, the progressive raising of average allowances lagged somewhat behind the increases in incomes and consumer prices.

Other transfers played only a minor role: daily indemnities whose share in France[35] has increased with the extension of sickness insurance, unemployment pay and other transfers where scholarships and pre-salaries constituted a relatively small proportion, despite the increase in the number of beneficiaries and the amounts of scholarships. It can be noted that in France the allowances granted to persons repatriated from Algeria after 1962 had for a while represented 1 to 2 per cent of cash transfers, but their role had become negligible by 1969.

When collective funds are regrouped by functions[36] it appears that, in the first place, public expenditure in the health sector has increased rapidly, mainly in France and Italy, and that it absorbed one-fourth of collective funds allocated to

---

[35]The number of unemployed registered in public labour exchange offices was, in France: 140,900 in 1959, 142,100 in 1965 and 223,000 in 1969; in Italy (including first job-seekers): 1,117,000 in 1959, 721,000 in 1965 and 663,000 in 1969; and in Switzerland: 1,690 in 1960, 473 in 1965 and 343 in 1969.

[36]The functions were defined according to the following regrouping by categories of needs: function health = medical goods and services (9.00), function social services = social services (10.00), function education = education and research (11.00), function culture-information = culture, information (12.00), functions sports and leisure = sports, leisure and entertainment (13.00), other functions = food, beverages, tobacco, etc. (1.00 + 2.00 + 3.00 + 5.00 + 6.00 + 7.00 + 8.00 + 14.00). Cash transfers have been divided by function according to the following principles: daily sickness pay and invalidity pensions under the function "health", family allowances, unemployment benefits, old-age and war veteran pensions under the function "social services", scholarships under the function of "education", other cash payments under "other functions".

households in 1969 (25 per cent in France, 27 per cent in Italy and 28 per cent in Switzerland). This was due simultaneously to the strong increase in medical consumption and to the extension of social coverage in this field which also involved an increase in the various types of collective funds devoted to these needs.

With regard to social services, nearly 90 per cent of collective funds were allocated in the form of cash transfers. In spite of the rapid growth of pensions and certain non-market consumption categories, both in value and proportion, the decidedly slower expansion of family allowances in France and Italy has checked the rate of growth of expenditure in this category; their proportion of public expenditure declined from 52 to 46 oer cent in France and from 56 to 53 per cent in Italy. In Switzerland, where total family allowances and pensions had increased at a similar pace, social services accounted for a virtually stable 43 per cent of collective funds allocated to household consumption.

Expenditure on education maintained a fairly stable proportion in Italy and Switzerland (15 and 16 per cent in Italy and 16.5 and 17 per cent in Switzerland) but it rose in France (from 12.5 to 15 per cent), mainly on account of the supplementary subsidies granted to private teaching since 1960. In all three countries more than 95 per cent of public expenditure in this field was devoted to the production of divisible public services if one considers that subsidies granted to private education in France contribute to its assimilation of public instruction and renders the former virtually free.

For all other categories taken together, intervention by the public authorities, except for France, represented a smaller share of collective funds in 1969 (25 per cent in France, 4 per cent in Italy and 12 per cent in Switzerland). It was also more dispersed and concerned:

- in France: agricultural subsidies, various transfers and allowances to housing, telecommunications and public transport and general administration costs of the Ministries of Culture, Youth and Sports;

- in Italy: agricultural subsidies, benefits in kind of leisure and services of the general administration of cultural activities;
- in Switzerland: subsidies to agriculture, housing and public transport and indemnities for losses of income during military service.

In conclusion, it can be stated that an analysis of the structure and development of the financing of enlarged consumption in the three countries during the 1960s is more instructive than a study which is limited to market and non-market forms of the satisfaction of needs. The former requires an explicit statement of the various forms which the collective funds have taken in the financing of consumption and it thus throws light on the following issues:

(i) The proportion of the collective financing of consumption has increased very markedly between 1959 and 1969 and has reached 42 per cent of the total in France, 35 per cent in Italy but only 27 per cent in Switzerland, the relatively low figure in the latter country being due to a less highly developed social legislation.

Nearly 50 per cent of the collective funds were absorbed by cash transfers in 1969. However, despite the growing weight of pensions and daily sickness pay, the share of cash transfers tended to decline in France and Italy because of the very slow progression of the total amount of family allowances.

Benefits in kind represented about 20 per cent of collective funds in France and Italy but only 15 per cent in Switzerland in 1969. In all three countries this proportion tended to increase, mainly on account of medical consumption and the extension of social coverage in this field.

Table 3.15

Structure of collective financing on behalf of households by "function" (in per cent)

Functions	Year	France Cash transfers %	France Benefits in kind %	France Subsidies %	France Public di-visible consumption %	France Total %	France Value 10⁶ FF	Italy Cash transfers %	Italy Benefits in kind %	Italy Subsidies %	Italy Public di-visible consumption %	Italy Total %	Italy Value 10⁹ LI	Switzerland[b] Cash transfers %	Switzerland Benefits in kind %	Switzerland Subsidies %	Switzerland Public di-visible consumption %	Switzerland Total %	Switzerland Value 10⁶ FS
Health	1959	23.3	69.3	5.0	7.8	100	9668	36.2	48.7	na	15.1	100	934.5	24.3	31.3	5.0	39.4	100	1093
	1965	27.2	63.3	2.8	6.7	100	27,134	26.1	59.6	na	14.3	100	2108.8	na	na	na	na	na	na
	1969	23.7	66.9	2.9	6.5	100	44,314	26.5	58.7	na	14.8	100	3358.1	30.0	36.1	7.7	26.2	100	3507
Social services	1959	91.5	2.2	0.7	5.6	100	25,659	88.0	5.2	na	6.8	100	2145.4	86.6	10.1	–	3.3	100	1731
	1965	91.9	2.2	0.7	5.2	100	54,984	88.7	4.2	na	7.1	100	4316.9	na	na	–	na	na	na
	1969	91.4	2.1	0.6	5.9	100	81,489	88.8	4.2	na	7.0	100	6626.6	87.6	8.9	–	3.5	100	5366
Education	1959	4.8	–	10.3	84.9	100	6204	11.4	–	na	88.6	100	571.4	–	–	–	100.0	100	667
	1965	5.0	–	13.5	81.5	100	15,730	1.2	0.7	na	98.1	100	1453.6	–	–	–	na	na	na
	1969	5.2	–	13.4	81.4	100	26,502	1.7	0.8	na	97.5	100	2006.7	–	–	–	100.0	100	2115
Culture-information	1959	–	10.3	11.3	78.4	100	533	–	–	na	100.0	100	45.9	–	–	–	100.0	100	26
	1965	–	3.6	20.4	76.0	100	889	–	–	na	100.0	100	84.6	–	–	–	na	na	na
	1969	–	3.3	16.7	80.0	100	1316	–	–	na	100.0	100	137.4	–	–	–	100.0	100	100
Sports-leisure	1959	–	1.8	23.8	74.4	100	340	–	45.6	na	54.6	100	20.4	–	–	–	100.0	100	10
	1965	–	0.4	24.6	75.0	100	820	–	41.1	na	58.9	100	60.3	–	–	–	na	na	na
	1969	–	0.3	24.1	75.6	100	1843	–	48.5	na	51.5	100	88.5	–	–	–	100.0	100	37
Other functions	1959	11.8	34.8	38.5	14.9	100	6891	–	83.7	na	16.3	100	116.8	12.5	16.3	60.2	11.0	100	510
	1965	9.4	27.2	50.5	12.8	100	13,986	–	82.1	na	17.9	100	211.9	na	na	na	na	na	na
	1969	10.8	24.8	56.9	7.5	100	21,666	–	75.1	na	24.9	100	293.5	16.5	10.0	66.2	7.3	100	1295
Total	1959	54.5	18.7	8.3	18.5	100	49,290	57.1	16.8	4.5	21.6	100	4013.4	45.3	14.8	9.0	30.9	100	4037
	1965	52.9	19.6	9.4	18.1	100	113,543	51.0	19.1	4.4	25.5	100	8618.1	na	na	na	na	na	na
	1969	50.1	20.8	10.3	18.8	100	177,130	51.2	19.0	5.9	23.9	100	13,291.8	48.1	15.0	9.1	27.8	100	12,420

[a] Benefits do not include subsidies.

[b] Switzerland: 1960 instead of 1959.

na: not available

The total amount of subsidies constituted no more than about 10 per cent of collective funds in France and Switzerland and 6 per cent in Italy. Their proportion, both in public funds and in the financing of consumption, increased slightly on account of the raising of subsidies to agriculture (in all three countries), to hospitals (in Italy and Switzerland), to private education (in France) and to housing (in France and Switzerland).

Major items in the consumption of divisible public services were education (in all three countries), hospital treatment (in Italy and Switzerland), social services (in all three countries) and expenditures of the general administration of social insurance institutions (in France and Italy). Their relatively greater importance in collective funds in Switzerland (28 per cent in 1969) was due mainly to the smaller share of other collective allocations in the form of transfers in cash and in kind. These represented 24 per cent of the total in Italy and 19 per cent in France and have slightly increased during the period, mainly because of larger expenditures for education, the administration of social security institutions and, in Italy, medical treatment.

(ii) With the exception of pensions, Switzerland devoted a much smaller proportion than France and Italy to transfers directly allocated to households in the form of family allowances, benefits in kind for medical consumption, scholarships, allowances for housing, etc., during the 1960s, all of which generally aim at income redistribution. If this disparity appears to be due mainly to a less highly developed social legislation, this is no doubt because income differentials and the inequality of disposable incomes seem to be smaller than in the other two countries.[37]

(iii) The growth of collective financing of consumption appears to have been—directly or indirectly—very sensitive to demographic developments in the three countries, particularly to the ageing of the population, which influences

    (a)   medical consumption and hence Social Security benefits;
    (b)   the bulk of old-age pensions;
    (c)   the agricultural population whose incomes have been supported in various ways;
    (d)   the decline in the birth rate and the entry of children born after the Second World War into progressively higher age groups, thus increasing the expenditure on secondary and higher education but reducing the share of family allowances.

(iv) The extension of compulsory coverage of the risks of sickness and old age to a growing number of households, as well as that of benefits and conditions for granting collective insurances, has marked the development of "para-public" Social Security institutions in France and Italy, of local authorities (regions, cantons and communes) in Italy and Switzerland and, to a lesser extent, of mutual insurances in Switzerland. This expansion occurred at the expense partly of private insurances financed from individual precautionary savings and partly of the State, whose intervention is now largely concerned with education and assistance to the poorest classes of the population, the protection of public enterprises and the control of prices (agricultural, medical, housing, energy, public

---

[37] See   Incomes in Postwar Europe: A Study of Policies, Growth and Distribution,
United Nations, Geneva, 1967.

transport and certain cultural services and leisure). Such a decentralization of the functions of the State in favour of more autonomous institutions generally took place within a national legislative framework, guaranteeing a homogeneous social protection to the whole population[38] (at least in France and Italy) but did create some difficult financing problems.

(v) It is mainly in education, health and social services that each of the three countries operates the most extensive systems of social coverage, both with regard to expenditure and the risks of losses of income. Each country used varying combinations of instruments and institutions, depending on its economic and social structure. But, as has already been stated, it is certainly not by accident that, even in Switzerland whose economic system remains more liberal than in the two other countries, collective funds are of considerable importance in these three sectors: they play a fundamental role in the creation and preservation of human capital. On the other hand they have an important short- and long-term distributive effect, their "Consumption" involves different individual gains and collective advantages and, finally, it is increasingly unacceptable that the satisfaction of these needs be dependent on the level of household incomes or social status.

(vi) There is every reason that the range and forcefulness of the means adopted, particularly the considerable importance of cash transfers in the three countries, the selective allocation of subsidies in France and Switzerland and the contractual control exercised by the public authorities over the production and financing of medical treatment in France and Switzerland, reflect a policy which aims to correct the effects of the market mechanism without at the same time unduly changing liberal production structures by maintaining certain aspects of competition and preserving the freedom of consumers'choices. But, conversely, such interventions bring in their wake a dependence of the functioning of market sectors on the allocation of collective funds at several levels. The forms and development of demand functions result to a large extent from the amount and nature of collective resources allocated to households; and the complex connections between market and non-market sectors, or public enterprises, create conditions of complementarity or competition with certain consequences on income distribution, redistribution and the possibilities of satisfying household needs.

3.6   THE FINANCING OF COLLECTIVE FUNDS BY HOUSEHOLDS

From the point of view of economic policy, it is not enough to state that the share of public financing in the consumption of the population is relevant and increasing. Such a development, which is now widespread also among the most liberal developed countries, must be confronted with the modalities of the financing of collective funds by households. Only then is it possible to assess the extent to which the whole fiscal burden imposed on households does or does not balance the benefits they receive in different forms from the redistribution of public funds. Unfortunately, however, no estimates by categories of households are so far available which would single out the categories of "net losers" or "net gainers" from the global interplay of redistribution. By a limitation of macro-economic data one avoids the thorny problems of the real incidence of collective tax retentions[39] and of a precise knowledge of incomes by category of population, but this means that an evaluation of such balance sheets must be limited to only[40] two broad institutional groups: the State and the insurance institutions,

---

[38]See Section 3.6 below.

Tables 3.1 and 3.16 show the total taxes and Social Security contributions which have been directly deducted from household incomes or consumptions:

a) They have risen fastest as a share of GNP in France (from 20.5 to 26 per cent between 1959 and 1969) compared to an increase from 19 to 23 per cent in Italy and 22.5 to 26 per cent in Switzerland:[41]

b) They differed in structure between the three countries in 1969. The French fiscal system favours social security contributions (49 per cent of taxation) and indirect taxes (33 per cent) while household taxation of income and capital played a minor (18 per cent). In Switzerland, by contrast, social security contributions (39 per cent) and direct tax receipts (37 per cent) quite substantially outweigh indirect taxation (24 per cent).[42] While Italy had a similar tax structure to that of France at the aggregate level, it occupied an intermediate position with respect to the taxation of households: social security contributions accounted 47 per cent of total tax receipts, indirect taxes for 28 and direct taxes for 23 per cent.

In France the development of the fiscal system was marked in the first place by the extension of Social Security to new household categories and the partial "deplafonnement" of the calculation of social security contributions from 1967 onwards, and in the second place by the simplification in 1968 of the system of indirect taxation through a generalization of VAT and a recasting of rates. Compared with this, the legislation on progressive taxation of household incomes has not varied during the period apart from some modifications of detail. Finally, the increase in the share of tax receipts in national income stems partly from economic factors, that is from shifts in the consumption structure towards more highly taxed expenditure items which slightly raised the burden of indirect taxation, but mainly from institutional factors connected with the extension of Social Security to larger population sectors.

---

[39] It must be noted, however, that Social Security contributions paid by employers are considered as taxation of households (as income earners or consumers) and not as a curtailment of enterprise profits.

[40] Thus ignoring the scarce and unreliable data on transfers and reallocations of private administrations and enterprises.

[41] Compared to the global ratio of taxation of GNP which averaged between 1965 and 1971: 35.8 per cent in France, 30.1 per cent in Italy and 23 per cent in Switzerland; the share of taxes and Social Security contributions which weighs directly on households was considerably higher in Switzerland (85 per cent) than in France and Italy (between 75 and 80 per cent). See Statistics of Public Receipts of OECD Member Countries, 1965, 1971, OECD, Paris, 1973.

[42]

Structure of public receipts
(Average 1965-71 in per cent)

	Social Security contributions	Indirect taxes	Direct taxes	Other	Total
France	36.3	39.2	15.7	8.8	100
Italy	38.5	36.1	18.3	7.1	100
Switzerland	28.0	23.0	40.2	8.8	100

Source: OECD, op cit.

Table 3.16

Transfers between household, the State, Social Security and private institutions[a]

	France (10⁶ FF)					Italy (10⁹ LI)					Switzerland (10⁶ FS)			
	1959		1965	1969		1959		1965	1969		1960		1969	
	Social Security	Total	Total	Social Security	Total	Social Security	Total[b]	Total[b]	Social Security	Total[b]	Private Institutions	Total[b]	Private Institutions	Total[b]
(1) Social Security contributions of which:	100.0	46.4	52.1	100.0	49.5	100.0	45.5	47.2	100.0	47.4	100.0	39.0	100	38.5
(11) contributions from dependent and independent employed persons	(21.0)	(10.5)	(14.5)	(28.4)	(14.5)	na	na	(12.9)	(25.6)	(12.1)	(42.4)	(18.2)	na	na
(12) contributions from employers	(79.0)	(36.1)	(37.6)	(71.6)	(35.0)	na	na	(34.3)	(74.4)	(35.3)	(57.6)	(20.8)	na	na
(2) Indirect taxes	-	33.6	29.5	-	32.5	-	30.9	28.0	-	27.7	-	26.6	-	24.3
(3) Direct taxes	-	20.0	18.4	-	18.0	-	20.7	22.6	-	22.6	-	34.4	-	37.2
(4) Other current transfers	-	-	-	-	-	-	2.9	2.2	-	2.3	-	-	-	-
(5) = 1+2+3+4 Total %	100.0	100.0	100.0	100.0	100.0	100.0	100.0	100.0	100.0	100.0	100.0	100.0	100.0	100.0
Value	24,608	54,793	114,462	91,439	189,716	1682	3697	7822	5577	11,756	2200	8189	5136	20,681
(6) Current cash transfers	70.6	55.5	53.7	63.9	50.9	72.1	51.5	45.9	67.6	46.2	71.5	45.3	59.7	28.1
(7) Social benefits in kind	23.5	19.0	19.8	30.7	21.1	20.2	17.2	19.3	26.1	19.6	28.5	14.8	40.3	15.0
(8) Divisible public consumption	5.9	19.0	18.4	5.4	19.1	7.7	25.9	28.5	6.3	27.4	na	30.9	na	27.8
(9) Subsidies to production	-	6.5	8.1	-	8.9	-	5.4	6.3	-	6.8	-	9.0	-	9.1
(10) = 6+7+8+9 Total %	100.0	100.0	100.0	100.0	100.0	100.0	100.0	100.0	100.0	100.0	100.0	100.0	100.0	100.0
Value	26,613	48,357	111,879	174,300	174,300	1902	3352	7704	7144	11,575	320	4037	3262	12,420
(11) Ratio 10/5	1.08	0.88	0.98	1.09	0.92	1.13	0.91	0.98	1.28	0.98	0.60	0.49	0.64	0.60

[a] Excluding transfers to households in cash or kind by enterprises and foreign administrations.

[b] State, local authorities, Social Security and, in Switzerland, private insurance institutions.

na: not available.

In Italy, even more than in France, the development of the fiscal system took the form of mainly an extension of Social Security to new population groups. The Italian system, which was characterized by a multiplicity of direct and indirect taxes, has otherwise not been substantially modified during the period, that is before the tax reform of 1974. The only change was that in January 1960 the general tax on receipts from retail sales (I.G.E.), that is imposed at the last stage of distribution and hence on consumption, was abolished.

In Switzerland also the fiscal system has not been subject to any notable institutional change during the period. With regard to Social Security contributions, the proportion derived from incomes from dependent and independent employment was very much higher than in France and Italy (40 compared with about 25 per cent). The increase in the proportion of tax receipts in national income seems to have been due mainly to higher direct tax receipts in a period of constant increases in income and wealth, owing to progressive tax rates which have been modified very little between 1960 and 1969. Further, the improvement and extension of social insurance resulted in a more rapid increase in contributions than in national income.

The relationship between the total reallocation in favour of households and their total collective tax burden differs slightly between France and Italy, on the one hand, and more substantially between both these countries and Switzerland, on the other.

Total benefits paid out by Social Security in France and Italy amounted to more than the sum of contributions received. This was due to the fact that in France a part of the Social Security system is financed from central taxation, that is from transfers from the State budget in favour, notably, of social regimes in agriculture.[43] Similarly in Italy the State participates in the financing of Social Security: subsidies to cover deficits of health insurance, contributions to the social funds for invalidity and old age of non-wage earners, and partial annual subsidies to family allowance funds. Such systems thus superimpose two redistributive mechanisms: one among all contributors and the other, superimposed on it, a partial redistribution from the State budget. In Switzerland the excess of contributions over the payments by private institutions derives from the fact that a part of the latter ("caisses de prevoyance") functions on the basis of a system of capitalization which blocks considerable sums until contributors reach retirement age-a system which is the opposite of that of distribution operated by Social Security in France and Italy.

By contrast, total direct and indirect tax receipts of the State and local authorities in each of the three countries were very much larger than the benefits in kind allocated by them to households.[44] The ratios reallocation/taxation were as follows in 1969: in France 76 per cent, in Italy 70 per cent and Switzerland 59 per cent; the State and the local authorities therefore ran a surplus which was mainly destined for the provision of indivisible collective services. Compared with this, Table 3.16 shows that Social Security registered deficits in France and Italy because their out-payments exceeded the contributions they received. However, at the global level and including all administrations, total taxes

---

[43] Budget Appendix to <u>Prestations Sociales en Agriculture</u> (B.A.P.S.A.).
[44] In France the under-estimation of both taxation and reallocation for local authorities should not substantially modify the ratio between total reallocation and taxation.

received from households in France and Italy practically balanced total benefits of all kinds which contributed to the financing of enlarged consumption. It can therefore be assumed that public expenditure on economic interventions (subsidies to equipment, public investments, etc.) and on indivisible consumption (justice, foreign affairs, national defence) have been covered from other fiscal resources received from other economic agents (taxation of company profits, taxes on investment, etc.). In Switzerland, on the other hand, the excess of levies (or taxation) over reallocation can be explained not only by the fact that "old-age" contributions are capitalized and not distributed, but also that in the Swiss fiscal system the incidence of taxation, notably of income taxes, falls essentially on households and that social legislation is less extensive than in the two other countries so that tax receipts from households have to finance the major part of public expenditure.

Thus two kinds of conclusions can be drawn from this aggregate comparison:

In the case of France and Italy, where the total fiscal pressure attained already is nearly one-third of the National Product, it seems that the tax ratio is soon likely to reach its upper limit, at least if it is assumed that the two countries maintain a predominantly market and liberal economic system. This means, in other words, that all increases of public expenditure on behalf of households will fairly rapidly come up against the capacity of enterprises to finance Social Security and the capacity of the more heavily taxed income groups to pay taxes, except, of course, if the authorities find new means by restricting indivisible and unproductive expenditures or resort to indebtedness. It must also be noted in passing that indirect taxation, which is generally regressive, and Social Security contributions, which are at best proportional, offset the progressiveness of direct taxation so that the global tax system may become regressive. In these conditions there is every reason to believe that the combined effect of collective retentions and reallocations of public funds does not succeed, or only very partially, in reducing primary income inequalities.[45] Therefore all attempts to achieve a more efficient income redistribution, with more or less constant total tax receipts (or global tax pressure) would presuppose structural changes in the fiscal apparatus or in reallocations, or both, particularly in the field of Social Security and education.

In the case of Switzerland it appears that, if a supplementary effort is to be made on behalf of households, notably by reducing the dispersion of incomes, there is more room for manoeuvre. The extension of social protection and benefits granted to the consumer should not be checked by a corresponding increase in fiscal pressure. Nevertheless, nothing justifies the affirmation that such a two-way increase of taxation and reallocation would be achieved without a profound alteration of the present legislative and institutional framework, in particular so as to ensure a harmonization of benefits to the whole population at the reallocation level.

---

[45] For France, see Un Premier bilan de la redistribution des revenues en France. Les impôts à la charge des ménages en 1965. A. Foulon, H. Hatchucl and P. Kende, Consommation, 1973, no.4.

3.7 CONCLUSIONS

At the end of this analysis it can only be regretted that the information available has not permitted more detailed comparisons which would take into account the effects of the mechanisms described on the structure of consumption and incomes of different household categories. At the highly aggregate level the comparisons raise more questions than they provide answers. However, even a greatly simplified analysis reveals the characteristic tendency of increasing public intervention in the structure and financing of household consumption.

The fairly similar development of the enlarged consumption structure in all three countries
shows that the modifications in the population's way of life during the 1960s depended on a common set of demographic, economic and social factors. The dialectic relationships between changes in demographic components (age, size, urbanization, etc.), the relations and motivations of the market and non-market productive sectors, as well as the allocations of collective funds to household incomes and consumption, create complex and interdependent links between the various economic agents. In this sense the growth of the share of collective allocations in household resources-less important in Switzerland than in France and Italy-must not be considered as an autonomous or exogenous phenomenon in the functioning of the whole; it is certainly both cause and effect through an interplay of political and economic mechanisms which cannot be entered into here.

The public authorities have increased their role with the help of various instru-ments at their disposal: production outside the market, taxation, subsidies, legislative constraints, collective insurance of expenditure, public enterprises, etc.
A more detailed analysis would be required to reveal the objectives pursued
in each field. But the analogy of the instruments used in the three countries, if not of their forcefulness, leads one to suppose that the authorities were inspired by similar preoccupations:

  (i) the formation and maintenance of investment in human resources, that is education and health (in all three countries);

 (ii) the redistribution of incomes for population categories which are at the margin of the market economy, particularly of old people, large families (mainly in France and Italy), handicapped persons and workers with low salaries;

(iii) the control of prices in socially and economically important sectors, notably agriculture, medical care, public transport and, to a lesser extent in each of the three countries, housing;

(iv) the dissemination of information, in particular through radio, television and telecommunications.

In each of these fields, public intervention is entirely or partially justified by the requirements of public services, the collective coverage of risks of large population groups and the need to ensure a minimum coherence in the functioning of the global system while at the same time avoiding an excessive development or failure of the market and unduly sharp socio-political tensions.

This does not mean that the objectives aimed at are in fact attained or that the various formulae adopted by each country are necessarily coherent. On the contrary, notably in France and Italy, the multiplicity of ways and means for financing consumption and for correcting income distribution in facour of the poorest strata of the population, does not necessarily represent a harmonized policy but rather a juxtaposition of measures which separately affect income or consumption inequalities in each of the fields considered. This is reflected in sectoral economic and social policies on behalf of large families, the sick, the elderly, etc., which only rarely take into consideration the interdependent and often cumulative factors underlying these inequalities. Thus the French and Italian fiscal systems decidedly favour taxation on expenditure and employers' Social Security contributions whose effect on income is regressive. It is therefore legitimate to conclude that if there is to be redistribution, the allocation of collective funds to households, in France and Italy at least, is somewhat contradictory.

The comparison of the different forms of intervention of collective funds on behalf of households has also revealed great similarities between the three countries. It is remarkable that despite the lower level of economic development in Italy and a much less marked interference by the public sector in Switzerland, the development of the structure of public expenditure should have so many common features:

(i) the determinant influence of structural factors, the most important of which seems to have been the change in the age distribution of the population, notably its ageing;

(ii) the decline in the capacity, or desire, of households to acquire services on the market which are identical or comparable to those freely supplied by the public sector, particularly in education, health and certain services in the field of culture and information;

(iii) in France and Italy households benefit much more from collective redistribution through legislation and action of Social Security institutions than from "divisible" services produced by other public administrations. In Switzerland private and local authority insurances have played a growing role in the allocation of these benefits. Similarly in the field of health, social services and the allocation of cash transfers, social legislation operates increasingly (mainly in France and Italy) through decentralized institutions of a semi-public type often financed through "para-fiscal" mechanisms which manage public funds of growing importance side by side with the State.

However, a more detailed study of the instruments used by the public authorities shows that there have been some divergencies in the socio-economic policies pursued by all three countries. In Italy the tendency to increase the non-market sectors of production is reflected in an expansion of benefits in kind and of divisible public services, particularly in fields where regulation through prices meets strong resistance from the parties concerned (doctors, hospitals, private schools, etc.). Conversely, in France and Italy one observes that the policies pursued during the 1960s have tended to limit the direct assumption by the State of non-market production for education; by contrast, the growing intervention in the form of subsidies, of cash transfers which are not assigned to particular consumption categories, of price controls and contractual relationships between the public authorities and producers emphazise the desire to control market mechanisms without undue interference with the preferences functions of the consumer. In other words, it would appear that social policy in Italy during the 1960s sought to reconcile individual choices with the satisfaction of preferential needs by progressively orienting public intervention towards non-market spheres, whereas in each of the two countries such a reconciliation aimed at checking the market mechanism through a complex system of market controls. It would still be important to estimate the extent to which such interventions help to ensure greater equality of consumption by different population groups in the most important fields; or whether, on the contrary, the redistributive system, in spite of its relative efficacy, is not in the last resort only an excuse to justify and render more acceptable the sometimes considerable inequalities in primary income distribution in savings and in access to certain consumption categories.

One might thus conclude that social policy and the structure of public expenditure on behalf of households could certainly be improved and better managed in varying degrees in all three countries; and that in Switzerland it might well be further developed with the help of traditional methods, that is of price control, tax reform, the allocation of transfers in kind and in cash and the production non-market services. However, the control and coherence of such policies in a still largely liberal economic system cannot be guarenteed unless they are closely integrated with policies for production and income distribution.

CHAPTER 4
A Tentative Comparison of Consumption Patterns in Some Eastern and Western European Countries*

4.1 OPENING COMMENTS

Various kinds of difficulties complicate the comparison of consumption patterns of the populations of Eastern and Western European countries. Let us briefly recall them here.

A. Institutional factors

It is clear that, as far as sources of collective financing of household consumption are concerned, the very wide disparities in the structure of public institutions in the various countries under study bear directly on their economic mechanisms. The reader should always keep this heterogeneous institutional background in mind while interpreting the results of this research.

B. Policy factors

It is also clear that State interventions in the field of economic activities are aimed in quite different directions and with a specific intensity in each country: priorities and policies can vary widely in this respect. Consumption structures of national economies are inevitably influenced by these differences.

C. Price factors

Price formation and structures, as well as price mechanisms, are of a different nature in socialist and capitalist countries. This obstacle, formidable when comparing economic activities in Eastern and Western Europe, has been put aside rather than overcome in this study. But we mention in the following pages, whenever possible, the influence of this factor on our results.

D. Information channels

We refer here to the channels of information capable of shaping, orienting or changing consumer behaviour. These channels are obviously very dissimilar in the countries under review and the impact of them is difficult to measure.

E. National accounts definitions

Disparities in the definitions used in the national accounts of the participating

*This chapter has been prepared by J.N. Du Pasquier and L. Solari

171

countries are well known. This problem is described in sufficient detail in Chapter 1 of this survey to make it unnecessary to describe the disparities again here. But it should be stressed once more that the aggregate of consumption used for the purposes of this chapter does not benefit from any coherence in Western European countries, either in terms of the system of values of market and non-market consumption or at the accounting level, as it results from the addition, on the one hand, of private household consumption at current market prices and, on the other, of divisible collective consumption assessed at factor-cost.This process leads to duplications, the extent of which must not be under-estimated. To illustrate this point, it is sufficient to compare the figures shown in the present chapter with those appearing in Chapter 2. It is hoped, however, that the disadvantage of using aggregates of this type will be more than compensated by the fact that they are presented similarly for all the countries under review, this being the obvious precondition if these comparisons are to be meaningful.

It is equally superfluous to revert to the disparities in the definitions of certain items of household consumption. As regards the listing of functions of consumption, these have been harmonized as far as possible within the constraints of the available statistical sources.

Finally, beyond the various difficulties mentioned above, we should like to add a last comment related to the problems of East-West comparisons. The patterns of household consumption-we are tempted to say the ways of life of the inhabitants-vary widely from country to country on the continent of Europe and even within areas which are limited geographically and thought to be homogeneous. It is often difficult to identify quantified indicators which are capable of conveying faithfully the extent and refinement of such disparities. Later in this chapter there are some results pointing to similarities and divergences in habits of consuming or of organizing consumption in the various countries. It would be both precipitous and presumptious to conclude, on the basis of such results, that there is a trend towards similarity, or towards greater divergence, in the modes of living and social organization of these countries. The purpose of this study is more limited and is deliberately confined to a confrontation of data relevant to household consumption in countries with differing social systems.

4.2 STRUCTURES OF ENLARGED CONSUMPTION

Household enlarged consumption grew strongly during the 1960s. As will be seen in Table 4.1, this growth-calculated on the basis of series at current prices- is mainly evident in Western countries, where average annual growth rates of the order of 8.5 to 10 per cent are observed, compared with rates of 3.5 to 7.1 per cent for the Eastern countries. These figures should not, however, be given undue significance, as they are largely the consequence of factors listed in the preceding section and especially of the movement of prices in the various countries.[1] Section 4.4 includes some comments on the problems raised in establishing series by volume or at constant prices.

---

[1] See Chapter 2, p.32 and Chapter 3, p.129

Table 4.1
Enlarged consumption. Values at current prices

Country		Enlarged consumption: total					Enlarged consumption: *per capita*		
		Currency unit	Value	Annual growth rate,%	Per cent of national income[a]	Population (million)	Currency unit	Value	Annual growth rate,%
France	1959	10^9 F	180.6 ⎫		74.2	44.7	10^3 F	4.0 ⎫	
	1965		312.4 ⎬ 9.8		72.0	48.8		6.4 ⎬ 10.9	
	1969		460.5 ⎭		70.7	50.2		9.2 ⎭	
Italy	1959	10^{12} L	13.8 ⎫		78.0	49.4	10^3 L	279.6 ⎫	
	1965		26.2 ⎬ 9.9		74.6	51.6		490.7 ⎬ 9.2	
	1969		35.6 ⎭		73.9	52.8		673.5 ⎭	
Switzerland	1960	10^9 FS	24.0 ⎫ 8.4		72.5	5.4	10^3 FS	4.4 ⎫ 6.9	
	1969		49.6 ⎭		70.0	6.2		8.0 ⎭	
Hungary	1960	10^9 Ft	115.5 ⎫		72.1	10.0	10^3 Ft	11.6 ⎫	
	1965		140.2 ⎬ 5.0		72.5	10.2		13.8 ⎬ 4.6	
	1968		170.5 ⎭		68.4	10.3		16.6 ⎭	
G.D.R.	1960	10^9 M	63.8 ⎫		76.7	17.2	10^3 M	3.7 ⎫	
	1965		73.3 ⎬ 3.6		74.0	17.0		4.3 ⎬ 3.6	
	1969		87.5 ⎭		72.6	17.0		5.1 ⎭	
Poland	1960	10^9 Zlo	292.8 ⎫		69.7	29.7	10^3 Zlo	9.9 ⎫	
	1965		398.2 ⎬ 6.5		66.9	30.8		12.6 ⎬ 5.4	
	1969		517.9 ⎭		68.1	32.6		15.9 ⎭	
U.S.S.R.	1960	10^9 R	117.0 ⎫		72.9	212.4	10^2 R	5.5 ⎫	
	1965		158.0 ⎬ 7.1		72.6	229.6		6.9 ⎬ 5.8	
	1969		217.1 ⎭		73.8	239.6		9.1 ⎭	
Czechoslovakia	1960	10^9 CR	120.9 ⎫		69.5	13.7	10^3 CR	8.9 ⎫	
	1965		147.3 ⎬ 5.5		78.3	14.2		10.4 ⎬ 4.7	
	1968		185.6 ⎭		66.9	14.4		12.9 ⎭	

[a] For differences in the definition of national income between Eastern and Western Europe, see Chapter 2, Table 2.1 and Chapter 3, Table 3.1.

A more significant finding is that the share of enlarged consumption in the national income is of roughly the same size in all the countries considered. It will be noted, however, that this share diminishes markedly during the period under consideration in all the countries except the U.S.S.R. It is also noticeable that there is no internal homogeneity within each of the two geographic groups of countries: Italy, the German Democratic Republic and the U.S.S.R. have an enlarged consumption share of over 70 per cent of the national income; France and Switzerland a share of some 70 per cent; and Czechoslovakia, Hungary and Poland have shares below 70 per cent. (These figures relate to the end of the period of observation.)

The following tables throw some light on the components of enlarged consumption, namely, direct household purchases on the market (Table 4.1) social benefits in kind (Table 4.3-the sum of these two amounts total private consumption as understood in this study[2]-and divisible public consumption (Table 4.4).

As regards the average annual growth rates of these three aggregates it must be repeated that since these rates are very closely linked with the different social policies and the movement of prices in each country, undue weight should not be attached to the gaps revealed between the two groups of countries.

The share of enlarged consumption taken up by direct household purchases on the market is very similar for all the countries considered. This significant result of our study contradicts a common idea current among economists. For 1969, the share for each country falls within a band of 85-90 per cent, the G.D.R. alone standing at 80 per cent.[3] It will also be noted that this share fell slightly in every country during the period under consideration.

There are sharper differences between countries when we turn to social benefits in kind and to divisible public consumption. A first glance at these figures will lead us to conclude that Western countries have held social benefits in kind at the same high level as divisible public consumption, unlike the countries of Eastern Europe which give the latter category a very strong advantage.[4]

Such a statement is nevertheless subject to exceptions and qualifications. Thus, the level of social benefits in kind, in Switzerland is closer to that in Eastern countries than to that found among its geographically close neighbours, whereas the G.D.R. illustrates the opposite. With respect to divisible public consumption, the gap found between Eastern and Western countries at the beginning of the period tends to narrow progressively owing to a very marked growth of this type of public expenditure over the period in France, Italy and Switzerland, such growth being mainly attributable to the rapid expansion of expenditure in the field of education due to demographic pressure (related to the post-war birth boom), increase in secondary school attendance rates and increase in the unit costs of production in this sector.[5]

---

[2] Cf. Chapter 1, Table 1.3.

[3] For an explanation of the higher proportion of consumption financed by collective funds in the G.D.R. during the period under review, see Chapter 2, Section 2.2.3.

[4] The main reason for this stems from institutional disparities in the health sector: collective financing of health expenditure is considered as a social benefit in kind in France and Italy (Social Security system), whereas it is included in divisible public consumption in Eastern countries and Switzerland.

[5] The increase of unit production cost is attributable, in varying proportions in each country, to: (a) an increase in relative nominal wages; (b) an increase in the number of teachers per pupil; and (c) a shift towards higher and more expensive levels of education.

Table 4.2

Aggregates of enlarged consumption. Direct household purchases on the market

Country		Total				Values at current prices per capita		
		Currency unit	Values	Annual growth rate,%	Per cent of enlarged consumption	Currency unit	Values	Annual growth rate,%
France	1959		162.2		89.8		3.6	
	1965	10^9 F	275.8 } 9.5		88.3	10^3 F	5.7 } 8.3	
	1969		400.7		87.0		8.0	
Italy	1959		12.7		89.2		257.1	
	1965	10^{12} L	22.4 } 9.5		85.4	10^3 L	434.1 } 8.7	
	1969		31.4		84.6		592.8	
Switzerland	1960		22.1		92.3		4.1	
	1969	10^9 FS	44.3 } 8.0		89.3	10^3 FS	7.1 } 6.3	
Hungary	1960		102.0		88.3		10.2	
	1965	10^9 Ft	122.1 } 4.8		87.1	10^3 Ft	12.0 } 4.4	
	1968		148.6		87.2		14.4	
G.D.R.	1960		51.5		80.7		3.0	
	1965	10^9 M	58.6 } 3.4		79.7	10^3 M	3.4 } 3.5	
	1969		69.8		79.8		4.1	
Poland	1960		262.3		89.6		8.8	
	1965	10^9 Zlo	353.7 } 6.4		88.8	10^3 Zlo	11.5 } 5.3	
	1969		457.0		88.2		14.0	
U.S.S.R.	1960		101.9		87.1		4.8	
	1965	10^9 R	133.4 } 6.7		84.5	10^2 R	5.8 } 5.2	
	1969		183.1		84.4		7.6	
Czechoslovakia	1960		105.4		87.1		7.7	
	1965	10^9 CR	128.9 } 5.5		87.5	10^3 CR	9.1 } 4.8	
	1968		161.2		86.6		11.2	

Table 4.3
Aggregates of enlarged consumption. Social benefits in kind
(Values at current prices)

Country		Total				per capita		
		Currency unit	Values	Annual growth rate,%	Per cent of enlarged consumption	Currency unit	Values	Annual growth rate,%
France	1959	10^9 F	9.2 ⎫		5.1	10^3 F	0.2 ⎫	
	1965		22.2 ⎬	14.9	7.1		0.5 ⎬	13.3
	1969		36.8 ⎭		8.0		0.7 ⎭	
Italy	1959	10^{12} L	0.7 ⎫		4.7	10^3 L	14.2 ⎫	
	1965		1.6 ⎬	14.1	6.3		31.0 ⎬	12.2
	1969		2.5 ⎭		6.8		47.3 ⎭	
Switzerland	1960	10^9 FS	0.6 ⎫	13.5	2.5	10^3 FS	0.1 ⎫	13.0
	1969		1.9 ⎭		3.8		0.3 ⎭	
Hungary	1960	10^9 Ft	3.4 ⎫		2.9	10^3 Ft	0.3 ⎫	
	1965		4.8 ⎬	7.3	3.4		0.5 ⎬	9.1
	1968		6.0 ⎭		3.5		0.6 ⎭	
G.D.R.	1960	10^9 M	2.9 ⎫		4.5	10^3 M	0.2 ⎫	
	1965		3.8 ⎬	4.5	5.2		0.2 ⎬	4.6
	1969		4.3 ⎭		4.9		0.3 ⎭	
Poland	1960	10^9 Zlo	6.2 ⎫		2.1	10^3 Zlo	0.2 ⎫	
	1965		10.2 ⎬	9.2	2.6		0.3 ⎬	8.0
	1969		13.7 ⎭		2.6		0.4 ⎭	
U.S.S.R.	1960	10^9 R	2.8 ⎫		2.4	10^2 R	0.1 ⎫	
	1965		5.1 ⎬	10.4	3.2		0.2 ⎬	13.0
	1969		6.8 ⎭		3.1		0.3 ⎭	
Czechoslovakia	1960	10^9 CR	- ⎫		-	10^3 CR	-	
	1965		- ⎬	-	-		-	-
	1968		- ⎭		-		-	

Table 4.4
Aggregates of enlarged consumption. Divisible public consumption
(Values at current prices)

Country		Total				per capita		
		Currency unit	Values	Annual growth rate,%	Per cent of enlarged consumption	Currency unit	Values	Annual growth rate,%
France	1959		9.1		5.0		0.1	
	1965	10^9 F	14.4	9.7	4.6	10^3 F	0.3	17.5
	1969		23.0		5.0		0.5	
Italy	1959		0.4		3.1		8.3	
	1965	10^{12} L	1.3	14.9	4.9	10^3 L	25.6	14.0
	1969		1.8		4.8		30.7	
Switzerland	1960	10^9 FS	1.2	12.6	5.2	10^3 FS	0.2	13.0
	1969		3.5		7.0		0.6	
Hungary	1960		10.1		8.8		1.0	
	1965	10^9 Ft	13.3	5.8	9.5	10^3 Ft	1.3	5.2
	1968		15.8		9.3		1.6	
G.D.R.	1960		9.4		14.7		0.5	
	1965	10^9 M	13.3	3.9	15.0	10^3 M	0.6	5.4
	1969		15.8		15.2		0.8	
Poland	1960		24.3		8.3		0.8	
	1965	10^9 Zlo	34.3	7.7	8.6	10^3 Zlo	1.1	6.4
	1969		47.2		9.2		1.4	
U.S.S.R.	1960		12.3		10.5		0.6	
	1965	10^9 R	19.5	9.2	12.4	10^3 R	0.8	7.0
	1969		27.1		12.5		1.1	
Czechoslovakia[a]	1960		15.6		12.9		1.1	
	1965	10^9 CR	18.4	5.8	12.5	10^3 CR	1.3	5.6
	1968		24.4		13.2		1.7	

[a] Social benefits in kind included.

When we consider these aggregates and their trends as a whole, we note striking similarities among the various countries in respect of direct purchases by households on the market, whereas the contribution of public administrations to household consumption varies quite sharply between the two groups of countries. In this respect, and if we concentrate on the redistribution of wealth which results either from the grant of social benefits or from the production by public administrations of non-market or semi-market goods and services, it would be interesting to determine to what extent and with what effectiveness the different policies of public authorities have contributed to a true reallocation of a country's resources. We shall revert to this issue later, in Section 4.4.

We must now inquire whether these very broad conclusions remain significant when we break down the magnitudes of enlarged consumption into their component functions, in other words when we examine the structure of consumption by categories of needs.

A first synthetic picture of such a structure emerges from a marshalling of the functions of consumption by rank. On Looking at Chart. 4.1 it is at once apparent that the food-and-drink function leads the field by a wide margin in every case. Housing easily takes second place in the Western countries, where controls over land prices, rents and speculation have been restricted to a minor part of the housing market, while in Eastern countries the whole sector is under the strict control of public authorities, giving no room for speculation, and a big part of financing from State resources at stable factor costs diminishes the total expenditure. This is closely followed by clothing in the G.D.R. and Hungary, while in Czechoslovakia, Poland and the U.S.S.R. the positions of housing and clothing are reversed. With regard to clothing and shoes, Charts 4.1 and 4.2 show that their share is generally higher in Eastern countries due to the lower status of housing and probably also to the higher relative prices of textiles. The remaineder of the hierarchy shows fewer points of similarity or divergence, inasmuch as the gap between functions tend to narrow progressively. It is to be noted, however, that except in the case of Hungary-a special instance-education occupies a much more important place in household enlarged consumption in the Eastern countries than it does in the West. This is the direct result of the relative numbers of young students, who are far more numerous in the various types of secondary schools in all Eastern countries as is shown in Table 4.5.

Table 4.5
School attendance rates

	France	Italy	Hungary	G.D.R.	Poland	U.S.S.R.	Czechoslovakia
Age	6–14	6–14	6–14	6–15	7–14	7–15	6–15
1960	96.1[a]	83.8[a]	98.3	100	7–13	100	100
1969	99.2	88.0	98.7[b]	100	99.7	100	100
Age	15–18	15–19	15–19	16–18	15–17	16–18	16–19
1960	33.2[a]	16.0[a]	47.7	31[c]	14–17	–	43.9
1969	46.9	32.9	60.6[b]	53[c]	67.2	80[d]	47.3

a 1959
b 1967
c Only secondary schools; not including professional or technical schools.
d Secondary education is compulsory up to the age of 17.
    Sources: Western countries: U.N. Statistical Yearbook
             Eastern countries: Chapter 2
e From 7 – 13 years
f From 14 – 17 years

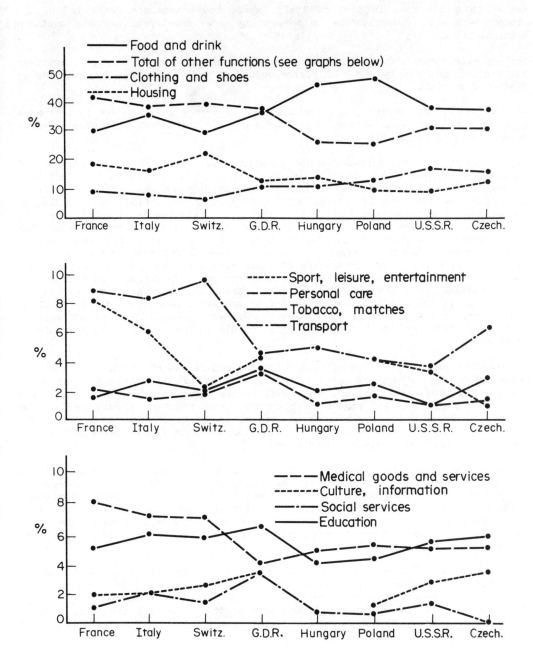

Chart 4.1 Hierarchy of consumption functions.

Another atypical case is that of Italy, where low attendance rates in the age group 15-19 are evidently due to persisting under-development of the southern areas of the country.

The opposite comment can be made with regard to the category "transport", and this is readily explained by the much higher volume of individual travel prevailing in Western countries.

We now turn to the evolutionary trend of each category of needs and to the share taken by non-market consumption[6] within each category. Chart 4.2 illustrates these developments in respect of each function.

With respect to the food-and-drink function, we note in all countries and throughout the period a decline in the share of this item within enlarged consumption as a whole. In the light of economic growth and of the resulting improvement in standards of living which have marked the period, this finding is not surprising and confirms Engel's Law. Taking the relative level reached by this category in each case, the countries can be arranged in fairly homogeneous groups: the first consists of France and Switzerland, where the share of food-and-drink in total enlarged consumption reaches a level of some 30 per cent at the end of the period; in a second group, consisting of Czechoslovakia, the G.D.R., Italy and the U.S.S.R., the share varies between 36 and 39 per cent. In Hungary and Poland, the less urbanized countries, it lies in the neighbourhood of 50 per cent. Within the same category, the fraction consisting of non-market consumption is low-from 1 to 5 per cent-in the countries of Eastern Europe and insignificant in the Western countries, where the low percentages refer mainly to food supplied to patients in hospitals.

The relative importance of categories "clothing-and-footwear" on the one hand, and "housing",on the other, varied very little in any of the countries considered during the decade. Nevertheless, sharp differences begin to emerge between the two groups of countries with regard to both the level reached by each and to the fraction ascribable to non-market consumption. It may be of interest to point out that collective consumption in the field of housing is highly developed in the East and virtually non-existent in the West.

The remaining categories of goods, for which private consumption by households is predominant by tradition, call for no particular comments. These categories include "tobacco and matches", "personal care", "transport", "telecommunications" and "sports, leisure and entertainment". Details are shown in Charts 4.2 and 4.3. With regard to "sports, leisure and entertainment", however, it should be noted that the disparate nature of definitions and nomenclatures renders comparisons between countries largely illusory.

However, some attention must be given to those categories of goods for which collective consumption plays an important role. An example will be found in Chart 4.4. We have considered it best in this context to view the "collective" element of household consumption from the standpoint of the collective financing of such consumption, that is to say by adding social benefits in kind to divisible public consumption.

---

[6]Divisible public consumption and social benefits in kind or in the form of services.

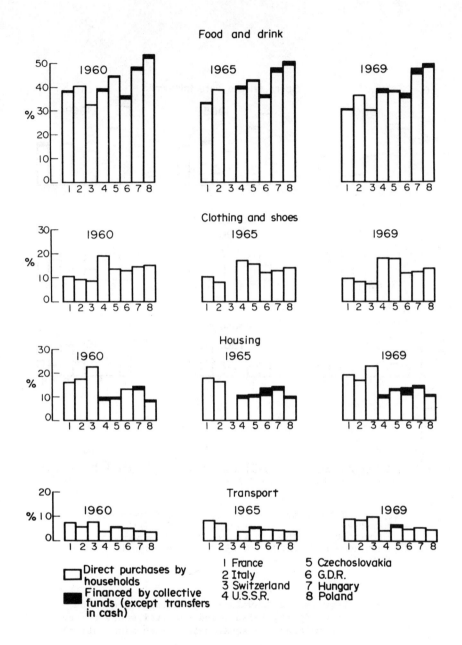

Chart 4.2   Structure and evolution of enlarged consump-
            tion (Food and drink, clothing and shoes,
            housing, transport).

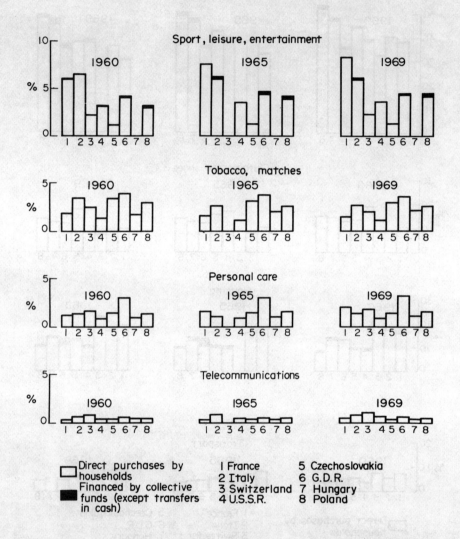

Chart 4.3   Structure and evolution of enlarged consump-
             tion (Sport, leisure and entertainment, tobacco
             and matches, personal care, telecommunication).

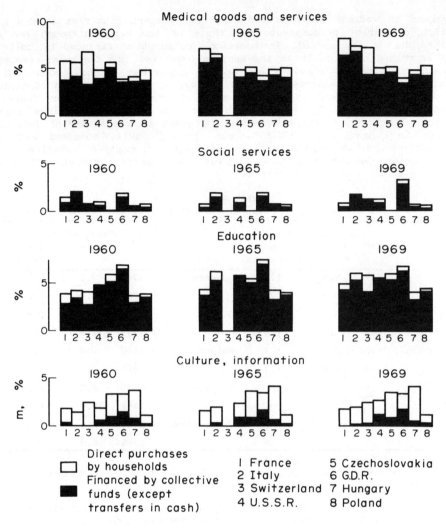

Chart 4.4   Structure and evolution of enlarged consump-
            tion (Medical goods and services, social ser-
            vices, education, culture and information).

With regard to medical services and supplies, Western countries show a higher proportion of market procurement than those of the East, although the ratio diminishes during the period. In addition, consumption financed by collective sources increased appreciably in the Western countries, and the total consumption of medical supplies and services has accordingly risen in those countries to a level higher in relative terms than that prevailing in the socialist countries at the close of the period. Table 4.6 makes a comparison between degrees of satisfaction of needs for medical care on the basis of various physical indicators. The higher rates and faster increases in the number of doctors per inhabitant in Hungary, the U.S.S.R. and Czechoslovakia, compared with lower proportions of health expenditure in enlarged consumption relative to the situation in the Western countries, suggest lower factor costs of medical goods and services in the socialist countries.

Table 4.6
Medical goods and services: Physical indicators (per 1000 inhabitants)

		Hospital beds	Doctors and dentists			Hospital beds	Doctors and dentists
France	1959	9.8	1.3	Hungary	1960	7.1	1.5
	1968	10.3	1.7		1968	8.0	2.2
Italy	1959	-	-	G.D.R.	1960	11.9	0.9
	1968	10.3	1.8[a]		1969	11.2	1.5
Switzerland	1960	12.6	1.3	Poland	1960	7.0	1.2
	1970	11.2	1.3		1969	7.3	1.8
				U.S.S.R.	1960	8.0	2.0
					1969	10.6	2.7
				Czechoslovakia	1960	7.6	1.6
					1968	8.0	2.2

[a] Dentists not included
Sources: Western countries: *WHO, World Health Statistics*
Eastern countries: Chapter 2

The situation in the field of education is somewhat similar, with the difference that at the start of the period considered, Czechoslovakia, the G.D.R. and the U.S.S.R. accorded greater weight to this category of consumption than did the capitalist countries, whereas by the end of the period this divergence had pratically disappeared because of a sharp increase in consumption financed by collective funds in the capitalist countries.

The "culture and information" category is also marked by clear distinctions between two groups of countries which are in themselves relatively homogeneous. For this category the non-market element is virtually insignificant in the Western countries, while it is more prominent in the East. In addition, the Eastern countries (but excluding Poland) give this function a higher place in the hierarchy of enlarged consumption than do the Western countries.

4.3 FORMS OF FINANCING OF ENLARGED CONSUMPTION

The chief point of interest here is in the financing of enlarged consumption out of collective resources. The main features of this mode of financing are given in Tables 4.7, 4.8 and 4.9.

Table 4.7
Forms of collective financing the enlarged consumption (values)

Country		Currency unit	Social transfers in cash	Social benefits in kind	Divisible public consumption	Total
France	1959	10^9 F	28.6	9.2	9.1	46.9
	1965		62.8	22.2	14.4	99.4
	1969		92.7	36.8	23.0	152.5
Italy	1959	10^{12} L	1.9	0.7	0.4	3.0
	1965		3.8	1.6	1.3	6.7
	1969		5.7	2.5	1.8	10.0
Switzerland	1960	10^9 FS	1.8	0.6	1.2	3.6
	1969		6.0	1.9	3.5	11.4
Hungary	1960	10^9 Ft	8.3	3.4	10.1	21.8
	1965		12.6	4.8	13.3	30.7
	1968		17.7	6.0	15.8	39.5
G.D.R.	1960	10^9 M	6.3	2.9	9.4	18.6
	1965		8.2	3.8	11.0	23.0
	1969		10.1	4.3	13.3	27.8
Poland	1960	10^9 Zlo	23.1	6.2	24.3	53.6
	1965		32.9	10.2	34.3	77.4
	1969		47.7	13.7	47.2	108.6
U.S.S.R.	1960	10^9 R	10.4	2.8	12.3	25.5
	1965		14.9	5.1	19.5	39.5
	1969		21.6	6.8	27.2	55.5
Czechoslovakia	1960	10^9 CR	20.0	15.6		35.6
	1965		24.3	18.4		42.7
	1968		30.9	24.2		55.3

Sources: Chapter "West", Table 2.12.
          Chapter "East", Tables 2.2 - 2.4.

The various forms of collective financing of enlarged consumption can be broken down as follows: first, those that earmark collective resources to meet clearly specified needs; and second, those that do not involve such earmarking. The first group includes social benefits in kind and divisible public consumption. The second group consists of social transfers in cash, which provide to households money that can be used freely on the market to satisfy the various needs of the beneficiaries. We may consider, somewhat arbitrarily, that the totality of social transfers in cash is earmarked for consumption, as such transfers are, for the most part, directed to low-income and large families.

With regard to the structural aspect of the collective financing of enlarged consumption, countries of Western Europe favour transfers falling within the second group, while the Eastern countries—with the exception of Czechoslovakia—tend to prefer the methods included in the first group.

Referring more particularly to the modes of financing relevant to the first group, it will be noted that the socialist countries and Switzerland give the most weight to divisible public consumption directly financed by central or local authority budgets. In France and Italy this mode of financing, globally considered, is roughly on a par with the grant of social benefits in kind. It is hardly worth recalling here again the important role performed in these two countries by the Social Security system as a separate public institution, almost entirely financed by households' direct contributions. In the field of social benefits in kind, Social Security in these two countries is mainly aimed at the satisfaction of medical needs. Such a system does not exist so far in Switzerland.

Details regarding the various types of social transfers in cash will be found in Table 4.10. These types are closely dependent upon institutional structures and governmental policies in each case, and little homogeneity can be expected to be found in this respect in either of the two groups of countries.

Pensions[7] undoubtedly represent the major type of transfer in cash in all

Table 4.8
Forms of collective financing the enlarged consumption (structure)

Country		Social transfers in cash	Social benefits in kind	Divisible public consumption	Total
France	1959	61.0	19.6	19.4	100
	1965	62.2	22.3	14.5	100
	1969	60.8	24.1	15.1	100
Italy	1959	63.4	23.3	13.1	100
	1965	56.7	23.9	19.4	100
	1969	57.0	25.0	18.0	100
Switzerland	1960	50.0	16.7	33.3	100
	1969	52.6	16.7	30.7	100
Hungary	1960	38.3	15.4	46.3	100
	1965	41.0	15.6	43.4	100
	1968	44.8	15.2	40.0	100
G.D.R.	1960	33.9	15.6	50.5	100
	1965	35.7	16.5	47.8	100
	1969	38.8	15.5	49.0	100
Poland	1960	43.1	11.6	45.3	100
	1965	42.5	13.2	44.3	100
	1969	55.8	12.6	44.2	100
U.S.S.R.	1960	40.8	11.0	48.2	100
	1965	37.7	12.9	49.4	100
	1969	38.9	12.2	48.9	100
Czechoslovakia	1960	56.3		43.7	100
	1965	56.9		43.1	100
	1968	56.1		43.9	100

Sources: see Table 4.7.

[7] Namely retirement ex-service and invalidity pensions.

countries. Nevertheless, there are conspicuous differences between Switzerland and the G.D.R., and the other countries: for Switzerland and the G.D.R.pensions account for over 80 percent of total transfers in cash, whereas in other countries this figure is about 70 per cent (Italy, U.S.S.R.) or 60 per cent (Czechoslovakia, France, Hungary and Poland). In Switzerland, the main explanation of such a high proportion of pensions stems from the virtual non-existence of other forms of cash transfers and does not mena a high level of per capita pensions. In the case of the G.D.R., this high proportion is the result not only of the minor role of family allowances (largely replaced by services for children provided by public bodies), but also of the larger proportion of elderly people in the population, as shown in Table 4.11.

Table 4.9
Forms of collective financing the enlarged consumption
Share of collective financing in enlarged consumption of households
(per cent)

Country		Social transfers in cash	Social benefits in kind	Divisible public consumption	Total
France	1959	15.8	5.1	5.0	25.9
	1965	20.1	7.1	4.6	31.8
	1969	20.1	8.0	5.0	33.1
Italy	1959	13.4	4.9	2.9	21.2
	1965	14.5	6.1	5.2	25.8
	1969	15.4	6.8	5.0	27.2
Switzerland	1960	7.5	2.5	5.0	15.0
	1969	12.1	3.8	7.1	23.0
Hungary	1960	7.3	2.9	8.8	19.0
	1965	9.0	3.4	9.5	21.9
	1968	10.4	3.5	9.3	23.2
G.D.R.	1960	9.9	4.5	14.7	29.1
	1965	11.2	5.2	15.0	31.4
	1969	11.5	4.9	15.2	31.6
Poland	1960	7.9	2.1	8.3	18.3
	1965	8.3	2.6	8.6	19.5
	1969	9.2	2.6	9.1	20.9
U.S.S.R.	1960	8.9	2.4	10.5	21.8
	1965	9.4	3.2	12.4	25.0
	1969	10.0	3.1	12.5	25.6
Czechoslovakia	1960	16.6	12.9		29.5
	1965	16.5	12.5		29.0
	1968	16.7	13.0		29.7

Sources: see Tables 4.1 and 4.7.

Daily allowances for sickness appear to play a more important role in Eastern than in Western countries, in so far as this comparison remains valid given the marked divergences in the legislation of the various countries. In the West, for example, the absence from work due to sickness may be met either by daily allowances or by continuance of the salary paid by the employer; but in the latter case the amount involved is obviously not debited to sickness benefits of Social Security institutions in the national accounts. Finally, it will be noted that the proportion of family allowances in the total of transfers in cash has diminished

sharply during the period of observation. This diminution may be ascribed, subject
to particular conditions in each country, to the impact of the following factors:

-demographically, through lower birth-rates and increased numbers in the higher
 age-groups;
-faster growth of the volume of other allowances, particularly of pensions;
 amendments to legislation, e.g. in France where allowances are subject to variations governed by the number of children.

Table 4.10.
Social transfers in cash, by type (structure) (per cent)

Country		Family allowances	Sickness benefits	Pensions	Other	Total
France[a]	1959	30.9	4.7	54.0	10.4	100
	1965	24.3	7.0	59.3	9.4	100
	1969	21.0	6.6	62.8	9.6	100
Italy[a]	1959	29.4	4.0	60.9	5.7	100
	1965	25.2	3.5	67.5	3.8	100
	1969	19.1	4.6	73.8	2.5	100
Switzerland	1960	2.0	11.7	82.7	3.6	100
	1969	2.4	8.2	85.8	3.6	100
Hungary	1960	17.1	20.2	54.9	7.8	100
	1965	12.5	18.0	61.2	8.3	100
	1968	16.2	15.7	58.3	9.8	100
G.D.R.	1960	3.5	15.2	74.4	7.4	100
	1965	3.0	10.5	81.6	4.9	100
	1969	1.3	9.6	84.1	5.0	100
Poland	1960	35.9	9.6	47.9	6.6	100
	1965	28.2	10.1	53.4	8.3	100
	1969	18.1	11.1	61.4	8.0	100
U.S.S.R.	1960		25.0	69.2	5.8	100
	1965		23.4	71.0	5.5	100
	1969		24.6	69.4	6.0	100
Czechoslovakia	1960	23.3	12.7	56.6	7.4	100
	1965	22.7	12.9	62.6	1.8	100
	1968	22.1	14.7	61.8	1.4	100

[a] The heading "Other" includes unemployment benefit.

Sources: Chapter 3, Table 3.14.
           Chapter 2, Table 3.7.

Table 4.11
Population over 60 years of age in relation to total population

	France	Italy	Switzerland	Hungary	G.D.R.	Poland	U.S.S.R.	Czechoslovakia
Census year	1968	1971	1970	1970	1971	1970	1970	1970
%	0.19	0.16	0.16	0.17	0.23	0.13	0.12	0.17

Source: *U.N. Demographic Yearbook.*

4.4 CONCLUSIONS: SIMILARITIES, DISSIMILARITIES AND OPEN QUESTIONS

Even if it remains superficial, the comparison which this study has made possible between household consumption in various European countries of the East and West leads us to a number of results which deserve attention and which do not always match currently held opinions in this field.

In the first place, what is the character of household consumption? It is here that the most marked differences arise between Eastern and Western countries. In the West, in accordance with Engel's Law, the aggregate of those items of consumption which are traditionally regarded as of "prime necessity" (i.e. food, clothing and housing) is less than that of so-called secondary items, in contrast to the situation in Eastern countries (excluding the G.D.R.).

A comparison of the composition of household "baskets" of acquisitions is conditioned by the relative prices of each category of goods and services in the respective countries. Although this study has not taken the problem of relative prices into account, its influence is easily perceived, for example the fact that housing and transport occupy a higher place in the "baskets" of Western households than in those of Eastern households, while the opposite is true in respect of the category "clothing".

Turning to those categories of goods for which the non-market method of consumption prevails, comparison leads to results of a more unexpected nature. It might at first sight have been assumed that in view of a higher degree of development of the non-market sector, these categories would-in terms of enlarged consumption-have occupied a higher rank in socialist than in capitalist countries. Yet the quantified results of this study show that this is not true for health, education and social services. These results are all the more surprising because the human and material resources, as well as the policies, directed to the satisfaction of these needs are as fully developed, if not more so, in the socialist countries, as evidenced by the few physical indicators we have quoted (school attendance, teacher/pupil ratio, doctors per 1000 inhabitants, etc.). We have to seek an explanation for this in two directions, which are, in fact, interconnected. On the one hand, since we are comparing the relative proportions of each consumption function, the greater weight given to "prime necessity" functions in the socialist countries must reduce the apparent weight of other functions by the same amounts. On the other hand, there are significant disparities present in respect of both the production costs of these services and of their institutional definitions and operational mechanisms between socialist and capitalist countries.

The second central issue is that of the financing of household consumption, either privately or collectively. Here again our findings are unexpected, since they reveal fewer differences between socialist and capitalist countries than would at first be expected.Thus France, Italy, the G.D.R. and Czechoslovakia give a markedly higher role (some one-third at the end of the period) to the collective financing of consumption than do Switzerland, Hungary, Poland and the U.S.S.R.(between one-fifth and one-quarter at the end of the period). Even though the annual growth of this aggregate, no doubt as a result of the increase in costs already noted, has proceeded faster at current values (and indeed much faster in the case of Switzerland) in the Western than in the Eastern countries, the sharpest difference is nevertheless to be found in the methods used to ensure collective financing: the socialist countries give far greater weight to divisible public consumption,[8] thereby bearing witness to the important role played by public administrations in household consumption, contrary to the situation in the capitalist countries which, for their part, favour social transfers in cash(chiefly in the form of pensions and family allowances) together with social benefits in kind (sickness and invalidity insurance), which are largely dependent upon specific institutions of a Social Security type.

We should also note that if the trends observedbetween 1960 and 1969 were to continue into the future, then the collective proportion of the financing of private consumption in Western countries would rapidly overtake the corresponding proportion in Eastern countries, as indeed was already the case in France in 1969. In fact, the events and institutional changes which have occurred since 1969 have probably affected these relative trends, though it is difficult to say with what effect: as an example, we note in Czechoslovakia after the close of the period a much faster growth of collective financing of enlarged consumption,[9] while in France coverage for the medical expenses of the liberal professions was instituted from 1970. Lastly, the crisis which the Western countries have undergone since 1973 has doubtlessly affected the trends observed from various angles in this study of the preceding decade.

If we look, for each category of goods and services, at the market and non-market forms of consumption we shall again find many more points of similarity than of divergence between the two groups of countries.

Accordingly it can be seen from this study-and this is part of its interest-that the disparity of the socio-political systems of the countries considered affects only fractionally, and only in specific sectors, the behaviour of consumers and the structure of the economic mechanisms of consumption. It also emerges that the role of the non-market channel of consumption, historically more limited in capitalist countries, has developed more quickly in those same countries, thus leading to a certain similarity between Eastern and Western countries as regards the respective proportions of the market and non-market forms of household consumption.

On the other hand, if we turn from the global aspect of these aggregates to examine in more detail the various categories of goods and services, together with the forms of collective financing, we discern a number of significant disparities and divergences between the two groups, particularly in the housing, transport and health sectors.

Lastly, the analysis undertaken here and the results that emerge bring to light various lacunae and limitations due to the method and instruments used in the process. Their mention here is designed not so much to lessen the significance of the results obtained as to draw attention to some approaches likely to improve and enrich this field of inquiry.

---

[8] The proportion of divisible public consumption in the total of collective financing varies from 20 per cent to 30 per cent for Western countries and from 40 per cent to 50 per cent for Eastern European countries.
[9] Average annual growth rate: 0.7 per cent between 1961 and 1968, 2.6 per cent between 1968 and 1972.

DATE DUE